ch–ch–ch–changes

Interviews by John Reardon
Edited by David Mollin and John Reardon

artists talk about teaching

ch–ch–ch–changes

> 'Teaching is first of all not a question of methods or techniques, but of personality; lasting influence is personal radiation …'
>
> Josef Albers, from an untitled paper presented at the Museum of Modern Art, New York, 9 January 1940

The often repeated claim that good artists don't necessarily make good teachers offers some solace to those who found their way into the world of art via the door labelled 'art teaching' and also presumes there's something to teach when it comes to art. This isn't to say that the average artist teaching in art school today is by virtue of being average, a good teacher. It's that one of the consequences of having average artists teaching is that sometimes they tend to consider as Michael Craig-Martin says, '… the world of the artist, as it exists, to be vulgar, mercenary, too much involved with money, too much involved with success […] But the reality is; *that* is the art world and it's not the other pure one. And, of course, it's infinitely more interesting because of that.' Who are best able to do this work and how they should act within the world of teaching is far from clear though it's likely to do with how fearless or risk-averse they are.

Maybe good artists are good teachers not because of what they say or don't say but because of what they do, what they represent and it falls to a particular kind of art teacher to believe that teaching art can be separated from the world of art, can be done by bypassing the world of art for the world of teaching – that teaching or being taught is useful and necessary to those would-be artists who may have something to contribute to the world of art. Something that the art teacher who entered the world of art via the door labelled 'art teaching' will never be able to contribute – this is not to say that the average artist teaching in art school today cannot be a good teacher.

When I began this book, I had an idea that teaching was the thing for me. That was about two years ago or about the same time I asked Michael Craig-Martin whether he'd agree to do an interview. I was interested to talk to him about teaching because when you teach art the assumption is often made that you know how to teach art and if you don't then you kind of pick it up. Thomas Bayrle, who taught at the Städelschule for close to 30 years, says:

> When I started teaching, I quickly found out that I'm not the guy who has the answers [...] It seemed all my colleagues were using another method, as if they knew something, and they stood there and dispensed this to students. I was the only one who was like, yeah ... in the wind. The result of this was that the students decided, 'OK, if he doesn't do it then we have to do it', so they took advantage and gradually I found out that this was actually a very productive position. While other professors deliberately tried to make them take a position, in my class it happened because students thought I was a kind of yeast-like thing, a kind of fermentation that didn't have a lot of mass, a kind of nervous ingredient.

ch-ch-ch-changes is a book of interviews with artists who teach. The interviews – while not a definitive collection – take place mostly with artists teaching in the UK and Germany. They are about human endeavour and human folly as much as they are about education or art, and while these left me less sure about the value of things like teaching art, fine art departments and art education, they left me more sure that a lot of good work is done by people not so convinced by things. The interviews provide a glimpse into the world of teaching as well as the individual character and anxieties of the teacher – their attempts to survive within the world of art education, or merely survive the world of art education. Perhaps survive what Jon Thompson calls 'the mechanisms of academic surveillance and control', which left him so frustrated at Middlesex. Thompson says:

> I know how to operate as a teacher, I don't need to be told. I've been doing it for God-knows how many years – 40 years or so, I think – and then there are all these rules and regulations ... you have to see students, whether it's useful to them or not. I mean you can say the right thing to a student 50 times, but if it's not the right time, you may as well forget about it, it's no use.

Walter Dahn takes up Thompson's concerns and talks about how he approaches teaching in a way that allows for the kind of ad-hoc, out-of-hours encounter with a student, an approach which also says something about the Klassen system. Dahn talks about his students as a collective saying, 'we try to be as autonomous as possible, and I find the niches beyond rules and regulations where more things are still possible. Most of the time, I try to be with the students, as autonomous as possible.'

Karin Sander supports Dahn when she talks about the mobility of the Klassen system: 'In the academy, or any other kind of institution, there are certain rules or rhythms to it, and to break these is very important to your art practice.' Sander would regularly teach in her studio, and says, 'All the conversations and discussions I've had with students here [...] have had a totally different concentration than those at the academy.'

One of a number of conversations that cut across these interviews seems to be about a form of intensity, and how this is present or not in an art school, how it is recognised, named, nurtured or destroyed. The implication seems to be that an over-administered space is a space of less intensity and less creativity. Liam Gillick talks about being a student at art school at a time when '...there was clearly still the legacy of trying to retain the feeling that teaching was a student-centred enterprise [...] What's happened over time is, as one gets further and further away from the political dynamic that changed those hierarchies, and changed those power structures, that the staff themselves have become less proactive and offer less. So you have a student-centred and student-orientated system that still exists, yet the structuring of the way it operates doesn't put enough obligation – and I'm not talking in terms of administration – put enough obligation on the people teaching, or being involved on that side of it.'

Gillick, for example, would have staff present their work alongside students 'in order to create a true debate and shift the potential hierarchical nature of the students to critique'. This shift of focus and intensity may also be related to what Michael Corris talks about as 'an antidote to the kind of pluralism that I think most people feel is their lot.' When talking about working with graduate students who 'come out with the idea that they have their own voice', Corris feels that it is his job to 'thrust them back into a situation that is much more collective'. As an example, he mentions the *Annotations* project he participated in, in New York in the early 1970s

> ... as a way of tackling what it is we have to know about theory, history, or any kind of method to reflect on one's practice critically. That works very well, and all of a sudden we have this kind of self-organising group and students experience a good deal more autonomy with respect to their learning, their intellectual interests. They're taking a very active role in shaping the discussion, so in a way it's recreating – without nostalgia – what seemed to be a fairly interesting conversation or situation in the past, and bringing that into the university as a way of teaching. And that means that I get involved too, so it's not about me imparting what I know, it's about me learning from students and also engaging with them and becoming a co-participant.

Here Corris also speaks directly to Dahn and Sander, and to the kind of collectivity and focus that forms such a vital part of how they work, while Gillick's desire to expose staff to the same scrutiny as the students has echoes of Bayrle and the courage he demonstrates in putting himself before students in a condition of 'not knowing'. This attitude stands in stark contrast to the kind of 'not showing' and 'not telling' still so prevalent among artists teaching today and which seems to be as much about preserving a certain kind of authority as anything else. Gillick agrees that this is indeed the case, and for good reason, because as he says, '... you could have a breakdown of authority, of moral authority. Or just authority in the loosest, weakest sense ...'.

A number of artists who appear in this book suggest that art schools provide or should provide protection from the world of art though its not always clear who or what they should provide protection from and whether teachers more than students need protecting. Because here the teachers authority is at stake, and authority, often mistaken for insight, can sometimes be bound up with maintaining this distinction between the world of teaching art and the world of art, allowing many of the people working in art schools to avoid running the risk of exposing themselves and their work to the world or putting themselves in a position where they're having to defend their work before their peers. According to Corris '… outside of the major urban areas where there are art markets, the majority of people teaching in the US and in the UK have this very same relationship to their practice' – a relationship that is risk-averse. In other words, maybe because many of these people end up as career teachers, they have a real sense of there being something to protect.

One of the most common requirements for artist's involvement in the world of teaching is they have what is variously called a 'practice' though there's no knowing either what that qualifies them to do or to say, nor whether anyone will even benefit from this. Liam Gillick thinks 'practising artist' is actually the wrong term when talking about the kinds of people art schools like Columbia focus on trying to employ '… people who are visible and seen to be taking part in the network of exhibitions, and so on'. Gillick adds a rider – which he's found, creates 'genuine anxiety' for practitioners – that this form of engagement 'has to be in the recent past'. And as I've already mentioned, he also thinks that teachers should be obliged to run the same risk as students, to expose their work to scrutiny in the same way students are obliged to.

For Guillaume Bijl it's clear that the world of teaching and the world of the artist are connected and that an artist's progress in the world of art is directly related to their ability to teach. Bijl says that 'an artist who has only got so far in his career […] is severely limited in terms of his ability to teach'. In Belgium for example he says, 'they don't have such good teachers […] They have middleweight teachers, not really artists. Frustrated artists who teach and then become teachers'. The problem for Bijl is that these very weak artists who are teaching cannot help a younger artist 'because they only went so far as […] a mediocre Brancusi. They cannot evaluate, they don't know whether something is good or not.'

In contrast, Martin Honert who studied under Fritz Schwegler wasn't drawn to Schwegler by his work as an artist. Honert says:

When I started in his class, the artist Fritz Schwegler wasn't so important
for me. I really only understood his work very late on, at the end of my own
studies, so the decision to study under him wasn't a case of, 'oh, he makes
wonderful things and I want to learn from him'. No, it was more the person
and the way he interacted with us … this was really special and really
interesting. I learned this from Fritz Schwegler and use it today as a
teacher.

And Christoph Schlingensief is probably no less effective as a teacher because,
as he himself admits, he doesn't have the first idea about teaching: 'Nein, nein!
I have no idea how it works', nor is Schlingensief even that interested in looking
at the students' work:

> I want to show students my films, tell them how they happened and that's
> all. I'm not very interested in looking at their work. I'm really not. […] In
> the beginning I thought I had to sit there for hours and hours in order to
> understand what they want, but now I look very quickly […] if students
> want to work with me, then they have to come with me and work wherever
> I'm working'.

And yet a good deal of mediocrity still comes through the doors of art schools,
people who fundamentally misunderstand art schools as places in which to
protect themselves above anyone or anything else. People who mistake teaching
 art for making art – being in proximity to people making art but without the
problems and responsibilities that come with making art – brings a sense of
urgency, usefulness and singularity to the world of the art teacher, a feeling of
being involved, of being in the world of art so to speak. However to live out this
'being in the world of art', the art teacher needs to be able to sustain the conviction
that being an art teacher is in fact being an artist and to do this, to sustain this
conviction, must disavow the world he now believes he belongs to, through
separating the world of art 'as it exists' from the world of teaching art. Because
in the world of art – the 'vulgar mercenary world' – he may be found wanting,
he may have little or nothing to say whereas in the world of teaching this lack

can be made up for through a focussed intensity fuelled by the demands that are made on his generosity, time and commitment to art, the kind of commitment that makes him a valued contributor to the work of those people making art and to the world of art.

re: the verbal nature of teaching art David Mollin

When John Reardon asked me to help him edit his book, he sent me the interviews as straight transcriptions from the recordings he had made. Nothing of the dialogue had been left out and nothing tidied up. He had even left large gaps in the text representing silences and hesitations. I found John's generous, if not slightly obsessive, transcriptions of his interviews to be key to the editing process of a book of artists talking about teaching.

I equated the chance to both work from and preserve this initial open form that included all the mistakes and confusions of the dialogue between two people with a possibility for misunderstanding, something that I believe to be part and parcel of the verbal nature of teaching. If the texts were left as close as possible to what was on the recordings, then maybe there would be a greater chance of similar misunderstanding, allowing for a broader inference from what was said. Much can be lost in the transition from talking to text by thinking one knows what is said, and going about reducing the sentences and paragraphs to just that and nothing else. This is when the dialogue starts to look like a text, quite different in character from the original conversation. One only has to compare the conversational aspect of teaching art with certain other elements of teaching art, for instance the lecture, the paper given at a conference, or the statement of intent in a prospectus, to see what we were trying to avoid in this book.

Having more, or even complete, control over the text that emerges from a conversation suits some people more than others, particularly if they feel the responsibility of telling 'how it was' to be a very specific and important part of history, rather than in the more general history of the kind espoused by the aural historian Studs Terkel in books such as *The Good War or Working*. If you are a specific, named part of history, the last thing you want is to be misunderstood – there's a lot at stake, after all. When one needs to set the record straight, one cannot allow any kind of sloppiness to infringe on what is far more important than idiosyncratic concepts, or ways of making a book more interesting for the editor. What is being said in the clearest way possible is what is important, and goes, paradoxically, above and beyond the individual named character. Some people would argue that such clarity is what teaching is all about, thereby linking the process of teaching to the achievement of greater goals, hard to guarantee, but nevertheless an idea.

In the case of published interviews, where what has been said during conversation – the same unguarded, verbal form that is part and parcel of the day to day machinations of artists/teachers talking to students – is written down, another problem occurs: some people don't like the sound of their own voice when it is played back in the form of a text. One artist had interviewed candidly, and very much in keeping with the spirit of their own teaching philosophy. A fellow teacher and collaborator sat in the background on their computer, googling information for the artist. They sat at a table that was a symbol of the 'open plan discussion' encouraged at the college, a table that they had built and varnished together, made for one of their previous collaborative events, but now taken to heart by the students. The open plan nature of that particular school was well illustrated in the freely spoken interview. They sent back the text reduced down to a couple of pages, not even a table-leg. We sadly dropped that interview, as the artist was not willing to publish anything vaguely resembling the original.

Maybe I misunderstood some of the transcripts in the job of getting them 'punctuated', organised. I hope so. Then at least there is a chance that they can be misunderstood by the reader also. Not unlike teaching situations in art schools where one can talk about anything, and possibly late at night if that's what it takes, and still things happen. It's not always what's said. Often what was of help wasn't even said at all, not even inferred, but imagined or overheard, or part of a ventriloquist's act, a voice thrown over white painted partitions, or even something witnessed. All of these oddities either have a firm methodological structure around them in the teaching studio, or are kept in check, or denied completely as a powerful element of teaching. Consensus is the goal at the end of the day, and the various methodological frameworks that have replaced the teaching of craft and technique and rid the place of the belief that everybody is an artist allow some kind of consensus to be reached periodically throughout the year. We have not tried to draw out a consensus within this book. We have tried, in fact, to do the opposite, as this was a goal that appeared more achievable.

This whole question of punctuation is an odd thing and causes a lot of distress if it is in the wrong place, to me, John, the interviewee, the reader, even the publisher – all of us. I was never sure if I had put these dots and semi-colons and commas and dashes in the right place. I am not talking about a comma wandering off into the middle of a word or an apostrophe missing, and green wiggly lines nagging me up and down the page, I mean just where the hell does that full stop go? Could be anywhere sometimes. But you pick up on the characters talking and they take you there to a large degree. I started thinking about Richard Rorty (easy to feel that kind of pressure when reading interviews on the subject of teaching). Rorty talked about punctuation. He described things that 'fall out of the semantic pale': things that don't necessarily make sense but do something, are there, have effect, are like odd punctuation, or a slap in the face. They have an effect of us wanting to bring them into meaning, to produce. And when you have a transcript like the one John sent then odd, or no punctuation, and a few slaps in the face, abound.

To overly dwell on misunderstandings, or moments that fall out of sense, would in the end be subversive and destroy the interest that these interviewees had in what they were formulating in front of John's microphone. This is why much of the editing was a balancing act of these 'things' that fall out of the semantic pale, that abound in a straight transcription, that might be interesting (maybe what Dr Seuss would call 'Thing 2 and Thing 1' in their possible potential for destruction) and the striving for coherent sentences that produce an idea of what people actually said, or at least meant.

Another reason why the straight transcriptions were key to the editing process was that they gave access to the distractions and literal interruptions that occurred during the interviews. This made me aware of the rooms within which the interviews took place and helped me understand something more of the characters. Rainer Ganahl, for example, requested that his interview take place in front of an audience of his students and his replies were projected. Walter Dahn played rock music to John all the way through his interview, and talked over the music. Jon Thompson had the weight of his own experience insulating the points he made from other disturbances. Liam Gillick was interviewed in a busy coffee shop near the main train station in Amsterdam. His ideas were relentlessly delivered in transit, not that different from Erwin Wurm's coffee shop in Vienna – the previous haunt of Thomas Bernhard – but much closer to the station. All this helped me, to a certain extent, imagine the tone of their speech.

I also liked breaks in the flow of the conversation, moments when the interview was diverted by something external, breaking the train of thought and sending it in a different direction, or into forgetfulness: a phone call, a request for directions, an assistant bringing tea from China, or a large delivery of wood. It takes all sorts. This is the other 'thing' present in John's transcripts that was not odd punctuation but the sound of the building. It is the sound of the room within which the interview took place, and sometimes it is the sound of the building evoked when the subject of teaching is discussed: the building as a structure within whose constraints an artist/teacher must think, constraints on sentences and constraints reflected in body language. Sometimes it is the constraints of not hearing yourself think. So we have chairs scraping, beeps and bobs, phones ringing, the trees outside and in, traffic, venetian blinds going up and down, opening and closing, office tip-taps, a London bus, Dutch coffee cups; the fiddling, coughing, tension, the um-ing and ah-ing of both the interviewee and the interviewer, loud as day.

Finally, always present in the transition between ideas for the book and the final draft is the question of ambition. Ambition shaped the final draft and in the end it is more interesting to have a book shaped by the various ambitions that come into play at every stage – from the moment anyone opens their mouth, in fact – than by some preconceived idea of what makes a good book.

One of the questions that John's interviews raise is about the role that these artists' own ambition in their work and careers play in teaching, which, for some, is so intrinsically linked to their practice. It is a question of focus. Can one teach successfully when one is a successful artist, and fully focused on one's own practice? Is this a case of teaching by example? Or can it be a source for recruiting little helpers to realise one's own institutionally subversive, or institutionally exclusive, projects? What does such a teacher see when they look at a student's work? What about the person who merely wants to be a good teacher out of love, devoting all their time to the activity? Have they anything to bring to the table if they have no practice, as some would claim? Or no research points, as others would put it? One is also left to wonder if a person who wasn't even an artist might not be better qualified to teach art? Someone not involved at all in the business. This would be a logical step perhaps to the bureaucratisation of art education, and an odd managerial twist (or even coup) to the claim still popular that one can't really teach art.

A solution to what some people see as the over-professionalisation of teaching and its feared consumption of an artist's precious time, is to curb one's teaching ambitions and keep a distance, keep one's coat on during tutorials, make sure the car isn't blocked in the oversubscribed university car park. It's a long drive home through 50 mph restrictions and that needs to be kept in mind, even on a short-term contract. If you need to leave early, do so. Money and prestige is a real carrot, and what with an office to boot, it's what many of us always wanted. But then what? Move the family down here, or over there? Would you? Could you? In a box? With a fox? In a house? With a mouse? Maybe it is a generational thing and some people still treat teaching as something that you kind of do, with one foot in, one foot out. In some ways the decision to at least try to keep the incoherencies of a conversation present in a text is the sole justification for this book being titled as it is, even if these incoherencies end up getting lost after everyone's had their say. It is these moments of incoherence that are the struggle, from the recording to the page. They are initiated in the directly spoken opinions given in the face of one's own investments being often or always subject to change, and which move through a process of others' own collapsing investments. Change itself taking place can only be present in moments of incoherence and collapse, odd moments. It is this that we tried to emphasise, perhaps only symbolically, in these interviews: a stuttering change embedded within the necessary certainty needed to teach.

What one is hopefully left with, after all of this, are specific artists talking specifically about their work as teachers, professors, without the deadening uniformity that would come from boiling things down to just ideas.

interviews

John Armleder — in a non-descript building in Lucerne, Switzerland — a warm June afternoon.

How long have you been teaching, and where are you currently teaching?

I started teaching on a permanent basis 10 years ago. I don't remember exactly when it happened … I started in two academies: l'Ecole des arts de Lausanne, ECAL, the academy of fine arts I think it's called in English, and the HBK in Braunschweig, where technically I have a class under my name, although I changed the name to 'Team' – the *Yellow Pages* project for example is done by John Armleder and Team 404: this stands for a changing team and is made up of the students from the class. We conduct all sorts of projects like that … so it's been 10 years.

They sign up for your class?

Exactly. The academies in Germany have classes taught by one artist, professor, or whatever, as opposed to Lausanne where I'm one professor among others and we all teach the same students. The academy decides on the students and we accept them. I have really no idea who is under my supervision, I just see everyone. The class in Braunschweig is supposed to be a painting class so there's a studio space for my class. Theoretically there is also one for me as a professor, though I give this up to students which is something I'm not actually allowed to do … there's been a lot of discussion about my activities in Braunschweig. One of the students acts as a tutor who is like an assistant and gets a small payment for this. The tutor gathers the class together whenever I come in. We have meetings and we do different projects.

And OK, I started to change things in Braunschweig in the sense that instead of having a class of between eight and 15 students, I would accept anyone who applied to my class. So it grew into a class of 50 students, much more like a forum. And I also pushed a lot of students to take classes with my other colleagues, which until then hadn't been common practice, that students would study with more than one professor. When I started doing this, it was controversial in the school. I had problems with the director because of my way of doing it. The other thing that was controversial was the problem of credits – of grading students and of deciding 'how good the students are'. I don't believe in all of that. Basically, so long as people are there and take part in the projects, I consider them students of my class and they should get the grades and da, da, da, da, da, da. But if you think of what Joseph Beuys did years ago at the Düsseldorf Kunstakademie, that was exactly the same thing.

And in Beuys's case didn't the academy have to intervene?

Yes, and they were going to do that in my case too. But of course, it would have been a bizarre replay, and they wouldn't have gone that far because of this. Most of the work in my class is about doing projects, so student's own individual work is just mildly discussed. We normally invite other artists to take part and if students want to show their work, they show it, we talk about it and that's it. I'm not directive in any way. I would never tell a student he'd better do something. He should work with more colours, or larger, or more often.

When you say the work is project-based, what do you mean by that?

I don't know when the first project was … It was a series of shows and other events organised by a small group of students in the class. We began by inviting artists from all over the world, to take part in the project by sending us proposals. And then the students built the proposed work of these different artists, as well as their own work, which they also included. The projects were shown in the class, or elsewhere, usually elsewhere. We've just come back from Shanghai, where we did a show.

The student isn't responding to a brief?

Well, no. We'll discuss collectively how we want to conduct the project, and we'll decide on a theme, or format, which we label in such a way that it can be understood. This will then be dispatched here and there to artists we know. It's usually open-ended, so artists can also contact us and submit a piece that fits this format. There have been very famous artists in our different shows, very established artists, and some people whom we don't even know today who they were. So they're the kind of projects we do. To make it easier to understand; the first project we did was on the invitation of the director I'd had that problem with. He sort of tried to arrange things and said to me 'well, since you're an international artist and know a lot of other international artists, why don't you organise a show with your students?' And that's what we did. Since Braunschweig is near Wolfsburg, where they make Volkswagen cars, we said 'let's do a show about cars'. Volkswagen had a big hall on the ground floor that we could use, so we borrowed 50 cars from different garages, which funnily enough actually lent them to us. Then we sent an invitation to 50 artists I knew, and they all designed work that would be constructed in or around the cars. The work was to be constructed by the students if the artists weren't available. So the students produced the actual designed artwork for them, while some of those invited came along and produced the work on site. That was the first project. The next project was the *Yellow Pages* project. I can show you a book …

[Pause while John Armleder gets out a book.]

I think I read about this …

You can have it.

This is artist's …

… submissions. The collection is now in Geneva. It was another project where the class were invited to take part, and it started with an awkward place to show which we didn't know what to do with, and I said 'well, let's use it to launch a project, which will turn out to be a book'. We sent an open invitation to artists to submit a one-page piece in A4, which would be printed on yellow stock like a Yellow Pages directory. The only thing we said was that the page would be produced in black and white, on top of the work of someone else chosen at random. So on each page there are two artist's works on top of each other. We showed it in an actual Kunsthalle, in Basel, and then in MAMCO, in Geneva.

How did the artists get to work on top of each other's work?

They didn't. They just submitted their work individually and we printed it. Everything was scanned and then overlapped without a graphic design purpose. It was like chance, just one on top of the other, which is, of course, the reverse of what the Yellow Pages are about. There were 500 or more artists involved, and some very famous, or established, or whatever, and some we don't know who they are. A few were from the old Fluxus days.

Can you tell me how you think about teaching in relation to your own practice, particularly because of the kind of Fluxus background or tradition you come out of?

Well, the first thing is that I'm not trained in an art school. I only ever spent six months in an art school in Geneva.

[Tea is served by an assistant. A variety of Chinese teas are offered.]

Since we're just back from China we're experimenting … I quit the art school in Geneva very quickly. As a matter of fact I originally planned to go to Düsseldorf academy, to Beuys's class, where I had been accepted. I was 18 years old, or something like that. At the time I was engaged in some political activities here in Switzerland. Military service was compulsory and I refused to do it, so I went to prison, which was the normal procedure then. I spent seven months there. And when I came out of prison there was no point in going to art school. As a matter of fact, I had missed the beginning of the class so I never … I only served time in prison, not in an academy. A few years later we invited Joseph Beuys for a project and I told him how I should have been one of his students, but that I'd spent seven months in his colour-scheme anyhow, so I thought I'd graduated! He sort of looked at me in an awkward way. But anyway … so, yeah, my background is without academic training, which makes it bizarre, being a professor. I conducted a lot of workshops in Iceland. I just don't know how to teach other than understanding it in terms of working with a group of people and using the – it seems new age – but let's say the *energy* of this group and the different points of view, to understand more about what you're doing yourself. So I'm in exactly the same position as the students when I'm working with them, because I'm discovering things as much as they are. And, as a matter of fact, I take much more out of it, because there are more of them than me.

But what about the power relations, you're there as a professor, they're there as students, and you're within an academic framework?

That's conflictual, particlarly in Braunschweig at the beginning, because they give a lot of credit, especially in Germany, to the professor. They believe in professors. Here in Lausanne it's a bit different, because for a long time you were teaching basically because you couldn't make a living out of your own art – you *had* to teach. In Germany it was always considered an achievement, and you were called Herr Professor and all those things. I don't believe at all in any kind of power relationship in any situation, and certainly not in art, so I never consider myself as knowing more than students do. I just know it differently, because I have a practice and have shown as an artist. And most of them have not as yet.

But it's there institutionally, isn't it?

Yes. It is the pressure and the nonsense from the institution that sort of puts you in that bizarre role.

So you have a certain polemical relationship to the institution?

Well, most typically is when you come to this bizarre moment when you have to give grades. That's always extremely conflictual for me, because my only way of getting out of it is by ignoring it and by systematically giving the students the best grades possible. And that doesn't really work because I'm not the only one giving the grades! Depending on the school there are different problems, but I always run into some kind of problem in those discussions, and it always ends with me being called up by some committee that says, 'by the way, you have to decide your position about the grades', and so on. I do make my point, you know? But this just goes on and on, and nothing comes out of it. Whether you finish your studies with good marks or bad marks doesn't change anything if you're an artist. It maybe gives you a chance to teach or it gives you a chance to maybe get grants, which are all reasons to give good grades to a student – it's just being helpful. But as far as the quality, the engagement of the person as an artist is concerned – good grades, bad grades, no grades, they don't change anything.

So can you teach art?

Well, I don't know if it's teaching, I mean ... I'm involved as much for myself, as I am for them in trying to understand what we're doing. So my involvement with the students is more experimental, much more like a laboratory where people get together to understand a bit more about what they're doing, and what they want to do. Of course, because of my long-time practice I have some kind of knowledge. And because I'm someone who's been interested in art for a long time, I do have that kind of knowledge, not as an art historian, but as an artist, which, in a way, I'm very happy to share. Because if you give something out like that, it will be assessed critically by the people who are listening to you, and given back to you in a different way. So it's reviewing from both sides. And because most of the students are people who are just trying to find out if they want to do art or not, and I'm a person who has been doing art for a long time and takes for granted that's what his life is about, but who still doesn't know why, it's a discussion. An art school is a very privileged place for that. You won't find that again elsewhere, so that's something.

Why are you in an art school if you can survive economically without teaching?

I don't know if I have a good answer, because I don't know if I have a good answer to why I'm doing art. I'm teaching on a permanent basis in both academies. I didn't apply for my own sake. I wouldn't have done it. It was only because people there asked me, people who were friends. In Lausanne, it was a new director who was an old friend. He wanted to arrange the school on different terms, and he was very excited about it and I said 'OK'. It just seemed normal to go along with him, but I had no plans to teach. In Braunschweig it was a Swiss artist who called me one day, Thomas Hüber who was there then, and he said 'oh, by the way, wouldn't you want to come to Braunschweig to present your work?' I didn't understand completely what he said, because it was in German, although I speak German. And I sort of said 'yes, he's a friend, I'll go for it!' When I got there, I discovered that the presentation I was making was for a job, for the post of professor! I only found out when I got there, and then I was accepted. After I had done the general presentation, there was a committee, and they said 'OK, it's very interesting what you said. Now, how do you see your teaching?' And I said 'what teaching?' Then, of course, I explained my position as an artist who worked a lot with other artists – who had created cooperatives and so on. And I said that teaching for me was the same thing. I don't know why they went along with it, but they did. I would never have thought 'oh, I would like to be a professor, I would like to apply to the school'. All the workshops I had done were because other artists thought, 'oh, it would be interesting, fun, or whatever, to have you around'. Economically, for me, it's more of a hindrance than anything else, because it costs me a lot in travel expenses. And when students don't have the money for projects, I usually give part of my wages. So in Braunschweig I don't earn a cent, I'll spend all the money on the projects, to do a book, or something like that, because the school doesn't pay for them. So the economic part doesn't exist at all in my case. On the other hand, I like doing it because I like working with other people. I'm not the kind of artist who believes he has a single mission as a person, and who is going to go home to his studio and do the perfect artwork. That's a position I have as an artist; so it's just quite normal.

I know a lot of artists who would never want to teach because it would be distracting for them. I know a lot of artists who are not 100 per cent engaged in their work and want to start teaching; all their activity swerves towards academic activity. They can be good professors and not such good artists. This idea that one has to be excellent everywhere is problematic. Art schools have suffered from having a lot of artists teaching who are bitter because their careers went wrong, and their only chance now is because art schools have a kind of credibility in the art community again. It is true that some schools are attractive, in the sense that they try to get famous artists in. So an artist who is not so famous becomes a famous artist *de facto*, so there's this kind of reward.

Is there something of this reflected in the current interest in teaching and schools, the rise of summer academies, panel discussions about teaching, and so on?

Yes, and I don't know how much it really makes sense, or how problematic it really is. There are a lot of artists who get together and create their own academies, or pseudo-academies, like Rirkrit Tiravanija, for instance. And there are many others who've also already done that. It's a way to contradict the normal institution and at the same time to recreate it in their own way. Another thing that's always been discussed is how young artists should know a lot about art, especially about what's happening today. So you have a lot of schools where the teaching about art of the twentieth century, or contemporary practice, is fairly intricate, is fairly well addressed. But very often the history of art in a larger sense is completely forgotten. So you have very few people with a specific knowledge about Gothic in our countries, or about the Chinese Ming period. That's a bit bizarre, because we've lost a lot of knowledge, though we've gained a lot of other knowledge. And we think it's important that a young artist when he is quoting something in his practice, knows what he is quoting, but I don't believe in that at all; if someone is using something he finds useful, that is an efficient tool for whatever he is producing, and he has no idea where it comes from, that's good. No one would claim that a young musician who's into sampling music should know exactly what he's sampling. That's what we do in our world, I think.

Is there a sense that to be an artist today one needs to go to art school, or is OK not to go?

Of course, of course, because even if you do go it doesn't mean that you know more. You have other tools. The more you learn things, the more you forget things. You forget only because you know. If you don't know, you can't forget. So it's a choice. Look, I have tons of books. I love reading things about art, but I don't have an academic knowledge about it at all. My reading is totally different to an art historian's. Or even … I don't know … Daniel Buren would see all these books in a different way than I do, and use them for something radically different. Or he could be reading only science fiction. So there's no single way. You could just be happy knowing about botanics, or not even knowing, but just looking at flowers. Take paintings of flowers; there are those you like because you can see how organically the flower is made, and there are those you like because of the colours, and you can't say one is better than another. It's about something else. It's the same thing in life in general, and certainly in art.

When a student enrols with you, I wonder if they believe they are buying into part of a network?

You could see it from the other end. In the art world, if someone asks what you've done, and you say 'I went to Goldsmiths', for example, they'll say 'oh well, then, you must be interesting', which makes no sense. But you've always had that in one way or another. Before you would say 'ah, where did he show?' and someone would say 'he showed at Castelli'. Credentials don't exist in art, it's the work you're doing, and how it makes sense at the time you're doing it, or maybe later on. Even that is not decided, because some artists are very important at a certain point and time in history and make no sense whatsoever later on, and vice versa. There are different phases of interest. A lot of credit is given to knowledge, which was not the case before. You actually had the exact opposite; this idea that an artist should be someone who lives just out of feelings, and they could be quite un-knowledgeable, and through their energy, their force, their special character, they would come out with something extraordinary. So it was expected that artists would be a bit crazy and dumb. Now it's the reverse; if an artist doesn't know what he is doing, if he's not capable of quoting, then maybe he's not so intellectually fit to do it. In both cases it's stupid. It doesn't make any kind of sense. And in any case, no one was actually really that dumb or stupid. You could come up with the most outsider kind of person in the art world and find he knows a lot, at least about some things, if not many things. Today if you go and talk with an artist who is supposed to be extremely knowledgeable, maybe he knows some things very well, but then you maybe just move slightly out of that frame and he's lost – he has no knowledge at all. I don't think people have to have universal knowledge but it's true that everyone has a very specialised field, and if they know a lot then they usually know a lot in very few domains. And even their perception of that knowledge is very restricted.

You said earlier that you're in exactly the same position as the students when you're working with them, because you're discovering things as much as they do. At what point do you know teaching is doing the kind of thing you want it to do?

There are so many different positions if someone is teaching. When teaching etching, the teacher knows when he's performing well or not, the student knows what he's talking about, and he will find out if that student follows his instructions and if there's a transmission of knowledge. That's teaching in the traditional sense and that can still work in many domains of the arts, not only in practical making, but maybe also in understanding how to install your work, how to present it, how to discuss it, how to defend your position, and all that. In these cases you can feel that, if you explain your position, it gives students some tools, or some instruments or an asset, they will then develop. But I don't know if I really want to do that. I'm happy to give whatever I can so that someone has it to hand and gives it back to me, and then I know more myself what it's about. So the only time I know when something is happening, is when I'm learning more about it. It's really a mirrored situation. I know that the vast majority of the artists who have been in my classes in Lausanne and Braunschweig, or in other workshops, won't do art later in life. Statistically there must be, globally speaking, tens of thousands of students coming out of art schools every year. There are not ten thousand new artists on the map every year, so you know that in your class, of the people you're working with, there will maybe be one or two out of 20 or 50. It doesn't mean you're only addressing those one or two, it's not only those one or two that count. The others have got to have an experience, which is maybe as valuable, or important for society in general. Because they will have had an experience that will maybe be useful in a bank, or as a cook, or in whatever they will be doing later on.

Do you know the one or two in your class? Can you tell?

If I can see when it's happening from the beginning, you mean? Yes and no. Usually you can tell the one that is close, that has everything to be a challenging artist.

What is it?

I wouldn't describe it as this or that, but somehow you can see that they're engaged; they can discuss their work, and it means something to them. And they can challenge what they're doing in a critical way by talking about it, or by going towards other people who are doing things that have something to do with what they're doing. You can see very quickly that most of the other people do something else, they don't have that kind of tight relationship with their work. Within that group some will end up doing the kind of art that I have no relationship with, because I'm not teaching them a style or a type of art. I'm not at all in favour of Conceptual art, or Fluxus art, or Constructivist painting, or whatever. I don't think there is any form that I would be able to favour in my discussion with them. If you're in a much more academic subject, if you teach them how to make good landscape painting, then you can see who has the expertise.

Josef Albers believed that you can't teach art, but you can teach other things; certain skills, ways to develop, to scrutinise objects and the world. The art, however, goes on in the studio, or wherever, and this is the artist's business …

It's right. But it's organised according to a world which is probably not working on the same terms today, because it's now much more intricate and complicated. This is a sort of post-Bauhaus definition of an art school. But I suppose the way I do it is not so different from that in the end, because my position would be that students in an art academy should have access to all the studios and workshops to learn different skills or different kinds of recorded knowledge, history of art, or science, or whatever. And the more that is available, the better for everyone. In that sense, art schools in America connected to a universities are very good, because students have access to a lot of information or knowledge. Of course, they then have to sort of pay back in a very academic way, because they have to get credits on all the subjects they're using … I'm not sure if that's needed, but maybe it is – I don't know.

John Armleder teaches at the Ecole supérieure des beaux-arts (ESBA), Geneva and The Hochschule für Bildende Künste, Braunschweig.

Phyllida Barlow — at home in North London —
early June.

In a recent article, Mark Godfrey introduces you as 'one of the most influential teachers and artists working in Britain today'. With a career spanning 40 years ... you grimace?

I don't think that's true.

Why do you think Godfrey would say that? Is it simply down to longevity, or do you bring a special kind of focus to teaching that produces particular kinds of results?

It is a very expedient remark that tries to raise interest in the article, otherwise there would be no point in him writing it. From my point of view, I don't quite know where he would get that information from, other than rolling the credits of a few names that I've obviously had contact with over 40 years. I feel that my kind of teaching – and there are a lot of us around – is that every day is a new day. You feel you have no history as a teacher, you almost feel you have no history as an artist. You enter the studio and the tutorial almost starts from scratch each time, and therefore you're in a process of constant renewal. I suppose that's the excitement of the teaching experience; that people like myself don't know how to use their own history. And it doesn't necessarily stand one in very good stead. It's unreliable, in as much as I don't have anything to rely on, everything is always different.

Why do you think that is?

Because I think there are so many changes with each decade, or five years, or even quicker now – two years. Each group of students is bringing an entirely new life cycle. If you just want to depend on something that happened to you over 40 years, that is not anything I'm particularly interested in doing. I am genuinely interested in the here and now and how that then relates to a whole history of knowledge and attempts to understand from the past. But I don't think the past leads, the individual leads.

How do you keep it from becoming predictable? How do you go in there every day and start again?

Unfortunately every teacher has their predictable emotional, passionate luggage, and the students are the first to recognise this. They know I might say something like 'take it outside, go and put it on a street corner', 'take it down to Euston Station', 'why not do

this as a performance?' 'Why are you videoing it, why not do the performance live?'
They know I will say these things, or 'why have you put it there, why not stick it on the
ceiling?' I can bore myself with my own repertoire of things, but I suppose that's directly
connected to how I would treat the process of making in the studio. You know that
nothing is reliable, you know an idea isn't reliable.

**In a conversation with Sacha Craddock about the making of *Peninsula*, the work you
did for the Baltic Centre for Contemporary Art, you explained how the students you
had working with you constantly reminded you of what you would say to them in their
studio, but would do the opposite in yours.**

Yes. Touché!

**You taught people like Rachel Whiteread, Steven Pippin, and so on. Did they require
much teaching?**

I don't think either Rachel or Steve Pippin would necessarily think of me as a particularly
significant teacher. That particular year in Brighton, where I met them first – at the old
Brighton Poly, before it became whatever it did become – there was an extraordinary
head of sculpture who was retiring. Which is why Ed Allington and I got this kind of joint
job there.

Who was the head of sculpture?

James Tower. He needs huge credit for his ability to select really interesting students.
If you look at the history of Brighton during that early 1980s era, the artists and the
students at the time who became well-known artists who went there, were astonishing.
A lot of these things go, they disappear without a trace and that's just the way it is. But
in that particular year at Brighton, there was Rachel, there was Steve Pippin, there was
another wonderful artist called Lee – gosh I've forgotten his name – Lee Andrews ... And
several others whose names have gone just for the moment. Alison Wilding was teaching
in this group of people at Brighton as well. It was an astonishing 18 months there,
and then the whole system changed. Polytechnics went, the new universities started
sprouting up left, right and centre, and that regime disappeared. A new regime came in,
but I was very lucky teaching with that team of people, to pick up that group of students

who'd actually been selected by someone else. We were very lucky to just be there at that particular moment. In fact Rachel was far more indebted to Alison Wilding, Ed Allington and Richard Wilson than me. She's become a good friend now, but at the time I was much more in a sort of supportive role than the sort of dynamic teacher. That has emerged later, actually.

Do you think someone like Rachel arrived with everything she needed? Did she need to be there?

Yes, I think so. Hugely so, yes. What the teaching context there gave was incredibly studio-based and produced a critical dynamic, between this extraordinary exceptional group of staff, and Eric Bainbridge was also in that group. It was a really extraordinary circumstance to bring these five artists together. It provided a kind of critical breadth. Whether those students then, or really successful artists now, would ever really credit that, I don't know. It was such a fertile environment for ambition really, and motivation, to do things with the work. I can remember Eric Bainbridge, whom I admire hugely – I think he's one of the most exciting artists and teachers actually – looking at this girl's work. It was very clunky and awkward and he just turned to her and said, 'well, why not stick all those bits together with bubblegum?' To make her completely rethink a way of doing something. He wasn't just being facetious; he was actually being really ahead of his time. If you think of what's happened to contemporary art since, you just know that that remark changed her life. Whether she became a famous artist or not, was neither here nor there – I don't think she did, I think she went off and did something completely different ... But you can see somebody's inspired thinking.

You were around at a time of some major figures in art education: George Fullard, William Coldstream at the Slade, Lawrence Gowing at Chelsea. Are there figures of that stature and creativity working in art education today? And, if so, where is their influence being felt?

The influence now is coming from the art world itself, and this is the most complicated part of art education today; art has become so successful out there that it's now impacting, to some extent, on what happens within art schools in a way that maybe hasn't quite happened before. The giant educationalists, who really had visions about art schools becoming dynamic centres for the exchange of ideas, processes and ways of thinking, both George Fullard and Lawrence Gowing and, in a strange way, Coldstream were like that. They didn't see them as places that manufactured finished artists who could be delivered straight into the art world ... they saw them as places where there could be an ongoing process of revealing and testing out, and changing and offering huge opportunity to people. Whereas now there is an intense pressure for young, emerging artists about surviving. That's very different from, say, 20 to 30 years ago. I wouldn't want to say it's a good or a bad thing; it's just a shift. You're looking at what's going on in the art world – outside of the art school – for information, for how to develop.

And what effect is that having on the art school and educational system?

It's making it incredibly economy-driven. It's making everyone very, very aware of the economies of being an art student, of how to relate that to economic survival after art school. I would say the running order when you leave is first how am I going to survive economically; then where am I going to survive economically; and, thirdly, how am I going to make my work? Whereas previously it was first how am I going to make my work; then, how am I going to pay for it?; and last where am I going to do that? 'Oh, in a shed in the middle of nowhere.' It's all reversed the other way, and this isn't a criticism; you can't blame people for that, because just trying to survive in London alone, as we all know, is a huge challenge.

Is this the same for teachers?

Yes, totally. The pressures, that is, for how to survive as an artist. Although the income from teaching does provide some kind of financial security but the responsibilities and accountabilities as a teacher are now under scrutiny in ways that were not so until comparatively recently. Teaching has offered a false security that has not done teachers, their work, or art schools any good. And in the end these accountability exercises were an inevitability to reveal complacency.

You mentioned to Godfrey that there was a time when art schools were seen as a form of patronage. 'There was less emphasis on whether you showed your work or not: it was about having the space and time to make work within your own studio, and teaching

afforded the means to do that. That whole culture of art schools being patrons has virtually disappeared without trace'. It now seems almost to be a career choice of a kind; you go to art school and you'll do the MA and PhD, and that's a way to continue being part of the system ...

Yes. I find it very difficult to talk about this aspect of it, and you maybe need to go to a higher authority, who really knows about it! The dogmatic feeling we have that there's the academic path, which gives you lots of job opportunities within academia and so you plod on through. You do your BA, you maybe have a year out, you do your MA and you do your PhD and then you're away, is deeply flawed as a concept for an artist. And maybe this has all come about through people actually saying, 'we don't have to call artists "artists" anymore, they can be anything ...' It's a slightly politicised thing; are they just like everybody else? Well, of course we're just like everybody else, it's just we have this desire to make visible things that usually aren't visible, and therefore it's a kind of useless profession. Trying to make it thoroughly useful through this academic trajectory seems to give it a kind of pretension, where there are problems with honing the artist into this highly academic being, while they're going to become enormously theoretical through this process.

At the expense of what?

At the expense of the risk that their work at the coalface might have to experience. Although PhD students struggle to survive – they're trying to get funding, they're trying to do this, they're trying to do that – they're also under this kind of protective umbrella, which I think is very make-believe. The other route, which is taking artists straight to the art world, and the hugely competitive thing that it is now and what that entails, and how they battle it out with galleries everywhere, and showing in your bedroom cupboard etc., that's sort of fantastic in a way. But it's also not without its problems, in emphasising the exhibition as a sign that you're alive, 'yeah, I'm alive, I've got a show.' And if you don't have a show you're dead. So both paths for me have huge problems. Just to finish this off without being too boring; the path towards the art world and showing your work and trying to get a job that just tides you over a bit, those artists who are succeeding in that, they are showing they do not want to do teaching jobs. They don't mind visiting, maybe doing something that's one day a week, but that's not going to pay for anything now. So you've got this huge rift building up, where the only real way that you can survive through teaching now is to do a full-time job. The part-time jobs don't pay.

Was there a time when you got a different artist coming in to teach, that wouldn't come in now, because of something to do with what you call the industrialisation of education?

Up to say the mid-1980s, the hierarchies in art schools were very much that there were these older people who were running the departments. They were rock-solid in their jobs and maybe the work had taken a back seat over the years. You could go around to Sheffield, or visit numerous art schools, and you'd find these very reliable, solid characters whom the students would often treat in a very paternalistic kind of way. Yes, they were usually men and what happened with the change in dynamic in art schools through the YBAS, through the whole rise of Thatcherism, the rise of an aggressive art market, is that educationally that whole system was challenged. So in answer to your question; I think the patronage thing went out of the window, because it had fallen foul of itself, it had shot itself in the foot. It was providing people with comfy incomes and stability, but it wasn't doing what it had set out to do originally 20 years earlier, in the 1960s, which was to foster this kind of huge creative resource. It sort of backfired on itself. And maybe there should never have been full-time jobs, maybe the patronage thing should have always been about three-year contracts, or something, so that it could have refuelled and revitalised itself. And the huge scrutiny that art schools are now under, or that education is under with the Research Assessment Exercise, although I think it's dreadful, there is a sense that you've got to be doing something in order to be able to teach it. That sleeping thing, where you had people who were really sleeping through education, who were running departments, but weren't doing any of their own work, has gone. That's been challenged in some way, maybe in the worst possible way. I don't want to sound as if I support the RAE, because I think these things are all cockeyed, but in answer to your question; the people who are visiting now are usually very successful artists that art schools are trying to get in. That wasn't what the visiting programmes were necessarily about so much previously.

Just on what you said about the RAE; would you agree that, as an artist, you need a practice in order to teach?

I think so.

In what state does the practice have to be in?

Good point. Very good point. The emphasis on the famous artist, who has zillions of exhibitions to their name, is obviously satisfying students curiosity, and it's important to satisfy that. But there is a whole raft of other artists who are working in all sorts of other ways. I met this artist I have a huge respect for, who's an ex-Goldsmiths student, Liadin Cooke. We just met the other day at The Henry Moore Institute, where she's got a drawing, and this one superb drawing had taken her two years to do. She's been an artist, but not within this kind of massive production way of showing left, right and centre. It's been a quiet, highly contemplative, very serious, intense activity, with a lot of thinking as well. Sometimes the London artist identity takes precedence over maybe many other forms of being an artist, some of which may be about not producing a single thing. And, my God, we should support that.

While I agree there is a variety of ways of working, we should also acknowledge what kind of condition a practice needs to be in, in order to have a certain kind of vitality and value. And I'm not just talking about some sort of commercial value necessarily …

It is a state of being. I would sum it up as that, where there is a deep sense of longing, and there isn't necessarily the product yet for that longing, but it's there and it needs that time and it needs that desire and it needs that process of deep introspection in order for something to then be catalysed. Those people can have a profound and lasting influence on balancing institutions and what goes on in them, but unfortunately at the moment they're a sort of breed that isn't evidenced within art schools. You see, it's not just about the rote production of work. A lot of these things that scrutinise education and judge it don't have a category for that, they don't know how to.

You've put your finger on something else that came up with Mark Godfrey around a question of failure. When he asked you about what you'd do if you could run an art school for a day – one of those kinds of fantastical 'what if' questions – and, to

paraphrase, you talked about acknowledging a certain kind of failure as being an implicit part of a process of working that's not so much acknowledged now.

Failure, and we've got to examine what that word failure means, because I see failure as a very positive thing, not as a negative thing. I see it as a whole process towards finding out about something. That if something doesn't work it carries an enormous amount of information with it. Whether you are then able to go on and make something work, I don't know, but that phrase of 'whether something works or not', is an extraordinary phrase: where does it come from? Does it come from the industrial revolution? Was it about discovering machinery? And the fact that it's the word 'work' that is associated with 'labour', in some way suggests there's a breakage when something doesn't work. I don't think there necessarily is a breakage. I think it's more that something hasn't fulfilled a kind of promise. That isn't necessarily an image in one's head, it can be as much a kind of sense of touch, or a driving towards something that doesn't yet have an image, or a visual identity, and that's what you're striving to discover. So the failure of it is that it hasn't quite happened yet, but I don't know what it should be. And that not-knowing state is often deemed a kind of failure; you must know what you want, you must know what your intentions are, you must know what your aims and objectives are. It's such a harsh, unforgiving language. And yet the not knowing can often be that, as an artist, you're not working necessarily with very vivid visual, cerebral processes. You're actually trying to find those, and that's why you want to make the stuff, or draw the stuff, or paint the stuff. So the failure thing to me is very much associated with that striving for, and that struggle. Two words that I know are very unfashionable. But there is something for me in the striving to find the visual thing that isn't yet in one's head. It just doesn't have a cerebral identity.

Can I read you something? It's part of a statement you made where you say '... teaching reciprocates my activities as an artist, as does my family (I have five children, now grown up). Sculpture for me has been ephemeral and temporary, and dominating my experience has been an experimental approach to making and exhibiting where I have prioritised an interventionist approach of the here and now ...' Looking across your work, there seems to me to be a number of themes that you constantly touch upon; the first, I would say, is the scourge of subject-led work, and maybe that goes back to the notion of failure. The second is how you got here. There's a certain kind of humility and self-effacement about how you got involved in this whole thing, and at the same time there's a kind of dissent, or scepticism, in your relationship to it. The third is sculpture as a theme, and the fourth is your family. I was just wondering what it all adds up to?

This is not going to answer the question, but I can remember when I did a talk at Goldsmiths, and I then did a talk at Camberwell, they were quite close together. I had had four years out, because of the children, and life had got extremely tough in all sorts of ways economically. When I went back in, I was quite startled by the changes in that brief time that had happened. I left Chelsea in 1978, and then the twins came along and that stopped me from going back into teaching. There were reasons I had to leave in 1978; one child was quite ill recurringly, and it was really becoming a nerve-racking process. So I left, and then the twins came along in 1981, and I then went back to teaching in 1984 at Brighton. By then I had five children, which was like a guilty secret, trying to not let people know this terrible fact of life. But I remember doing this talk at Goldsmiths, and then, when I got the job at Camberwell, it came up again, because I was describing how when the five of them were around it was very difficult to work. So I would go into the studio very late at night, and I actually hadn't got a clue what to make, so I'd turn all the lights off. I've described this many times in slide talks; it was a very, very pivotal moment, when making things not through an image, but through touch, which made me think about this whole issue of where the subject is in the work. Having described that when I did these slide talks, on two occasions students would say to me, 'well, what's more important to you: being a mother, or being an artist?' And I would just have to say being a mother. There was this recoiling in horror from the audience that one could actually say that – prioritise being a mother over being an artist.

But why were you being asked to make a choice in the first place?

Exactly. I didn't have the wits to say what you pointed out; it isn't about a choice, the two are actually reciprocal, although an impossible combination, and I wouldn't necessarily recommend it to anyone, because the split is a very cruel schism; they're both intensely creative processes, but they stand in absolute opposition to each other. One is selfish and the other has to be selfless. The mix is not good. But being asked by these students I felt so put on the spot, and it was like I had to tell the truth under those circumstances. Where you're maybe picking up the dissent is the fact that there was a kind of feeling of inhumanity about the whole role of teaching in an art school, that was rooted in how you portrayed the artist as this ruthless ambitious creature, which of course is true to some extent, in order to survive, and therefore anything else that might soften that was considered a nauseating, or slightly repellent characteristic. Now things are very different. Things have changed in that respect.

Is subject-led work still a scourge?

No. The way in which I might want to initiate work is still through trying to find something, trying to find a form, trying to find an image, trying to find how these materials can become articulate and coherent, and that I won't know what the subject is. At the moment I'm just making these endless folded forms and they look very sort of vaginal and lip-like and ear-like, or they look like folded cloth. And I hate that, because the image of them is too dominant. So a journey with them has begun, and I don't quite know where to make this folded form start to become absolutely itself, rather than having these other connotations. And maybe that shape is impossible without those connotations. So they're finding a subject and I'm reneging on the subject that they've found. Another artist would begin with saying, 'well, I want this very kind of inward-looking shape and it's going to be very bodily and it's going to be very visceral.' They would be very confident about placing those qualities at the forefront of the process. There was a time during the 1990s when the image-based, pictorial object was so dominant. That's what I was thinking about when I was talking about subject-led work.

Can you teach art?

No, but you can provide an endless process of enquiry and debate and discussion and conversation around it. But can anyone do that? No, I think that there are two things in that question; one is the object itself, and the other is the privilege of meeting the person who's made that object, who then enables you to question the object through them. So, there's this three-party thing; the object becomes a prompt and a prop for understanding that individual's deepest thoughts, and I think that does require a certain kind of knowledge of the histories that that object might promote. Whether it's an object that's referring very much to the here and now in terms of the galleries, or whether there's a bit of Arte Povera in there, or a bit of Minimalism, a bit of Victorian kitsch. Having that knowledge, you can bring it to the individual and maybe wake them up a bit about those things, or they might already know those things very clearly ... That might have come over as really kind of arrogant; I just want to qualify that. When I'm saying 'that knowledge', I'm not assuming that that individual doesn't have that knowledge as well, but that kind of pooling of knowledges becomes very revealing in how you can then find out about emotional expressions that might be trying to be communicated through this object that's in front of you. If you're going to talk about kitsch, or Victorian figurative art, and this individual says, 'yes, that's exactly what I was referring to', it becomes a point of contact in how one would want to do that now.

And what do you think is your responsibility as a teacher?

For me, it's to ensure that a student feels they have a working process with which they can leave their BA degree course, in order to set themselves up as the artist of their choice, as the artist they want to be. And are there enough methodologies at their disposal to be able to do that within the economic restrictions that they're going to have to endure. So you're not just promoting them to use polished stainless steel and incredibly expensive materials. You've actually said; 'try this out in all these other ways, so that you can at least begin to realise ideas and thoughts in your heads in a very direct, expedient kind of way.'

And the student's responsibility?

I've always thought the student's responsibility was to want to do it, quite simply. That was it. It's almost the question you might ask those incoming students: 'do you really want to do this?'

Can I ask you something about the relationship of the school to the world? I'm thinking about this in relation to your commission *Stack* for the Royal Festival Hall ...

Stack, for me, is a bit of a failure. I'm afraid it doesn't completely work; its base is too big and all sorts of things went slightly wrong with it, including having to cut off 60 centimetres at the top, so it doesn't quite go the height. But the location interests me, this idea of making something that big, which is then almost camouflaged into the Royal Festival Hall. What I'm almost suggesting with that work is that the public space is actually not just about a big glitzy kind of commissioned work. It's about an intervention, it's about drawing attention maybe to qualities of the space that wouldn't necessarily be looked at. Or using a space that's almost an unusable space, like a ship in a bottle, which is what the whole point of *Stack* was. So those kind of things would, I hope, enable me to talk to students in a very open way about the hazards of taking on a really full-on kind of public space like the South Bank, but still having a kind of flexible relationship with it, and trying something out that may not necessarily work, but to not be afraid of that. Several people have said to me that piece doesn't work, and that's fine. I'm glad they've been honest with me, because I don't think it works, and as I say to the students, 'I'd give myself a low 2.2 for that'. I'm very grateful to the South Bank for giving me that opportunity, but it was a hazardous experience. It was a real roller-coaster ride and I slightly lost my nerve with it. Therefore things, just at the last minute, went awry with it, and one has to live with that. You can't ask them to take it down again, so it's tricky. But I hope it provides students with a chance to be critical of their so-called teacher … if they ever wanted to talk about it, it would provide the context to say 'look this is a public work, and it hasn't completely worked, but it's interesting to have been put in that position; it's not just the protective space of the gallery.'

The more you talk about this, the more I understand that when you talk about failure, you're actually talking about learning …

Yes. It's so interesting, because when I was talking to Alison Wilding, about it not working, she said, 'no, it doesn't completely work.' But she said, 'isn't it wonderful that we can still be learning?' And she's absolutely right. I think that's part of the risk, and if I seem sceptical, it's because I don't entirely believe in the degree show system. It's a whole load of other things that are buried in that experience. It's great that they can put on these shows, but the show isn't the thing that's going to count at all, unfortunately it's going to be many other things. It's like being an athlete, isn't it? A fantastic athlete, except they've got this dodgy tendon in their ankle, and getting the athlete who's absolutely completely all-in-one and can run the 100 metres without hamstrings snapping and everything. The artist always has something. The very good degree show doesn't entirely convince me, because the sort of flaw that that person is going to have to overcome is the thing that's really interesting.

Why I asked the question in the first place was something that came up around subject-led work, and what you think got lost, or misplaced with the focus on subject-led work. You seemed to suggest that what got lost was an interrogation of context, or a set of relationships between the work and the world, so to speak. And somehow *Stack* made me curious about what kind of relationship you understand the art school should have with the world, and how this exchange should happen. How the world comes into the school and how you take the work to the world …

I saw the very dogmatic subject-led art as providing such a lot of equipment for theoretical semiotics, for semiotic language to be used. The object itself was just an equation for verbal language, providing a very fixed context, in which the object would be shown, for example in the white cube. So you got a whole cycle of things happening that were utterly dependent on each another. And then I began to see that the art school system, with the degree show as the culminating glory of that three- to four-year BA, or two-year MA thing, as absolutely reciprocal to that white cube orthodoxy. The object that went into it that would provide the theory, the verbal language, would provide the exchange. So something seemed to be going missing, and it seemed to be this huge territory between the art school and the gallery. Or it seemed to be about the process of thinking, or dreaming, or making, or imagination, trusting – a whole load of words – and the kind of flow chart that would come out of those words just seemed to be vanishing. It's not that I want every artwork to show its process – I don't – but it's as though something of how the artist would come to the position of being able to realise a work was getting less and less recognition, or acknowledgement. It was more the delivery and the end product that was important, and the best way of showing that – which is absolutely true, one can't deny it – is the white cube space. But it's not the only way, and it seems you don't always need a white cube space to do what you've got to do as an artist. It's been like trying to give students the breadth of experience that moves beyond and outside of that, that I think is very important. Which is why something like the challenge of the South Bank was important, because it's the biggest antithesis to a white cube in terms of space. Not in terms of people – the white cube space can attract huge numbers of people, and the South Bank has huge numbers of people going through it. But they're apparently very different groups of people, so that was the challenge.

And finally, how's the health of art education in the UK? Is it in robust health?

Yes, I think it is. The problem is getting the younger artists into the art schools to teach. I know some really fantastic younger artists and they will only visit. They're selling their work, they're kind of making ends meet through some other route. But intellectually and inspirationally and creatively, as people who can discuss work, they're fantastic. But they don't want that commitment, they don't want to be in that institutional framework. That is going to be an increasing problem.

Phyllida Barlow taught at the Slade School of Fine Art, London and is now retired from teaching.

Thomas Bayrle — early May — Frankfurt Hauptbahnhof.

You worked as an apprentice at the Gutmann factory in Goppingen before studying graphics and textile design at the Werkkunstschule at Offenbach, after which you co-founded Gulliver Presse. Who or what influenced you in terms of the artist or teacher you would become?

I was fascinated by this very old-fashioned technology of weaving. I was fascinated on the one hand by the rigidity of it, and, on the other, by its possibilities of diversification. You have different binding qualities, from simple ups and downs to all the fascinating thing of Jacquard.

Is Jacquard a card system?

Yes, it's a card system. It was a pre-computer experience. Now it's over 50 years old.

This was pre-Atari?

No, with Jacquard, we had to weave complex fabrics so on the one hand it was actually work, and on the other hand it was ornamentation, patterning, whatever. It was in the flatness – you have about 8,000 different threads per square metre. So I found out how diverse, how fantastic even a piece of cloth can be. But I didn't think of anything like teaching at the time. My aim then was to make patterns and ornamentation by weaving and by printing. I started with printing as it was easier. That was why I went to Offenbach. I just wanted to know what I wanted to print, what was interesting for me, but I still had in mind what it was for; it was not only a print on a t-shirt, or just a print on cloth. I always had the fabrication of the cloth in mind. The main thing was the weaving of the weft and the warf, and next to that was what was on top of it. But the best was if these two things were united. After that I started making books. I had a small press together with a friend, called Gulliver Presse. We published people like Artmann, and several Viennese writers, but mostly concrete poetry. The fascination with ornamentation – mass ornamentation – came early on. I already liked these huge productions in 1962. You'd find thousands of cars in front of a car factory. I was fascinated by that, it really fired me up.

You could say that the core of your practice was already established by then, the dot to the grid, superstructures, and so on.

Technically I knew it already. But there was a time when I made all these attempts to get away from it as well, you know ... to be free.

Free from what?

Free from all these technologies, from all the narrowness of techniques. So I tried out a little expressionism, I tried out what you have to try out. But I wasn't convinced by these things, so I got back to technology. I made excursions; book excursions, weaving, but also emotional excursions like jazz music – it was already in the weaving very early on. This machine rhythm, the sound of the escalator – tak, tak, tak, tak, tak, tak. Or the sound of slow country machines – big heavy machines. The sound and the rhythm were of the same importance as the knowledge of this weaving technique, so it ran in parallel. For a while rhythm became even more important because you could survive by jumping into the rhythm of these machines, not by being rational and trying to overcome them. It was very emotional and I was very interested in jazz at the time, especially black rhythm and blues, black music, because it came close to the machines, many years before techno. I was also fascinated by murmuring technologies; the murmuring of the rosary is kind of subterranean, beyond intelligence, a kind of half-dream la, la, la, la, la, like thousands of bees. I found the same in technology, in traffic jams. These things fired me up for several years and when you want to make something, you come back to these things but they're not always there.

At Gulliver Presse we made very small editions of books of up to only 50 or so. Hand-made, very well printed and bound, really perfect. We also did very cheap things so to speak; posters, one-day posters, like in 1968 we did a lot of agit-prop things that were needed at the time. Both sides – so-called very high and very low quality, very emotional, but very conceptual.

What I want to maybe emphasise is that we have this layer below all this technology, which is a kind of dangerous humming, breathing atmosphere on the one hand. But on the other hand it's a strength, it's where everything comes from. This breathing power is under us, this kind of melting, this jelly that is not formed yet. That is part of a vocabulary that I wanted to bring up in the interview because I thought about this the last few days ... what would be interesting for me to say here? Today we are too much involved in making products. It's a product time. As an artist you make a product. But one of the main things is being able to live with those muddy areas that you can't totally formulate, a kind of jelly. It can be firm, it can be soft, it's not clear. We need to stay with this not being clear, not being able to touch, and not being able to bring something into form immediately, or for a while at least. As I see it now, by the second or third semester students in art schools already try and produce products.

What do you think we're overlooking?

We're overlooking this uncertainty, of being in the condition of not getting everything, of being unsure … Being kind of soft or jelly-like ourselves. When you look at society today and you see all this news, you see all this mud, this wonderful mud! We can't just step in or fit in right there and make a nice product, something that just fits. We also have to fail; we have to stay for a while in this situation where we're on the edge of failing. Today is more about bits and pieces. It's hard work to stay with it and maybe it takes 10 years of not knowing why you do something, and after 10 years something comes together. It's like something bending … I'm thinking softer methods.

How do you teach that?

It taught me. When I started teaching I quickly found out that I'm not the guy who has the answers, students would have laughed at me after the first day if I'd tried to persuade them I did. So I decided to tough it out at the time. It seemed all my colleagues were using another method, as if they knew something, and they stood there and dispensed this to students. I was the only one who was like, yeah … in the wind. The result of this was that the students decided, OK, if he doesn't do it then we have to do it, so they took advantage and gradually I found out that this was actually a very productive position. While other professors deliberately tried to make them take a position, in my class it happened because students thought I was a kind of yeast-like thing, a kind of fermentation that didn't have a lot of mass, a kind of nervous ingredient. This realisation stimulated small groups like Tobias [Rehberger] and some friends, to take over because of my not being able to lead. That was the moment I could come back to them because all of a sudden there was an opposite.

What do you think your responsibility was as a teacher?

To be very true and honest towards myself and towards the students. To inform them I had some experience here, some experience there and in between no experience at all, so they'd have to make up for this lack. I had a lot of discussion about this with Beuys because he came to the Städelschule. Of course he was in a different position. He had five tongues when he talked, but he understood me, he understood this lingering. I wasn't this cool guy who takes risks; I was this conservative guy, and I was suffering through it. That's maybe what students felt; that it wasn't me trying to be cool. Some people tried to help by saying, 'oh, it's OK, everything goes.' Nothing went with me, it just didn't go. I was so red-faced when students approached me. I was embarrassed and I had to step aside. But after several years I found that wasn't such a bad thing and good students came into my class in any case. At first I thought maybe they came because I wouldn't bother them. But a dynamic grew around me, which wasn't my doing, I didn't shape it. But when it was there I could pretty much work with it, and it made me mature a bit. That had nothing to do with generosity, it had more to do with helplessness. I put this helplessness and uncertainty out there. I didn't try and hide it because they wouldn't have believed me anyway. After several years you develop something like a positive routine, and I had some very good colleagues, like Kasper König. He liked and accepted me like that, because it's how many artists are. They're kind of shy, they're not businessmen. Now Eliasson, nothing against him, but he knew what he was doing.

Who?

Olafur Eliasson.

With that attitude or approach you probably wouldn't get a job now ...

Yes! I'm too slow but then I learned. Of course I wouldn't approach it like that today, but then again, I am not the same guy anymore.

You're no longer red-faced?

I can't be and I don't want to be. So actually I was educated in the first years as a teacher by the circumstances in the school. Then I developed and they benefited.

This was at the Städel?

Yeah, yeah, this was the Städel. But I was also teaching a lot in Japan and in other countries.

Michael Krebber is your successor?

Yeah.

What does he inherit, or what's left behind when you go?

In a way I picked him and worked hard to get him into this position, because they need a guy like him.

What were you picking?

He's also a very divided guy; on the one hand he's very authoritative, and knows exactly what he wants. On the other hand, he's very unsure. Maybe we both have not very balanced personalities. The Städel has some very straight guys, so it needs at least one who's not so straight, and that's why I picked him. Nobody wanted him at first, they were all against him. So I said to Daniel [Birnbaum] he should watch out for the mediocre figure. If they'd all be like Krebber it would be impossible; you can only have one of his type. It's a real learning for the student, for the school and for the teacher when you enter an institution. They have to grow together. When I was visiting Goldsmiths, I looked down at the students from the balcony, and I was fascinated that Goldsmiths could do it like that.

What did you see?

I saw something like a zoo, or stage. It looked very tough. There seemed to be no place to hide any sort of weakness, because everything was floodlit, you know, but I wouldn't … I mean they have these examples like Damien Hirst, and there's no doubt this school has had a very important impact. The same as Saint Martins, but in a different way. We had a lot to do with the Slade. We had a lot of exchange with them, so I learned a lot about the English system. I like it, there's a lot of directness, which is very important. I worked in advertising and you can't work there like I did in the Städel. You have deadlines. You have to present. I had a business for four years, with five or six employees, so I know what that is, that world. It was very important that I knew that world too.

Jörg Heiser, writing for *frieze*, described your interests in terms of 'the oscillation between macro and micro, dots and networks'. You said 'when I concentrate on the detail the whole work becomes recharged.' I was thinking of this as a metaphor for a certain kind of relationship or connection between the student and the institution – the teacher and the body of students/individual student, and how this way of approaching things somehow enabled you to continue teaching; to be with this group and within an institution ...

That approach goes back a long way. My parents were both into ethnology, so China and other cultures were very present in our household. This metaphor, this Confucian cell-body-population, this zooming from micro to macro was always very clear to me. Even as a child I was fascinated by the idea of a single cell and the 30 billion cells that make up me. That each single cell can reproduce me and yet, that I'm unique and there's only one of me. But I also brought this fractalisation generally to whatever problem I had. I'd divide a problem into smaller problems. Which was a kind of cheap trick, but it worked. When I had a problem, I'd kind of divide myself schizophrenically so there was a lot of me's. I think this happened early in my life and it wasn't very well received. When I was a child there was a question of me having multiple personalities, which at the time was seen as a very weak thing because you had to be singular and whole.

Were these different personalities visible to other people?

I tried to hide them, but yes, they were visible. It was like putting something together and it falling apart, putting it together and it falling apart again. Very early on I had this metaphor for myself that I was like this meadow consisting of billions of little creatures, and each creature consisted of billions of elements. I didn't see the world vertically, I saw it horizontally. I could never work with this pyramid-shape because I knew it was weak. Everyone has a cock and they all want to fuck, it's very simple. It's a different approach to looking up and seeing somebody's feet. I think it's helped me, this scale change. And maybe it was only to escape, but I think it was also for getting close to and dealing with problems.

You once wrote 'my view of society is flat – horizontal – (electric) field / fabric / network. The vertical elements are plucked from the surface, like hay, grass in a meadow'.

In the class I didn't get it for a long time, I used to wonder what this or that guy was doing.

This 'not getting it' seems to be really important to you when you talk about the kind of 'unpleasantness' that you say 'is constitutive of a productive studio or student-teacher relationship'. And this 'unpleasantness' is related to what you describe as 'not understanding for a long time what someone is doing'…

That's right. It is a very good quality, which I had to learn.

That's quite a tough thing to live with.

Yeah, it's really tough. In the end it's tougher than pushing students until there's a result … Something hangs there, its not … It's not solved for a long time I think. That's what I brought to the class. It's like a kind of training; you want to have muscles but you don't have them yet, so you have to be patient, yeah, just patient … it's very simple … timeless.

You talk about your relationship with students as being based on an equality of rights or a 50/50 kind of relationship. What is this equality of rights?

It's built on them bringing something with them. They have their youth and experience and I think I've never tried to destroy that because it's of value; something that's not maybe developed yet but it's there. I've always thought that I'm the other half of something, so that we can negatively and positively combine this. It takes time and patience, as for a long time I don't get what they want. Like Sergei Jensen, who came to the school for an interview. He had a huge portrait of his mother, an oil painting that didn't fulfil any of the criteria. I just thought 'if he comes with this then we have to take him', because it was all that he presented even while he was asked to bring 40 pieces of work in A3 or a video or whatever else. It took the help of two people to bring this big thing in. I had to convince my colleagues to take this guy. I found out later it wasn't intended to be provocative or anything, it was very … honest. So I think I find my people by … I don't look for fashionable moods or whatever. No, its more this suspicion that there's a kind of reality and behind this reality must be powers that have caused this reality. You think there's oil or coal in that area but you haven't dug there yet. I'm not a mystic. I'm a very average guy but I know that one of the main qualities you want people to have in art school is something hidden. Not because they want to hide it but because they can't bring it out It's worth considering this quality as a new energy resource that you develop. You have this atmosphere in the class where all contradictions are allowed. Not out of some misplaced liberalism, but out of necessity. When they develop they'll produce some very strange plants. Teaching is a hard job. It's a bit like being in a hospital; you get different cases and some very big contradictions and you have to get along with them. I took people who were complete opposites or who maybe had a very old ability like drawing for example. Other classes are more streamlined and they wouldn't take people with such an ability, because they wouldn't fit. People like that maybe don't always fit in in a school, but there's so much these people can do. I'm very critical of our schools when it comes to this ability, this knowledge about materials. There was a moment when it was decided it wasn't necessary anymore, but there will come a day where they'll look for these 'idiots' who are skilled. I took them all seriously, and maybe we didn't understand each other, but it's like being in a band; you need this spirit in the studio. Art schools should also have very dull, normal people. It's necessary to have a broad range. I was always more a Venturi fan. I never really was a Phillip Johnson fan, but there are a lot of Philip Johnsons today in art schools.

You're talking about a kind of vernacular when you talk about what you call the dull or normal. You're talking about a kind of vernacular, which is what Venturi, and Scott Brown championed in *Learning from Las Vegas* ...

Absolutely. I invested a lot in teaching because I never saw it as taking away my time. The first few years I had to suffer, but then I saw it as very productive. It was really helping me at the same time as I hope it was helping students.

This began when you had the foundation year, because you didn't have your own class then?

That was very good. I had that for 10 years.

It seems that students ended up in your class ...

That was it.

So you got these odds and ends and probably the basis of something very interesting.

You're right. It was very good training, like training in the second division of a football league. How they fight to get into the first division; that is where the fight is, where it is toughest.

Tobias Rehberger said that you were 'always so awake, always open to a lot of things.' Given that you've been teaching for almost 30 years, I was wondering how you sustained that kind of engagement over time …

It grew, because there comes a moment when it's more than a job; it's part of your existence. One day I will die, and, like the old painters, I have a responsibility to be true to my work, not for the benefit of others, not to be able to stand before others, but to be able to stand before myself. That is why I maybe did a little more than others. I also liked it. But when you do it, you really have to do it or don't do it at all. I've often seen that people just took the job because it brought in money. Or, when the money wasn't such an issue, it brought a kind of status. But I've always thought of it as a part of my life, and you want to have a full life. I don't want to have empty years so that's why I did it. It has nothing to do with altruism, it has to do with the purpose of your life. It's not religious or anything, but you have to fulfil your things.

Can I go back a little bit and ask you what kind of engagement you think the art school should have with the world? I'm thinking of what Christine Mehring calls your 'double existence', she's referring to 1968, when you had the company Bayrle Kellermann. You've just explained that teaching was obviously more than just a job for you.

Yes, art is really important. Not because it's a second religion, as it's often called. No. It's a different machine; art is an organism, art is not only about a yes and no, but about many yes's and no's.

Does this go back to where we first started? In other words, that if you take art seriously, then it seems it has to be more than just a product that's being made?

Yeah, I can't fully express it and it shouldn't sound like preaching or religion but we lose a lot when 80 per cent of the people are treated as worthless. That is really bad for society. I see it as being about values and something that is of more worth than just getting the next lot of oil or the next year of energy sorted out. It's a real loss that we fail to use so many people's abilities, because they're not specified, because the problem is that we're looking for specified things. I believe deeply in this because I had abilities that I didn't regard as abilities, I didn't know I had them. In 10 or 15 years' time, lots of people will have abilities that currently have no value. In terms of our development it's very important in the broadest way.

And art can have something to say about this?

Quite a lot. It always has had. It has to do with wasting values, the kind which have been valued by people like Samuel Beckett, James Joyce or Flann O'Brien. They were modern people, and they weren't sentimental … It's about existence.

When Christing Mehring talks about your 'double existence', she's discussing the shooting of Rudi Dutschke in April 1968 and how 'this was a defining moment in German politics and culture, which separated right from left and revolution from the establishment.' You talked to her about having worked late into the night to produce a poster of Rudi Dutschke and how you 'cheerily went into work the next morning producing Mon Cheri' at the company you ran with Hans Kellermann. For Mehring, this encapsulated 'the slippery way in which your practice has long straddled the divides between agit-prop and advertising, commodity criticism, commodity culture, art and design.' I want to add; teaching and socialising, or teaching and community, something like that … would it be OK to add that?

Yes. Teaching has both sides, you're never really a hero. Maybe you're close to it once, but you're also very average. Like a mother with her children, she has to make sure that they go to school, that they eat. Seen from the Left, I did not have value, I was not the guy, I was of no consequence. There were two, or even three, worlds and I was somewhere in between. I was on the one hand making money with advertising and on the other hand I saw that these people were fighting for something very important. At a certain moment, you're asked to be this man of consequence, who joins this or that camp. I felt I was in all camps and none of them.

Is this something that a student should be encouraged to cultivate, this kind of double existence?

Yes, but not as a position of weakness. Two days ago I spoke with Chus Martinez and she made the distinction between being political and being ideological. I want to be political but not ideological. Ideological is too narrow, while being political is a responsibility. It's important, because you have to have a conscience; you have to be responsible for what you do, and for why you do this or that. But being ideological is different. Ideology is a very narrow thing, you go into this one channel and I think I always failed at it. I had several offers, but I saw I'm not um ... I'm very average you know, I'm just um ... I didn't want to be outstanding in this case ... more the average man who all in all has a wide range.

[Thomas asks if I want coffee – he returns with the coffee.]

An artist like Magritte goes straight through the whole sea of possibilities. If you go straight through life, it has wonderful and ugly sides. It's pretty good when we can master that. I was always fascinated by the whole disco thing, with John Travolta. There's something very beautiful and ordinary in reality, which passes through everything. That doesn't mean you're above anything, but you are in everything. To be hip is so specialised and outside this mass of vulgarity. Vulgarity is a powerful thing, like Venturi said. Now art is very hip, very trendy, it's making no mistakes, it's a little fearful. That's my impression.

Is that also the case at the Städel?

Even there I see it a bit, but it's more so in Düsseldorf, and these huge schools where they're afraid they don't follow the right track, and are always alert to making a mistake. I've made a lot of mistakes and I've also not been very successful all the time, but all in all I'm very happy with it now. I'm an old man who can say I was lucky enough to have experienced good and bad things, and they added up to being quite OK. When I started teaching I was aware I was not one of these superstar artists. I wasn't sad about it, but realistic. I didn't try to compensate for it but I did think I could broaden my teaching, create a broad base, a broad delta of possibilities, a network. I developed a network, not a line.

But you also need those stars like Gerhard Richter around you, if for no other reason than to deflect the attention, so it's on them and not you. Which leaves you to get on and do something in that space ...

Yes. I admire Richter, and I admire Polke. But you have to see that life is more than only competing in something very special. It's more important to invest in this network, its more subversive. I'm subversive in the way that I want to develop this underground network, because it's still a little bit anarchic. I believe in this network that is not only about looking at the result or at the symptom, but also about looking at where the symptom is grown, is cooked, as a strength. It's about looking beneath things, looking in the basement.

Does the Klassen system have this kind of network?

I see the Klassen system as a good thing. When I started, it seemed to me a little reactionary, but then it turned out to be a bit like being in a football team. The team has a trainer and they meet every Tuesday to kick a ball around. And that is what I did every Tuesday. Even if I had nothing to say that day, I was still there.

[Phone call for Thomas.]

It's a wonderful thing but it's also turning into a more boring reality again.

What is?

The whole art thing. Now it's so hip, and maybe it's coming back to this being average, which is not such a bad thing.

Did you miss teaching when you stopped?

This profession is fantastic, as it's so hard to bring creativity out in other areas; to do something fragile. But I didn't really miss it because I had a lot to do and I got kind of tired. Not exactly burnt out, but tired. You need to put a lot of energy into it when you want to keep it burning. They actually wanted to get me back recently because Daniel is doing the Biennale. They wanted to make me principal for a while. I can't do it now, because you'd have to bring a new energy to it, it has to develop. Now I'd put more energy into the so-called craft facilities, because so many artists need special assistance from people who have this knowledge. It's also fine if you use pre-fabricated materials, factories, and so on, you need factories. But that isn't everything; you also need to make your own mistakes, at least on a small scale.

You knew Helmut Pohl, he was a good friend and one of your first dealers. He was also a member of the Rote Armee Fraktion. Did you design, as has been rumoured, the RAF logo?

Well, it's one of my principles not to let it out as this has been asked so often. Not wanting to talk about it, but he served 22 years in prison. I met him when he came out and he was really a broken man. Sure I was interested in what they did, and I was also in it when it started to be… a real murdering … I would have been too weak to… and also not convinced. I'm not so … I thought about it … you have to approach a banker, you have to tell yourself he's a bastard, he's a bastard … you have to kill him. I knew Holger Meins and so on, but you know, you have to force yourself to be like … to act like a crook, this is so unnatural. You hurt yourself, and you hurt your psyche deeply and that's what made me stop and escape from it. You have a bad feeling that you're leaving them alone and that you don't help them. But, you fly through all these things, not sarcastically but also not driven into a special channel where you wouldn't even be master of it. You must see you're a weak and moody guy and these people were different. People like Baader, he was really the guy, the commander. You have to know where you are.

With the APO (Extra Parliamentary Opposition) and Rudi Dutschke it seemed to be about civil rights issues …

Yes, absolutely. I knew him well and I was with him at several demonstrations. He came from the intellectual side, he had this automatism, he had this machine-like rat-tat-tat-tat-tat-tat. But he was intelligent, because there were also stupid people involved. Sometimes it was like 'huh, what does he say, he's in my party, he's on my side but I can't share what he said.' In 1971, I helped organise a big children's fair here, there were 70,000 children involved over six weeks. I organised it with another teacher, who's since died. That was our escape – to go more into the children's thing, away from this fighting thing. Another friend, Burkhardt, escaped to England, to London. He's a Presbyterian minister now. He was helped by a Protestant leader to get to London, otherwise he'd have ended up in prison.

What you called the jelly-like substance, what brings people together and builds community around ideas whether they're more extreme in the form of the RAF and the church, or slightly more benign in the form of an art school; do you think the energy and motivation is similar, it just goes in different directions at a certain point?

In the beginning it's very similar yes, you're absolutely right. That is also the necessary danger art has. Art has a real anarchic power, and it would be 'undangerous' without it. It's important that it's on the edge of things. One of Sartre's first books was about the *Räderwerk*, this machine that is drawing you in. You're drawn into it and then it's important that as an artist you say its not my ... I wouldn't even say I'm too weak but it's not my thing. I'm not the right guy for it and this is not an escape. I've thought about this for a long time, because there's always people who'll say, 'you bastard, you escaped.' This thing is really like glue – a very strong glue, so that I know what it means ... political necessity. It also has something to do with art school, because if you can't build up a closeness like that, then something's lacking. Students have to feel it's really hermetic.

Thomas Bayrle taught at the Städelschule (Staatliche Hochschule für Bildende Künste), Frankfurt.

Guillaume Bijl — a studio on the Leonardo
Campus of the Kunstakademie in Münster,
Germany — interview late at night in front
of his students.

What characterises your class?

You have to ask my students. I don't know exactly what differentiates my class from others. I give the students a lot of freedom. I don't interfere too much. Sometimes they show me their work during the year, and I make some small intervention, or I give some tips – I give more a mental helping hand. I might also suggest things that I think should happen, but I leave them free to correct things or not.

Do you choose the students in your class?

Yes, I choose the students. First they go to the orientation class. There is a selection from incoming potential students by six professors. We select say from about 300 applications. We choose around 50 each year.

What are you looking for when you select a student?

Sometimes it's the way they draw, or the variation of expression, their creativity. Also the content. There are no rules, but you feel things going in a certain direction.

Can you teach art?

Can I teach art? There has to be a potential. You cannot teach art if there is no potential, or willingness, or attempt to express something. When this is not available in a potential student, you cannot teach art. There has to be a wanting to express something. If you took a casual passer-by in the street and you said, 'come on, I am an artist and I'm a teacher and I'm a professor, just come by and I'll teach you art', that's not possible.

And can only artists teach art?

[Long pause.]

It's the best way; artists, with some kind of experience, are the best placed to teach art. It might also be that some non-artists, who are very strongly connected to art in general, could also be good teachers. It doesn't mean that all good artists are good teachers, I don't believe this either, but it's most fortunate when a good artist is a teacher.

Are there clear distinctions between where your work stops and your teaching begins?

No, there aren't. I also don't feel so much as a teacher myself. I feel in the first place an artist who gives a helping hand, or advice, to my students. No, there's no big distinction, no big distance.

I ask you because your work plays with categories. According to critic Martin Spellerberg, your work falls under two categories …

Who?

Martin Spellerberg is his name …

What is he, a writer?

A critic …

An art critic?

Spellerberg claims your work falls into two categories; the non-real within the real, and reality within the constructed. You yourself have other kinds of categories for your work; *Transformation Installations*, *Situation Installations*, *Compositions Trouvées*, *Sorry-Installations* … can you put your teaching into one of these categories?

That is really not what I'm teaching. You also see this in the work of the students; it has almost nothing to do with my work. I started as an autodidactic painter and went through all kinds of influences and things like that. When I stopped painting I started to make projects and conceptual projects. And then I began to make installations, and I also make more absurd work, which are the *Sorrys*, so I started with a wide range. And my experience with material and dealing with the public, that is the basis from which I teach, my experience, the wide range of forms I used and use, and an ability to help and stand by young artists … I also don't use the word students so much; I regard them as young potential artists.

What's the difference?

The difference is that students want to learn something and I don't look at them from above, as a professor. I see them more like equals. I'm just an older artist with more experience. I see them as young, potential, up and coming artists who are a little bit less experienced, who have their own way of working, their own vision. And, the work they do in my class is completely different from each other, so I leave the individual that is in each potential artist. If you see my class, nobody's work looks like my work. I'm not teaching or pushing my own form, rather I do the opposite; I see the students as individuals, or as young artists. So in my class you won't see a lot of look-a-like Guillaume Bijl's, but completely different forms and styles and individuals.

It doesn't matter what it is to you, basically?

It doesn't matter what it is.

When you say you allow your students such freedom, is there sometimes a desire as a student to have some kind of limits placed on the work?

I sometimes point out some corrections to students, or I say what I like or don't like about the work. I'm also busy with material and the feeling of material, the feeling of composition, the feeling of fiction and reality, the feeling of the perception of the viewer, the feeling of presentation. I'm a lot busier with that, and for the rest it's their own individual world they create. I'm busier indirectly towards the students, whom I call individuals, or young artists; I interfere more indirectly.

Do you work with the students outside the academy?

Yes. In the last five or six years we've done some exhibitions outside, which I also find very important, because then they're in the reality of the art world and out of the school system. I try to get out with my students quite a lot and show in other places, in public places.

And do you make work with them?

Yes, I help them in presentation.

Do they help you?

Do they help me?

With your work?

No. Not much. Sometimes I ask some students to help me in a technical way. Yes, that happens sometimes.

I'm interested in your manifesto – this is going back quite a long time – calling for the abolition of art centres and replacing them with socially useful institutions …

No, it was a pamphlet I wrote, *The Art-Liquidation Project*. There is a 'By Government Orders'; they have to close all these art spaces and replace them with more functional places like hospitals, army departments, other kinds of ministries, or driving schools. Galleries are turned into driving schools, or into carpet shops, or travel agencies, or marriage offices, or whatever. That is still going on. It's a series that I later called *Transformation Installations*. I no longer use this text specifically, because it's visually evident that you come into an art space that has become a discount mattress shop. It's obvious that the Kunsthalle, or the art space, is transformed into another space, so it means that the business, or by city orders, the art space is closed, and it has become another kind of functioning space. I started in 1979 and I still sometimes do a *Transformation*. But I also do a lot of *Compositions*, and sometimes I do a *Sorry*, and sometimes I make a *Situation*. In the 1990s, I did a lot of small museums, like a lederhosen museum, or wax museum. I played a lot with cultural tourism. But towards my students, I'm not busy with my work, with disseminating my work through them, because if you look around, it's all different …

So how socially useful is the art academy?

How socially useful?

[Long pause.]

Art in general, and art academies in particular, are good spaces to let people be busy with some more un-functional things in society. It's better that a young guy of 22 comes to the academy to try to make art, or expresses himself in a completely other way in a capitalist society. It's better that he goes to an academy when he's 22 than he goes to the army and to fight in Iraq, or whatever. So the action, or the intention to make art, and to make good art, I always find a big step in somebody's life in a positive sense, in a pacifist sense. Art is a pacifist expression – more so than working in a bank, going into the army, working on Wall Street or …

But surely it's as capitalised as any of those professions. Art goes to war also as propaganda, social realism, and so on. I think you're choosing extreme comparisons.

To make myself clear.

Could we do without the art academy?

What?

Could we do without it? You didn't go to art school, you had no formal training …

Yes, you can, of course. If there is a potential, a will in somebody, then he will express himself at a certain moment, at a certain time. Writers, they're all autodidactic. There's no school for writing, or is there? Is there a school for writing?

There are literature classes and creative writing courses …

Are there? But it's also something you cannot learn, it's like art. As an artist you can help young artists, or young individuals; I don't call this teaching. It's like a guy who wants to write, who wants to express himself, there must be a potential writer in him; nobody can teach him. A lot of learning you do by looking towards what happened before, or by reading what happened before. You can teach making plaster, you can help with mixing colours, things like this, but that's more like craft. That can be good for some people, to express themselves later, but art teaching and art expression has to be a potential within the student. You can support this as a teacher, you can support this will, and you can make the potential stronger. An academy is a place to protect young potential artists, to give them a shelter, a shelter from society in general.

Why do they need it?

Why do they need it?

Yes …

Because you need time to develop your own individual work and therefore you need a place, you need a shelter, you need protection, to develop the kind of work you want to do in the future. That is one point; I don't say it's the only one. The academy is also a place for feedback from other artists, from more experienced artists towards younger artists. I see it as a shelter because I never went to an academy. I never had this protection, so I started quite late. I did my first exhibition when I was 33. I never had this shelter, or feedback, or protection. This is why I think it's good.

Do you think because you didn't have this shelter, feedback, or protection, something suffered in the development of your own practice?

No, it did not, no. It was a pain in the ass, but it was a pain in the ass in that period. On the other hand I think, you cannot change your life and you cannot change your past. I worked in a bank and things like that for some years, and this gave me more strength to understand that I had to express myself in another way than work in a bank for 40 years. So the opposite was happening with me; when I was 23, I stopped making art for five years, and then at 28 I had the force to start again. As a young guy, I was also in the army and I then went to work in a bank. Perhaps this is why I mention these two professions, they're autobiographic elements and they gave me strength to know what I should not do; I came back to art with more strength than before. This is my personal story, but it is good that academies exist for potential artists, and that's why I also say protection, shelter and distance, because I did not have this experience.

But, as you say, it may not have been a bad thing that you didn't?

No, not completely, because the type of work I made at a certain moment is surely influenced by not going to the academy.

Maybe by working in a bank …

Yes, it's like that. I wasn't in the academy, but when there's a potential it will come out.

Is the academy system in Germany in a good state?

I think it's in a good state. It's a completely different system in Belgium. They don't have such good schools, or such good teachers. They haven't evolved a lot, either; they're very conservative, the academies in Belgium. They have middle-weight teachers, not really artists. Frustrated artists who teach and then become teachers. In Holland also there are no real artists; they are something in between, like a different category – second-hand artists.

But they're in the school system and they're frustrated, so they can't communicate well with potential artists. On the other hand, some good artists who are teaching can also be too determining … too dominating. When this happens you have classes where you see signs of the professor's work. I'm quite proud that you don't see much Guilllaume Bijl around here, except these beers, but these are just beers, they are not my work! The problem is that very weak artists who are teaching cannot help younger artists. There are some young artists who are potentially much stronger artists than their teachers will ever be. With the large amount of experience that I've had as an artist, and also the different stages in my life – my artistic life, I can recognise immediately when they're at a certain stage, so I can help a little bit in this or that. You can see which stage an artist is at. You feel this immediately – you have immediate communication. These very weak artists that are teaching have the opposite, because they only went so far as, I don't know, a mediocre Brancusi. They cannot evaluate, they don't know whether something is good or not. They cannot evaluate anymore, so they let them do something, but without intervention, without correction, because they cannot correct. Because they're at this stage here and these young artists are busy at that stage over there; they cannot correct there because they were never there, they never reached that stage. Only someone who reached that stage can go and correct at that stage.

And this comes from experience?

What is very bad for artists is to stop when they are 30 or 35, because they have nothing going on. This is a stupid art jungle and a stupid art market with exaggerated prices, like with Damien Hirst or Maurizio Catalan, and young artists go blind from this. Sometimes they cannot criticise and evaluate. They think this is fantastic work by Matthew Barney and if they're quite weak they're going to make something like an epigone of Matthew Barney. But Matthew Barney's work is not so good, and young artists are not so critical, so they start to make something that looks like it. If you cannot hold them at a certain moment, they will see all kinds of things. And they're going to work like [Thomas] Hirschhorn or Jason Rhodes, and things like that, because, of course, young artists are influenced directly by what's going on and what's avant-garde. And then a teacher can offer a helping hand or correction if he also went through this stage.

What is the value you say of not giving up at 30 or 35. Is it a kind of persistence?

That's important, yes. A lot of things are important in becoming some kind of good individual artist. There are a lot of developments that don't happen in every young artist. It can also be a disaster for some young artists; wanting to become this artist, which they'll never have the ability to become. That is a disastrous life. If you're busy with this when you're 40 or 50, and nothing really happens, and you don't make a remarkable work, it can become a disaster, yes. So some would be better off stopping and going for something else. It's a very complex issue: who will become an artist? Who is an artist? Who is a good artist? Who is a real artist? And who is an unbelievable artist? I'm still surprised that I became an artist. I didn't want to say the word 'artist' when I'd meet, let's say, a girl in a bar, even when I was already quite busy with installations and things like that. It also took a long time before I sold something, because my work was really strange in the 1980s, with these realistic decors and things. I still worked in a bookshop part time, and when they'd ask me 'what do you do?', I'd say I worked in a bookshop. I could never say the words 'I'm an artist', perhaps because of being an autodidact. When I sold my first work, then I said the words: 'I'm an artist.'

Guillaume Bijl teaches at the Kunstakademie Münster.

Pavel Büchler — in his office at Manchester
Metropolitan University.

You were appointed as research professor at Manchester Metropolitan University. Is there a distinction between teaching and research?

If by research we mean the development of knowledge, or know-how, there is no way you can, at that sort of higher level of education, separate research from teaching, because if you don't develop knowledge, you've nothing to teach. However, in the current university environment, which is by no means completely homogeneous, but which has certain kinds of characteristics, there is a high degree of separation, which has to do with administrative convenience, it's to do with funding. It's to do with the way … even aesthetic production has to be epistemologically validated.

Before this you held a number of teaching posts? Did you choose to teach?

Oh, definitely. In fact I started teaching out of curiosity. I should preface this: I find teaching undergraduates much more rewarding and interesting than supervising PhDs, because of the kind of aspirations of the students. The main aspiration of a young undergraduate is still there, way before that ambition comes to be recognised in terms of being an artist, or whatever. And I find the contact with that way of thinking really crucial to a practice, which, in my own case, I like to think, is also founded in curiosity. Art is a kind of job that no one asks you to do. You become an artist for all kinds of reasons, but when I examined my soul, I think I've probably become an artist out of curiosity. And it is obviously important for any artist to maintain a kind of exchange with other people who are curious about things in a teaching situation … Ideally you are surrounded by curious minds. There is another reason why I believe that teaching is something for artists to do, way beyond just a kind of economic necessity – and I don't underestimate that economic necessity, but maybe I will get to that in a minute – while it's so difficult to define what the social role of the artist is, one of the ways of looking at it may be that the artist has the privilege, the opportunity, and therefore possibly a duty to maintain certain ways of thinking, in the environment of the western cultural world. That can be done through passing on the knowledge and experience that you develop in that practice in ways that differ from those which the art work itself can mediate, that experience. So the teaching situation gives you an opportunity to live up to that duty. And – and I don't want to underestimate this – when it comes to the economic necessity, or the economic dimension of teaching, there is a lot to be said for the way a paid job frees your practice from certain other considerations. That it may, depending on the practice, constrain that practice goes without saying, yes.

As an artist you say your responsibility is to 'make nothing happen'. How do you understand this concept, or approach, in terms of teaching?

The phrase 'making nothing happen' is shorthand, of course. It is shorthand for the way I understand the job of the artist, which, to me, consists of noticing those sorts of things that are already out there in the world, and the kind of spectacle we already participate in, and pointing it out to others. It's not quite the same as somehow reactivating the everyday. It's subtler than that. And I believe that one of the greatest cumulative discoveries of modern art is how little it takes to show something completely ordinary as being completely magical. Now, when it comes to pedagogy, my interest is really in finding out how to make students aware of that. It's not that doing less is more; it's that amazing thing of thinking, looking, reflecting, on the way the world is. In other words, imagination really is where the potential practice resides, rather than in the making. The paradigm of western art education has a certain genealogy. It's quite easy to trace initially. That is to say, maybe pre-Bauhaus, the model was founded in imitation; whether we are talking about imitation of nature, as it's sometimes called, or whether we are talking about imitation of the masters' work, or mimicking the metier whatever goes into the production of art. And the success or failure of that process was contingent on the notion of talent, and some sort of pre-existent ability, or gift. Later on, maybe with Bauhaus, the concept, or focus, shifts from something like imitation to something like, perhaps, creativity, or experimentation. And so does the condition of success, which is no longer entirely contingent upon talent, but on something like an attitude. And that shift continues obviously post-Bauhaus, until it reaches a situation in which we are now, where imitation is completely frowned upon and completely displaced by notions like originality. When I talk about experimental pedagogies of art, it may sound incredibly old-fashioned, because, in some ways, I want to go back, but look at it differently.

Back to?

Back to notions that bypass questions of originality, to a kind of experimental model. It's a kind of observation-based model, except that the modes of observation are different; they are not purely visual, they are not mechanical, they are not imitative in that sort of simple term.

Are they more reflexive?

They are reflexive, and they try to engage with the world as it is, rather than to merely imitate it. But I am not particularly interested in the way art education is generally understood these days, as a kind of individual-led 'you decide you are a minor artist, and you decide what you want to do, and you come to me and I tell you what I think about it'. I am actually interested in a practitioner/ teacher-led pedagogy.

Is this demonstrative in some way?

No, it's not demonstrative, because that would just be going back to the old academic paradigm. In fact, I actually find that this model still exists in current art education. For instance, when you look at the role of the art school gallery; every art school has something that would pass for a gallery, which may only be a corridor covered with an inch-thick crust of emulsion paint with hard-to-remove sticky tape. Where does that come from? That comes from the old academic model, where you needed a space to present the master works for students to copy. Obviously that no longer happens there, and it masquerades now as a kind of nearest simulation of an art gallery, a public art space. But, in fact, precisely because it masquerades as the nearest simulation of the public art space, this is where the imitative still resides, because it mimics cultural practices that can only be validated in their social destination, or in their kind of social environment, in an entirely academic context. In my view it probably does more harm than good to education. What I'm interested in is what you can learn from experimenting with the context and the function. If you have an empty space in an art school, where people can come and reflect on something; what it is you do with it, how do you engage with it, what forms of engagement – with the constituency, or the community, or the audience, or whatever you call it – would be appropriate? It's a kind of discovery-led process that I'm advocating.

And the student is as much artist as audience in that process?

Yes, both. Exactly. And I wouldn't even, certainly at the lower end of art education, at undergraduate level, want to separate the two. For artists that's an important point. The separation of the notions of production and reception in art education is not helpful. Artists have to be the exemplary viewers of art, it's something you learn as you go along, and it comes out of the same curiosity that I mentioned already. It comes out of the need to feed your work and place your work in relation to other work. That is something that really needs to be fostered and that's another thing that the dominant model leaves out. Where for example instruments such as the artist's talk, or the slide show seem to be used as the main vehicle for developing some ability to reflect on art, appreciate art, experience art, and so on … but we don't really have effective enough ways to make students feel that they live with art.

In the book *Speaking and Listening* published by Transmission, you say 'even the most hands-off approach that exemplifies my day-to-day practice is an act of interference with the way things are'. I was wondering how clear a distinction there is for you between teaching and practice?

I call myself an artist, it's more than a convenient shorthand, of course. But that practice combines writing, teaching and showing, or whatever. It's a practice that basically came out of circumstances, out of opportunities. I don't call myself necessarily an artist who also teaches, I don't make apologies about it. What I can say is that without the art making, or without that practice, I couldn't teach, that's true. I could practice as an artist without teaching, but …

It would be a different practice …

It would have to be tested, I don't know. The main precondition of being a good teacher, the main quality you have to have, is generosity. That is not the precondition of being a good artist. You have to desire your student to be better than you by whatever yardstick you measure it.

I'm interested in your 1997 work *What the Cleaners Found*. It is a set of 12 pamphlets, which comment on 'the twists and turns, ifs and buts, of institutionalised art education'.

I'm interested in this work in terms of how it seemed to be generated out of the environment and experience you found yourself in, and also because this appeared in the same year as you took up the post in 1997.

There are two sources to it. Artists work with what they have around them – I work with what I have around me. What I had around me from 1992 to 1996 was the bureaucracy of a good art school with an incredibly provincial mindset – Glasgow School of Art. Of course, the priorities of the management and bureaucracy were the immediate intellectual environment in which I existed as an artist. I don't know if you have seen the work, but it's basically re-workings of the language of various official documents, where I trace down the titles of the top ten 1960s pop songs in the text of an annual report, for instance, or 'discover' the word 'fart' in the School's *Disciplinary Rules and Procedures*. The language of the institution was the source of the material, but the work came out of frustration, and indeed anger, because, after a four-and-a-half-year spell as head of department, I got into a major confrontation with the management of the school. In some ways, it was my way of getting this out of the way.

It wasn't a pre-emptive strike against a certain kind of criticism that might be levelled against you for taking up an academic/bureaucratic role?

I can assure you that it was not, but I don't mind if it is interpreted that way! It actually came out before I took up this post. Ironically, it was brought out by a small publishing outfit at the University of Derby, by the Research Group for Artists Publications, which is part of that irony. When I resigned from Glasgow School of Art, I thought that I did not want to get involved ever again with an academic institution in this country. But the position I was offered here, and the way in which it was offered, was done with respect for my values. And, I must say, for everything else that this university may leave to be desired, I still feel that those values are respected here. I'm encouraged to do what I do.

I suppose I also asked you this because of what you said about academia in former-Czechoslovakia where you grew up, and where you were involved in Samizdat literature. You said 'progressive professors and lecturers were being replaced by those whose only ambition was their political survival or who had been frightened into passive compliance with the new bureaucracy and played brain-dead to save their academic skins'...

One needs Adorno's 'clown in the culture industry'. It may even be a slightly philistine sort of position if one sees it in that sort of instrumental way. It's like, 'Look, if you want me to work for you I can only do what I can do'. In other words, it's kind of demanding a certain privilege, which the logic of capitalist employment, the industrial logic of the contemporary university, etc., is not very good at understanding. Having said that, despite its industrial logic, or rationale, the contemporary academy is still slightly better at understanding this than some other industries. Yeah, there still is that concept of academic freedom, the concept of the value of independent thought and so on. But, just as Cambridge did not employ Wittgenstein to fill in forms and do self-assessment, I'm only interested in a position in the contemporary academy to the extent that you don't have me here to fill in forms. Being a bit more serious about it, the work, even though it's light-hearted, that sort of project, or that set of little artist's books, is an artwork in its own right. And it really is nothing much more than a work that came out of a certain environment. If you, as many artists do, go and try and live in that sort of quasi-anthropological fashion, with a certain community, or in a certain situation, and bring back a work which reflects something of the kind of basic conditions of that situation, you are doing more or less the same thing. It's a work that comes from a certain sort of situation where administrative convenience, managerial thinking – the industrialisation of education – are the basic framework for the experience as a teacher, as an artist, as a student. The experience of a contemporary art school, even a good one, even one which still verges on being an academy, as opposed to a university, like Glasgow School of Art, is still primarily an experience of the structure, rather than of the discourse, if you like. I feel rather disheartened by the way in which art needs to be dressed as research, for example, to be even tolerated in the contemporary academy. And I am very unhappy about the academisation of art at all levels within the academy, because I can see no meaningful role for academic art, other than strictly within the academic discourse itself. There may even be a case for training future 'academic artists', if you feel that somehow the academic environment needs the presence of that sort of discourse. But academic art is something else. You can probably send home 99 per cent of your students, because there is only so much academic art we, or anyone, actually need. And it's not only that art has to masquerade as research to be recognised as valid by the contemporary institutions, it's also that research itself is only valued for its economic and instrumental benefits, which takes the argument even further. The problem is part of a much larger cultural shift that we're experiencing, where the value of anything that constitutes culture has to be accounted for, is measurable, and so on.

You say 'if artists are to inspire, if they are to provide models of thinking of looking at the world, and models of taking up one's responsibility for what one does, we must reject this idea of regimented industrialised imagination and identity, and of useful work' …

The whole point in that is that, by definition, art is purposefully useless. That is why it is so necessary. And the more instrumental thinking, which focuses on usefulness, and so on, is at the heart of all decision making, and of all sorts of dominant cultural values, the more it is necessary to insist on the purposeful uselessness of art.

Pavel Büchler teaches at Manchester Metropolitan University.

Michael Corris — one afternoon in mid-November — The British Library, London.

What is the role of an art teacher today?

Well that's a big question and the only way I know of answering it is to talk about what I've done and what I've tried to do to help other people to do, and to stop other people from doing. It also depends on the level that you're talking about, because today there's so much structure imposed upon the practice of teaching, that pretty much anybody who wants to break out of that has to be either very clever or quite content with the idea that they're going to get fired, or won't be able to make any headway at all, because they'll face a tremendous amount of opposition. So you've got me on the defensive today. Given that the students are coming from a particular background, whether it's foundation or starting at undergraduate, their conception of art and what art practice is, is wildly different from anything that I would accept. Since I already have a problem with the idea of being able to teach somebody to be an artist, simply because it's about teaching them maybe to ignore things rather than to learn things, it becomes very … it becomes both difficult and easy. It becomes difficult because the expectations at a certain point are about what skills and techniques are required. It becomes easy because you can just circumvent that and actually get people interested in another agenda about art. First of all I see the role of somebody in that position as being a facilitator – and let's not sound overly managerial – but it's about first understanding where people think they'd like to go. The other issue that I'd raise very quickly is that it's difficult to get a critical mass together, from which you could actually present a course as a coherent point of view and push that forward. I see very little at the undergraduate level that indicates that people can actually create schools or compact communities in which everybody is moving in more or less the same direction. That would be useful as an antidote to the kind of pluralism that I think most people feel is their lot. In which they're really in a kind of an atelier-like situation, though I am aware of certain institutions where they're currently introducing things like that, simply to keep students interested and to get them to come.

Such as?

For example in Sheffield, they've broken large groups, first-year groups, into smaller groups that have a place in a studio, so they feel like they have a home, have a location.

What gives it the sense of home or location?

It's the social, the environmental effect, really. I don't think it's anything like a uniform conceptual or stylistic approach for making art; it's not like a school, it's not like an academy, and this to me is the big issue in the post-media world. Bureaucrats and administrators have understood the legacy of conceptual art as a roadmap for art education. It's very difficult to imagine that you could have something like an academy, where you could have sustained discussion, where people are actually sharing and learning from each other, because they're talking about more or less the same thing and more or less the same idea. So you kind of create environments that are a home for students. At graduate level it's a lot easier because I sort of teach from my own practice. I assume that these people have gone through this form of education in the past three years, they've struggled through it, and they come out with the idea that they have their own voice. Then it's my job to kind of thrust them back into a situation that is much more collective, and at that level I find it quite easy to use certain strategies and to develop projects around practices that I've been engaged in before. So, for example, rather than assign a series of texts to read, I've decided that we'll develop a project which is based on the *Annotations* project I participated in, in New York during the early 1970s, and use that as a way of tackling what it is we have to know about theory, history, or any kind of method to reflect on one's practice critically. That works very well, and all of a sudden we have this kind of self-organising group and students experience a good deal more autonomy with respect to their learning, their intellectual interests. They're taking a very active role in shaping the discussion, so in a way it's recreating – without nostalgia – what seemed to be a fairly interesting conversation or situation in the past, and bringing that into the university as a way of teaching. And that means that I get involved too, so it's not about me imparting what I know, it's about me learning from students and also engaging with them and becoming a co-participant.

You're also co-author?

A co-author as well, yes. There'll be some sort of material outcome at the end that will function as a kind of handbook of what they've thought, about what we've discussed and how people have interacted with each other. All this happens alongside the other things that everybody wants or thinks they need, which are group critiques, which is the endless parade of taking your work in, putting it up, talking about it, answering questions about how it was made, why it was … Then there's of course the demand that one understands something about the context of the practice, so right from the start there's this divide that I try to address in this way.

I take it you understand group critiques to be somewhat limited?

The question that's come up in my mind about that is: what is it preparing people to do? Is it like, 'now I know how to fill a sandbag and create a dyke and keep the world out?' Or is it opening their work up to some kind of critical revision? And more often than not it isn't, because the whole process doesn't really invite that kind of approach. If people are seen as being too critical, then you've breached some sort of decorum, and it's fraught with other kinds of emotions, because that's still part and parcel of what happens in the first three years of art education. People are thought to consider their outputs as precious, as off-shoots of themselves. Quite a lot of that is still going on, no matter what the work is.

What do you think students need to know and be particular about today? What is their responsibility?

Their responsibility is to learn what it means for them to be practising as an artist. Not to be professional necessarily, because the idea of professional studies, the thing that is supposed to teach people how to participate in the game of being a professional artist, that usually comes in the undergraduate curriculum, is not an answer. It's not an alternative to and it certainly isn't about anything other than how to manage your career in a way that conforms to the expectations of those who are already managing careers. What is the potential for unexpected things to happen, what is the potential for learning throughout every level? I can see the need for students to learn about the history of their practice and the issues, and the debates surrounding their practice, and that should somehow be much more integrated into what they do. So it should have some kind of impact on what they're doing, but really it's difficult to expect that much out of an undergraduate. You feel that people are quite young, they don't know enough, they're inexperienced, they could still have a different orientation, but it has to start right from the beginning. All I see now are these people who are very unsure about organising themselves. So very quickly any potential inroads into that situation are kind of stalled and you get distracted by banal operational details. Plus you just have to try to see how you can work against things like these student satisfaction surveys, these league tables, all these other pressures. So, teaching within the university is a tremendous struggle. There are maybe only three independent art schools left in Great Britain, and for the most part even the specialist schools are enmeshed in this academic university structure. In fact there are a lot of fairly good schools of art, departments of art embedded in mediocre universities, and yet they have to dance to the tune of the university and that whole structure. The unitisation of courses, the modularisation of programmes, has for a lot of people completely destroyed the unity of education of the arts.

There's a lot of nostalgia for the polytechnic amongst the people I've interviewed.

There is, yes. I've never experienced that. I've been teaching in Britain since 1990, so fairly soon after I arrived, the polytechnic I was at became a new university. I was teaching in the birthplace of British modularity: Oxford Brookes. The modular system was so complex that, like Einstein's Theory of Relativity of the early twentieth century, only a handful of individuals at the university actually understood how it worked! I had occasionally taught part-time in the United States before I emigrated, and those art courses had been unitised for some time, so I didn't understand what the problem was. Except that lecturers had more than 12 students, and they couldn't spend every afternoon in the bar doing their tutorials with them. The problem was that most of my colleagues were outrageously, scandalously unprepared to teach anything to anybody about contemporary art practice, as most of them didn't have art practices. I mean their work had the status of a hobby, as far as I was concerned. And where a practice was present, it was stuck in the era of late-Modernist painting and sculpture. But they all knew what they didn't like, and at that point what they didn't like was anything that smelled of Conceptual art, or anything that was attacking particular media-based practices, or anything that was attacking the sacred cow of self-expression.

Do you need to have a practice to teach?

Yes, I'd say that uneqivocally.

What constitutes a practice? Is it more than an annual exhibition?

Does the annual exhibition answer the question whether you are putting yourself in a position where you're having to defend your practice with your peers? What kind of critical feedback are you exposing yourself to in that case? The majority of people teaching in the US and in the UK have this very same relationship to their practice. You go to most universities in the US, outside of the major urban areas where there is an art market and sustained art practices, and you'll see people who have that kind of relationship to art.

Should the market decide then who teaches?

No. There are so many alternatives to the market that it would be really narrow-minded to draw on the conventional frameworks for production and distribution of art. Moreoever, the university itself has become the home for a certain kind of practice. I'm not advocating it without reservation, but this practice does represent a portion of artistic practice and is likely to increase in scale and scope when the US gets on the bandwagon. So, it's fair to say that right now you have a very interesting situation. I've been talking about this with Charlie Geer and thinking about it a lot, because I'm involved in supervising people who are doing so-called practice-led PhDs. I have my doubts about it, I am sceptical about it, because of the terms in which it's cast and the model that it ...

The social scientific model?

Because of the nature of government support in Britain, there is an entire stratum of people whose practice depends upon and exists almost entirely within the academy or the social realm that is supported by arts councils. So the market is no longer just the main focus. But it's interesting, because attached to the academic support of creative activity is the idea of accountability and assessment and also of the prefiguring of the whole issue of practice in a form that's amenable to the assessors of the Research Assessment Exercise. So from the very beginning, to be able to even partake in this funding, which trickles down to every level within universities, any kind of application for funding is couched in things like methodologies, outcomes, and this and that. It's not professional practice, it's research, and it's often a challenge to imagine what people are doing as 'research'. Because with research there's the possibility that halfway through, you could just turn around and throw everything out and start all over. You're susceptible to criticism, and theoretically criticism will transform the outcome. I don't believe that most artists work like that at all in an academic setting where the pressure is to produce 'outcomes'. I don't see any evidence that they do, but would welcome any that is forthcoming, because it would signify a mature and realistic attitude towards the academization of artistic practices. In the 'world', there's a long history of informal critical reflection; sitting and talking with friends, inviting people to your studio, having drinks with other artists. It's a model of sociality that can become a framework for artistic practice; it is close to the kind of socialising that was a central feature of my involvement with Art & Language. It may yet exist in some other collectives, but of course we live in a very different time and I wouldn't equate the one with the other. So the whole issue of research and teaching, the relationship of one's practice to teaching is complicated, because you already have these opposing frames.

You're always beholden to somebody ...

Yes, there's somebody out there. I don't know if the level of funding is sufficient to actually support some people entirely, but I do have colleagues who get a lot of money from funding organisations that are focusing on art and science initiatives, or art and urban development. In fact, they come to me, because I'm a professor and one of my jobs is to support the research of my colleagues. And they say, 'I'd really like to learn from you how I can get this work into galleries, where should it be shown?'

If you talk to people who can actually support themselves in the market then for the most part they don't look at teaching as a responsibility or an obligation. They don't feel that they need to impart anything to people who want to be artists. Personally, I feel more of an obligation. Given the overproduction of artists and the slim chances that one has to actually make a living as an artist, I feel that I have an obligation to say 'there's this possibility as well as that possibility', and to point people in other directions.

Do you have an obligation to teach?

For me it's very interesting, I try to learn something from it rather than just deliver something. It's not just about knowledge transfer.

What's it about then?

It's about community, but it's a very strange kind of community. You have to work hard to grab people, and you know you've only got them for a limited amount of time, and there's always the uneven relationship. Whatever your intentions are to break down those barriers, there's still the student-teacher relationship. I tried this early on; you fall over yourself trying not to be an authority, when in fact students crave direction, perhaps they also want you to be their father and their mother. I had a professor who said 'I'm not your father, I'm not your mother and I can't teach you anything you don't already know.'

[Laughs.]

He basically went on talking about his own life and his own practice for the whole semester. If you found it interesting, then fine, and I did, because here was somebody who convinced me that art could have a cognitive dimension.

Who was that?

Harry Holtzman, he was an interesting guy; the saviour of Mondrian and the editor of *trans/formations*: the first post-war publications to look at art as a form of knowledge, rather than simply as a means of expression.

It seems almost obligatory, if you're an artist teaching in an art school, to be at odds with the bureaucracy.

I totally go along with that. Artists in higher education are always at odds because they may feel they're essentially anti-authoritarian. There's the vanity, the narcissism of that, but they've also been subjected to mediocre management and have had to endure numerous, chaotic changes in higher education – and they are chaotic. Having worked here now for almost 18 years, I can't recall a single 12-month period in which some sort of external impetus to change didn't disrupt everything. People are constantly talking about change, and about being managed by people who know nothing about management, or about art. But everyone would agree that higher education is very poorly managed as a sector. Planning people are compelled to plan, they're asked for strategic planning, they're asked for this kind of organisation and yet they're never given the means to sustain it. You can't even depend on a budget for each year, so how could you plan? Now, all of a sudden these people who are complaining seem to have a point, no one I've ever worked with has not complained.

I want to go back to the beginning of the interview, when you said you have a problem with the idea of being able to teach somebody to be an artist, and ask whether you can teach art?

Can you teach art? That depends on what you mean by art. You can give people the opportunity to materialise their ideas, to develop visual forms for things, to engage in freewheeling discussion, to that extent you can provide the means for that to happen, for the learning to happen. The academy tried to teach art in a very particular sense and wound up with a lot of academic artists. Now the question is, how does the curriculum relate to what the reality of being an artist in the world is today? It doesn't relate very well for the most part, it certainly doesn't strike me as a curriculum that's there to support change. People go into art school, and not every one of them wants to be an artist, but every one of them feels that they have some kind of strong relationship to visual creative work, or what they understand as visual creative work. They may not have seen anything beyond an Impressionist painting once in their life, even that, or maybe they've seen Andy Warhol, or they know who Damien Hirst is or Tracey Emin, but they're totally outside of the culture of art. They're completely naïve, but they know they like art. Out of a crop of people who graduate, who is practising as an artist in some way five years later?

People like me tend to fantasise about what the ideal teaching situation would be, and it certainly would be more like Black Mountain and less like what it is now. But even Black Mountain worked because a lot of talented people went there, but they really didn't pay much attention to Joseph Albers. You can train someone to be a doctor, I don't know if you can create a brilliant doctor. You can give somebody education in art, you can teach them art history, you can teach them art theory, you could make philosophy and politics and everything available. And then you let them do what they want to do. The big problem in Britain, from my point of view, coming from the States, has been this excessive specialisation very early on. It comes down to the fact that the degrees are even identified and named very narrowly. You don't have that kind of narrowing down in the States. In a university art department in most institutions in the US, you have to take a wide range of courses drawn from the humanities and the sciences; you don't 'declare your major' until your second year of a four-year course. Clearly, the British system of education can't produce students as well-rounded. It's a scandal, really. At graduate level, the proliferation of specific MAs as in Britain is something that's completely alien. You enter onto an MFA in fine art, in the States. You can develop your practice in any field, you don't need to be doing an MA in video or painting or sculpture or public art; it's assumed that the course will be flexible enough to engage with a range of particular artistic practices.

It's a false particularity?

It has to do with some idea of marketing – proliferating options to attract more prospective students – and somehow with this notion that the university, as a public-funded institution, has the obligation to stream the optimum number of appropriately qualified people into society.

When do you think teaching transcends the conventional frame?

Probably when you 'get out' of university, in a manner of speaking; when you remove teaching and learning from the bureaucratic assumptions of management.

… at which point you're still teaching?

You have to kind of put yourself in another role if you want to develop; in a collaborative relationship. Then you have to stop. You don't stop telling people what you think, or imparting some information, but all of a sudden you've given yourself the room to be in a situation where someone is doing that to you. And you know it's a very good question, because when I started working with Ian [Burn] and Mel [Ramsden] in New York, and to some extent Joseph [Kosuth] – though nobody really worked with Joseph – there was the invitation to do things. There weren't many years separating us, in fact, Ian was quite a bit older, but Mel was maybe three years older than me, he was already another generation artistically speaking. The presumption that we were all in it together was there, but very quickly, as more people of my generation filtered into the group, the stresses in the group began to develop along generational lines. Not just ideological lines. It became increasingly paranoid and unsatisfactory after a while. Despite the eventual implosion of Art & Language, something important was accomplished through our collaborative work. When you ask: 'can you be a teacher in a different way?', I'd say 'you're a teacher and you take that role in a certain setting and you can take another role in another setting'. I have this framework that I set up …

The Invisible College?

That was something I was doing in Wales, which was really a means to get people to come and develop some kind of dialogue, some sort of discussion, in a place that was fairly isolated from those kinds of things. It was to expose my colleagues and some students to this and to see what happens. It turned out like any other kind of seminar or lecture series; people don't show up or they don't talk. In Sheffield, I organised another kind of framework; something that I called the Freedonia Salon: once a month people come to my place, I prepared dinner for around 15 or 20 people. We screened videos, we discussed them, sometimes there's no discussion at all … but a preponderance of graduate students attended these evenings and they liked the social situation; they responded wonderfully and it turned out to be a very positive and interesting part of their whole university experience. The salon idea will develop further, just as I hope to continue and develop the *Annotations* project in university settings. Aligned to this is the entire question of the nature and place of 'studio practice'. I tell the students: sometimes I have a studio, sometimes I don't. I ask them what does this mean, making things? How do you put things together? Where do you get your ideas from, what's going on? I'm an artist who works through contingency, always pressing things and with a certain kind of intellectual legacy and background different than yours. I came to it piece-meal, you'll come to it the same way. My experience was that some individuals were important to my intellectual development. I'm going to try and do that here. I'm just going to tell you what I'm doing. I'm going to show you how it happened. There's no great technique but there are intellectual skills to be learned. And if you do it on that level in a small enough class and with enough engagement so that nobody can hide, it works as teaching.

Has it changed much since the 1970s?

I didn't teach much in the 1970s. I literally taught three sessions for Joseph at the School of Visual Arts. I went on my first trip to an art school with Mel, to the Nova Scotia College of Art and Design, to do a lecture about our practice, which nobody understood, and very few people were interested in. We came back a few years later and developed a kind of a workshop situation with students there during the summer, which was more interesting. So I'm not too familiar with what the scene was during the 1970s. I came out of graduate school right at the beginning of the 1970s.

Having been a student not that long before, you were close enough to understand the kinds of upheavals ...

I still remember that, and what I tell everybody now is that if we now provided the same programme of study that I had, there would be uproar. If you had the undergraduate education that I had, that wouldn't be tolerated; people chain-smoking in classrooms, pacing back and forth chain-smoking, telling stories, like 'I was diapered by Paul Klee'. [Laughs.] It was great, I loved it. I think about what Ad Reinhardt said about how you teach art students. He said 'you put them in a position where they can watch artists arguing with one another, where they can listen to artists arguing with one other'. When you're really going to learn is when artists start arguing with each another, when you hear how they're defending their work and how they're being challenged. So for Reinhardt and that generation, by the time they got to the late 1940s or early 1950s and established the Club, it was all about people coming in and taking their knocks. When you're talking to students in a critique, you're always aware that you have to be supportive and constructive. You can't just say 'this is crap'. You can say that to a colleague in a certain setting, and they would know, you could say 'this doesn't work'. Artists and students in the 1970s, early 1970s, who were painters and who were still fascinated with late-modernist painting, had this expression; they'd look at something and if they liked it they'd say, 'it works', and if they didn't, they'd say, 'it doesn't work'. There was no long drawn-out narrative beyond that. Of course there must be qualification. You can't put people in that position. Very often these classes are taught alone, and I think it's probably a better idea to teach in tandem with somebody. A lot of people don't like that, but I think that's something that should be instigated. We mark in tandem, and we've institutionalised mistrust of our colleagues through double, and in some cases triple marking. The external examining system in fact is a kind of institutionalised mistrust in some colleagues' minds. I know what the rationale is, to maintain and assess quality across ...

Some kind of objectivity ...

... exactly, across the sector. But you're not going to tell me that a first coming out of Sunderland is the same as a first coming out of Goldsmiths or Chelsea or Central Saint Martins or Cambridge or Ruskin or whatever. Bullshit. But it's a first, OK.

[Laughs.]

What place do you think the art school currently has in the political arena and what place should it have?

I don't think it has any place in the political arena unless you believe that it's possible to breach the 'art'/ 'life' divide. That idea is quite 'avant-garde' isn't it? Some believe we have already done so. Should you teach artists to be socially engaged? People should understand the world and if they want to make it the subject of their art, if they believe the idea that their art is going to be instrumental in that, fine; then do it and put it up for debate. People associate me with the political left, maybe more than they should in a way. When my Ad Reinhardt book is out on the streets – you'll see me talking about an artist who was intensely politicised, who understood the politics of the world as well as the politics of art. And yet, he refused to use his work directly in that way and criticised people for doing so, and there were good reasons why he did that. It's worth looking at those again and not really assuming that it's such an advance to have work that embraces topical issues. But maybe that's not your question.

I think it's to do with the relationship between the school and the world, maybe in terms of what you call the Salon, which is an intrinsically political activity as well.

Yes, I intentionally use that expression Salon, with all the presumed elitism and separateness that it evokes, because I think art schools should be able to establish a difference, to really justify themselves as an independent and unique kind of practice, not an adjunct to business, to current affairs, to politics, to media or anything like that.

Whether or not it's even possible to conceive of art in those terms is open to question, but some of us carry on a practice that is always contingent in that way, always turning it's back on fashion. I don't see the fact that conceptualism or conceptual with a small 'c', which is now a household word, is a great victory, and maybe that's the problem. What's notoriously influential in the art world are either auction prices, or the fact that anybody coming along after you is going to turn you on your head as a matter of course. So where's the victory? I was talking about this the other day; when I started teaching you couldn't get a job if you were a conceptual artist; you couldn't get any support, nobody recognised it, so you had a position of some sort of appeal there, at least for that moment you were outside of something. But that's no longer the case, and maybe the whole idea of the post-media curriculum needs to be laid at conceptual art's feet. But there are many different kinds of conceptual art. I don't feel like I haven't been able to do everything that I've wanted to do, but I do feel that a lot of my time is taken up dealing with other people's agendas. I've made a decision about how I can fight them; that what happens within the classroom is privileged, insofar as it represents a condition of autonomy: people taking control of what gets done to them. Isn't that a value worth nurturing?

Michael Corris teaches at Sheffield Hallam University & Newport School of Art, Media and Design.

Michael Craig-Martin — a busy Sunday afternoon — his studio near Old Street, London.

Could you begin by saying something about the part teaching has played in your practice. I'm interested in particular in your experience at Yale?

First of all, the education I had at Yale was quite brilliant. I was well-educated in general in America. I had a 1950s education, and then going to Yale was just extraordinary. The most impressive were the 'Albers', because I had the full Albers courses. Even though Joseph Albers wasn't there, I had the full Albers courses. His assistants were teaching the courses that, presumably, he had overseen. There were classes, often with a lot of people in them, with two or three assistants teaching the same class. Some of them were taught pretty much as classes and others less so. Everything was based on the idea that only individual, personal experience of things mattered. You did things that were group exercises in order to achieve a personal experience, and somebody else's experience was irrelevant to you, frankly. Because the thing that really mattered was that you found it out yourself, it was about you. Which was very, very clever, because, in a way, it looked like it wasn't about you, because it looked like it had the structure of didactic teaching, whereas in fact it was a highly personal experience.

During the Albers talk you gave at Tate Modern you spoke about returning to the UK and Bath, which was in a period of revolt in the 1970s, and you wondered, how to bring what is essentially an authoritarian kind of system of education …

Very German …

… to a country that was going through a kind of liberation, so to speak, and throwing exactly this kind of thing off …

Yes, throwing all this off.

How did you reconcile this?

One also has to say that there was a great deal of unease among students, even in the early 1960s, about the Albers courses; that they focused on certain things and not on other things. Because all the courses made it very clear that this was not art, we were not making art, we were doing study work here. If you wanted to do art, you went to your studio and you did that. This wasn't, we were not. And so there was often a great disparity between the way you dealt with your work in your studio and what you did on these courses. There was often a very big gap between these two forms, and when I came to England there was no structure for doing courses. I actually tried doing the colour course, I tried doing this to begin with.

It didn't work?

It was hopeless; it just didn't work.

This was in Bath?

Yes. There wasn't the structure. You needed the kind of educational structure within which this made sense, and the structures were too loose. They were too personal. In a way, there was so much more emphasis on individual work at British art schools, from an American point of view. American undergraduate education was always seen as very general and very basic; you learned a generalised education for the first two years, you majored in something, which meant that you did more classes in that than you did in others, and you gained points. Then, if you had any serious study, you went on to graduate school. In Britain, undergraduate students were already as specialised as graduate students in America. So the first thing that struck me when I went to Bath was that I was teaching very young people, but they were dealing with their work, and their work was advanced to the level of graduate students, even though they were undergraduates. That completely threw me, but that's because they had already chosen; their other subjects had become minor subjects. They did a little art history, they did a little bit of psychology, which became less and less over the years. So you were really focusing on this one subject, which was fine art, and you were doing a few little minor things on the side. That's graduate school in America. That also meant that it was very difficult to do, and people did courses, and things like that at foundation school. When people went to BA courses, which were then the diploma courses, they expected something more independent, and the emphasis was on their independent achievement; in a way that was much more emphasised at undergraduate level here than it was in America. So the whole structure of how I had learned and how I was educated didn't fit this other model, and I struggled with that for a while. I became very interested in the idea of individual practice and students; that was what really intrigued me, which fundamentally had to do with my own practice. I found it very difficulty to understand how to assimilate the idea that there were artists whose work I didn't like, but I couldn't help but respect, because I really liked them and obviously they believed in the things that they were doing, in a way that I might not. I couldn't bring myself to despise people who did things just because they did things, which actually sometimes were in great contrast to what I thought myself, and I tried to understand that in terms of the students. I hated the idea that one's art should be based on the idea of dismissing other things. So how do you accommodate that? Then I realised that most of the bad teachers in this system were the people who only knew how to take what they themselves did instinctively, and who brutalised other people by forcing them to do what was not natural to them.

What you're talking about is a way to enable you to teach people regardless of …

What they do.

… what they make. You can engage with them and their practice as artists, but you don't have to like the work.

I don't have to like the work. I don't have to care about it. I don't have to understand it. I like the variety; I don't want them to be the same. I love the idea of going from one kind of work to another, and each one of them comes up with this completely different ball game. Whereas other people are trying to find a way to unify the thing, I'm not interested. I'm trying to readjust every single time to a different practice.

How did you make this step in terms of teaching?

I was kind of doing it instinctively, but it took me years to realise how best to make that function. How do you actually do that and not go crazy? How to go into a studio and how to be useful to people with different practices and how to teach people without feeling … I'm not an uncriticial teacher. I can be very tough, but I try to be tough because I try to be useful within the frame of reference defined by the student. And Goldsmiths was the absolute supreme expression of the student defining the terms of reference. I was partly responsibile for formulating this idea at Goldsmiths, but there was an aspect of it that was already there. But I was able to develop myself, and my ideas about teaching.

Was this with Jon Thompson?

It was principally through Jon. Jon had very similar ideas at that time – we came to disagree more as time went on – but on all those initial ideas we were very … I was just amazed at how he had thought about these things too and had come to certain … For instance, the idea that the art school should, in some way, be responsive to the world of art outside; you shouldn't act as though it didn't exist, or that it was 100 years ago. That we couldn't teach properly if we weren't true to ourselves; we couldn't respect the students if we weren't respected as artists. We had to respect them as artists, so we had to respect ourselves. You weren't asked to go to Goldsmiths to be a first-year tutor, or to be the drawing teacher, or to be the person who teaches etching. You were brought there to be you, and other people were brought there to be them. So if you hired one person who was very much like this, the idea was to hire somebody else who was the opposite. In those early days people loved teaching at Goldsmiths. We all loved it, because you just went there and did exactly the same as when you weren't there. Whereas other schools, you went there and you had to become something to fulfil the idea of the educational need of the school; you had to undo yourself in some way. While at Goldsmiths you could just literally be you, were paid to be you. I felt that suited my ideas about my own work; it was all part of a coherent idea, and I don't think I could have done it if it hadn't been. But I feel that idea came from Albers, because that's what Albers had done. He had found a bigger vision of education and that vision of education sat perfectly with his idea about what his art should be.

There's something in your practice that I would describe as an economy of means; a direct and uncomplicated approach to whatever context you find yourself in. Sometimes people want to complicate or obfuscate things. However what you do is almost the opposite; you try to make things very clear.

Yes, I hate jargon, and I can't stand people who think that complex ideas are best expressed in a way that's obscure or difficult. I think the opposite is the case. The people … the great people whom I've admired, like Wittgenstein and Beckett, they use an incredible economy of language. The things I'm dealing with in my work, the things I'm talking about, I always think they are unbelievably complex. They're more complex than we can ever cope with. So the idea is to find the simplest way of describing them. This is not to be simple, and it's not to make the thing simple, it's actually to reveal how complex they actually are. I'm not seeking to make everything the same, I'm not seeking to make it easy. But there are things that you can say, and they should be said too, and then other things – the complexity of things becomes revealed through that.

There's almost an inevitability in the process of you becoming a teacher because there is something fundamental in there about communication and engagement.

There was a time when artists thought much less about the idea that there was an audience than they do now. They do now because there is one, it's very visible and you're responding to it. Whether it is the audience that goes to Tate Modern, or it's the audience of collectors who buy things, or it's the audience of curators and critics; you are addressing somebody. There was a time when to be an artist was to address such a tiny amount of people that the artists themselves were very much foregrounded in this situation. I was always very conscious of there being this other person when I made the first work, with the boxes. The boxes opened and closed. The reason for the boxes opening and closing was so that the person would be forced to do the one thing you weren't supposed to do, which was touch the object; you were supposed to touch the art. Now it's in museums and nobody's allowed to touch it, including me! But the idea was to make overt the sense of that other person. The other person acts in order to … which was taking Duchamp's thing about the person completing the work very literally. So I've always done work that was very conscious of there being this other, which was also what happened in teaching. I became very conscious of my relation to this other person and what my proper role here was. To be honest, I ended up in a slightly neurotic … it's a slightly neurotic idea, but if I did a tutorial with somebody I would feel that I had failed them in some way if I didn't leave the room feeling that I left them with something to mull over. That partly came from the fact that I often wanted that from other people when I was a student, and they didn't provide it.

Given that you no longer teach, is there anything you currently miss about teaching or is this taken up in other ways within your practice?

It's come up, yes. I couldn't have done the teaching if I hadn't I enjoyed it. I enjoyed it because I made it interesting to myself. There was something I was trying to pursue with my own thinking which made it interesting. I really liked working all those years with young people. It took a lot of time and energy – I did more than I actually realised until I stopped doing it. I never meant to do it to the extent that I ended up doing it; that was not my idea. Every time I felt financially able to stop, I would stop, or I ran it down directly in relation to being able to escape from it.

Was there an amount of teaching responsibility you'd take on, and was there a cut-off point at which more was too much?

Yes.

You weren't running departments?

No, I never ran departments. Everyone always thinks that I did, but I never actually did that. In fact, the years when I was teaching, when I was most effective, were the years of Liam [Gillick] and Gary [Hume] and Sarah [Lucas], and all those people. I was actually teaching less than I had for the previous 20 years. I was teaching a single day a week. I came in and I saw six people, and I saw them over and over again. And that's what happened.

And that was it?

That was it. I didn't do a single other thing, I never even spoke to anybody in the department for a couple of years.

Is teaching for you about finding ways to enable or help students give themselves permission to do the things they really want to do?

That's my understanding of teaching. This sounds so simple, but it's actually very difficult for people to feel comfortable with that. It's not just that they feel it's bad, or naughty, or unworthy; it's often because the thing that you're best at is the thing you value least. So permission has to do with helping somebody recognise that this thing that they do, that's easy to them, is the thing that they should do. That it's OK to do it. In fact, they're unbelievably lucky, because they may be the only person able to do it just like that. In fact they are the only person who is able do it just like that. I found that my job in teaching is to help a person locate and then develop this thing that is truly theirs. And that's why

I'm opposed to an idea of teaching in which people come into school in order to be drained of their past, in order to be given a new way of looking. I don't believe that, I think that people arrive with a great deal. It's not that there aren't things that people can't be taught, that people shouldn't learn – there are. And there are things you can't learn except by learning. The thing I always felt was something that Jon felt very strongly too; one learns best when one needs to know something. It's like learning how to use the computer; there's no sense in learning Photoshop, you have to have something you want to do, and you learn the bit you need to know. As you do that, you start to discover that it does other things, but you have to have a context for knowing what to do, otherwise it's unbelievably difficult to learn anything. I think it is particularly true in art that there is nothing wasted, there is nothing that's a mistake. You do bad work, you learn it's bad work. You do good work, you learn it's good work. You do something that's inappropriate for yourself, you quickly realise it's inappropriate. How else are you supposed to find out what is appropriate?

But there's an idea that it can be found in the library.

That is a new and ghastly phenomenon. This is one of the reasons I stopped: I couldn't stand that.

I want to talk a little about you leaving in a moment, but first I want to return to the Albers talk at Tate Modern, where you answered a question about your time at Goldsmiths and your influence on artists, such as Sarah Lucas, Gary Hume, and so on. I was very interested in the reply you gave and how you described your part, or non-part, so to speak, in their development. So while there was, perhaps at the time, a unique constellation, individual energy, social and economic conditions etc., surely Jon Thompson and yourself created the environment which would allow for this constellation to flourish in the first place?

The people who really benefited from Goldsmiths the most are the ones who were there in that particular period, which was really the best period of Goldsmiths. Jon was dean. You never saw Jon. There were other times during those years, in the late 1980s, when Jon was around quite a bit. I was doing these seminars with groups of people and what Jon would do is ... Jon would just drop in, in the afternoon, in the middle of the seminar. And at that point, he and I disagreed about quite a lot of things, and we also had a very, very different way of approaching everything; our values, and our ways of doing things. So you had the students witnessing two very clever people talking about very important things, at a very sophisticated level, OK? That's what happened. To just have had me was really great. They were really lucky. To just have had Jon was really great, too. But to have this discourse going on ... That doesn't often happen in art school, where you get two people, who are actually playing with the most important ideas of the moment, and playing it out in a public sense, where the students are witnesses but also their work is the vehicle for this discourse of difference. Fantastic! That's a great teaching moment. Those kids were very lucky; they had a very good innings because of that. They got to see what that kind of discourse could be like, and they could see the tensions between us, they could see we didn't hide it. We weren't pretending that we were finding some consensus.

You did an interview with Jonathan Jones about the nature of the world students enter after leaving college, of what is expected of an artist. Is there the equivalent of a painting department out in the world, and the equivalent of a sculpture department out in the world? And your answer is 'no'. What were you thinking about?

Only that the ways we live in the world as artists, we don't divide things into categories in the way that art schools traditionally do. I always had lunch in the canteen with the students and I always thought I did half my day's work having lunch. We didn't talk about art. And even in the studio, we often didn't talk about art at all. We just talked about what movies we went to, or what books we'd read, or what nightclub we went to the night before, or something ... what clothes we were wearing; just anything. Just stuff. Just discourse. Just talking. And you need time for this; it is built on trust. And this is a very complex kind of discourse, and it's not to do with grand ideas. It's mixing those things in. It's having different kinds of moments. All these things about regular life are really very important and they're not secondary. To me, the problem is that art schools have become too fixed on the model of the university; it's too much to do with an idea of intellectual discourse, it makes art a kind of task, or a kind of worthiness, or something, instead of a pleasure. And also something that doesn't make sense. I found it awful, the idea that students had to justify what they did. I never thought anybody should have to justify anything; I don't understand that. The idea of being able to talk about what you do; that I think is interesting. But the idea that that equals justification, that's very different. I'm completely opposed to the idea. I met students in the last years I was at Goldsmiths who couldn't work, because they couldn't make a justifying case if they did it. So they didn't do it, which is terrible. It's the very antithesis of art, the absolute antithesis of art. And Goldsmiths was centred too much on that.

What happened?

To be honest, I think the model had run out. The model is dated. It's been running too long. Art school models have periods when they're the correct model, or are a really good model for that moment. That model is 30 or 40 years old – it's too old.

Is there a model that's appropriate for now?

If there is, I don't know. I'm not the person …

It's not out there?

It may be, but I don't know, and I'm not interested anymore. I had my time. It was a model that suited me and my generation and my experience, but I think that model may have run its course. What I see now, to the extent that I understand it, because I have nothing to do with it, is it looks like an academisation of what was originally an anti-academic idea. Now it's become formalised, and there are certain kinds of routine things that people say and that sound to me empty. It's total rhetoric. All the original ideas seem to me to have gotten compromised. My feeling was that, when I first arrived in Britain, the art schools were in this moment of blossoming in the 1960s, which was through the Coldstream report and all sorts of things that created the 1960s model of art school in Britain. The idea of that model was that instead of schools and professional teachers, which there had been up to the 1950s, there would be artists teaching in art schools, people who were practitioners. That's why they invented part-time teaching and all those kinds of things – that was the function of it. It seems to me now increasingly a return to the 1950s, where you will end up with a professional class of art teachers. It seems to me one of those cycles, a reversal of everything that was fought for in those days.

In the same interview in 2000 with Jonathan Jones, you talked about the insidious growth of academicism in art education. I was wondering whether our current interest in teaching and art school is a reflection of our attempts to think through and get out of a certain kind of academicism, or is indicative of a prevailing and growing academicism in art education, and maybe even art?

To be honest, I don't really know. But my instinct is … What Jon was really clever about was that he looked at the art world that he knew himself as an artist. And he knew that if he wanted to have good teachers, and he wanted to get the best out of them, he had to treat them the same way in the school as they were treated outside the school. Therefore, if we came in and we were there to teach, we were to teach in a way that made sense to us, with the lives that we lived as artists outside the school. There is an existing reality, there is an existing need. And it seems to me that so many of these proposals come from a world which is itself ill at ease with the world that artists actually exist in. And very often what happens in the art world is that the people involved in the world of teaching consider the world of the artist, as it exists, to be vulgar, mercenary, too much involved with money, too much involved with success, too much involved with all these things. But the reality is, that is the art world, and it's not the other pure one. And, of course, it's infinitely more interesting because of that. That's the thing that makes it real, and that's the thing that makes it dangerous and that's the thing that makes it vibrant. Those are the things that make it exciting and emotional. That's where everything that makes it important comes from. That doesn't come from finding the right moral route.

Michael Craig-Martin taught at Goldsmiths, London and is now retired from teaching.

Graham Crowley — his office — the painting department at the Royal College of Art, London.

I'm 56 by the way.

I know …

And you may or may not know that at the end of this academic year I'll leave the Royal College. I've requested not to have my contract renewed, because I intend to concentrate on my practice. I'm represented by Beaux Arts in Cork Street, I have lots of opportunities in Ireland where I'm currently resident … Very briefly put, I've been teaching as a visiting lecturer for about 30 years.

Since 1978 …

Yes, it would be. I left the Royal College of Art in 1974 or 1975 and I became a visiting lecturer here in 1978 or 1979 for Peter de Francia. I did a day a week and around 1981–82 I went to Oxford to do the fellowship, which involved very minimal contact with students at the Ruskin. I did very little visiting lecturer work during that year. Subsequently I have been a visiting lecturer in Leicester Polytechnic, Winchester Art School … It's probably easier to say where I haven't been.

Can you teach art?

I'm going to get straight to it and ask you what you mean by art, because to actually ask such a direct question … I admire the sort of sheer neck of it and I wished one could actually answer 'yes' or 'no' to that, and we could move on to the next question. But if you put art in a question and the question is *that* loaded … Are you asking me personally? Or are you asking if *one* can?

I'm asking you …

That's a very, very good question. I'll tell you how I have learned about art and how I now reflect that learning. Yes, that's about the most intelligent way of answering it, because I'm not too sure that you can't teach what you can't define, and I don't think that anyone has adequately defined what art is. That's problematic. What I've got to do is break down your question into 33 little parts! I was definitely not taught to paint. I've always had facility when I was at school. Even as a junior school kid I was always making things and drawing. It was my metier; it was what I was strongest at, it was what I chose to do when

I didn't have somebody telling me what to do, d'you get it? It stems from that, because I actually think you can't teach people anything unless they have a desire to acquire that knowledge. In my case it came by the most interesting teachers, the most charismatic were my English teacher and my art teacher. Those people actually reflected something; they displayed a form of engagement. And basically they made no bones about it. The English teacher said 'well, without literature, I think I'd just have become an alcoholic.' And the art teacher was probably much the same. They wouldn't know what to do with themselves. I don't want to start on the big 'what is there to do in life', because I was brought up in post-war Essex in what I regard as utilitarian, post-austerity. There was rationing in 1956 when I was a kid, because of Suez so I know about the utilitarian, the culture and society where art has no place ... does that make sense?

Yes ...

The people I'm talking about would not use the term bourgeois, but they would think about art as a middle-class or bourgeois pursuit. 'It's not for people like us' was the expression when I was a kid. But maybe that's part of the sort of softening, of the class transformation; lots of working-class blokes like me, or people from lower-middle class, working-class crossovers went to grammar schools because of the structure of education. We were not taught art. The best I can say of that is our enthusiasm and our curiosity were directed, that's all I can say about it. I've only ever had to be told about something that's aroused my curiosity and I've gone and found out about it. See what I mean?

So let me put it slightly differently: when you're standing in front of a student and his or her work, what are you doing?

First of all I'm contextualising it. Yes, that is a very important area ... sorry we're finished with the other bit, or it wasn't relevant to your question?

Well, not unless you've got something more to add?

The reason I was being so longwinded was because the way I approach teaching is borne from a vivid, and memorable, and extremely uneven experience of my being a student. I've not forgotten how unsatisfactory my education was here as a student at the Royal College, and at Saint Martins. Remember I was a student in 1968, and it must be said that there were institutional failings at the time … That changes the whole kind of mould, because I'm coming from a slightly different trajectory and that's why the whole preamble that I was giving you earlier was important. When I stand in front of a student's work, I do what we encourage all our students to do with their own work, and everybody who works here. We demonstrated this amazingly well to the pro-rector. He came in to see the short-listing process for the applications and we were unanimous about somebody's work and he asked us, 'Wow, what's going on here? You all jumped to the same conclusion'. And he suspected that it was about taste, or sensibility, or prejudice or patronage. It was none of those things. First and foremost, we went around the table, the students started: they gave exquisite and very different accounts of why they said 'no' to x, y or z. And all three, to a greater or lesser degree, reflected current discourse, in which the work would be located in terms of contemporary discourse, and the historical. And then, finally, most people notionally put that all together and asked of this work, 'is it good of its type?' I'm not looking for work that I like or dislike, I mean you get that right out the door, kick that right into touch. If I were to do that, I don't think I'd have to get out of bed, because I could dream the work I like. There is an assumption on the part of people generally, of people in art schools as well, particularly people that run them because they can't picture what we do; the nuancing and the complexity and the intellectual rigour … The visiting professor here is a philosopher, Jonathan Rae. He's not any old philosopher. This guy really comes at it, he's brilliant. This is the kind of department I run. It's not 40 or 50 people swanning around being arty. Or addressing how they feel, or which side they got out of bed, no way! My staff and I, we do not like or dislike any of the work here; what we look for at application, and all the way through is desire, is application. Basically, we're looking for the same damn criteria; the same qualities that my brother, who works as a manager in a factory, will look for among the people he employs to work for him.

But you wouldn't have your brother, the manager working here in an art college, would you?

Of course not, not any more than I could do his job.

So what can you teach when you teach art?

I teach, we all teach what's called a critical methodology, or some form of critical methodology. If you're anything like me, or even Peter de Francia, the professor before me … he said, 'God, I really need a good tutorial'. This is 30 to 40 years after having left art school, and that stuck. I suddenly thought 'yes, that's what we all need. What we really need is to know how to not beat ourselves up, not to get subjective about it'. We do more casual encounters socially. Critical methodology is to step back and look at the work, and apply an appropriate critical methodology. Those methodologies are available thorough various discourses; the critical methodology that surrounds someone who intends to make work that is perhaps surrealist in some ways will be different from the formalist, or the classicist. I can go on and on. You can break it down, so what you're doing is you're teaching through empathy. If you were a student, John, and let's say you were a Greenberg fan. The first thing I would do is I'd get you to talk about your work and ask in a straightforward way why you're making work that's so nostalgic, so academic. And that's the other thing that we've got to get clear; that academic art isn't about emulating the YBAs, as people were doing in the late 1990s and early twenty-first century. Academic art now is the whole discourse following on from the Richter/ Doig photographic appropriation. If every year 400 people apply, 300, let's say, basically make that kind of work, because that is contemporary academic work. Whether it's engaging or not is another matter. I don't like or dislike it. What you have to do, as an academic you have to go with this, and you have to make very hard decisions.

Are you saying that academic work is the thing that …

It's what academies approve of at any one time. I can tell you straight away, if you go around our studios I bet you 20 pounds you couldn't find what the house style is. You're talking to a guy who has worked in an institution where tolerance, pluralism, cultural complexity and diversity have actually been what the college is about. It has been really, really good in allowing those differences to nurture, to take root … in it not being an academy. And I don't mean that as in the RA. I mean academy in the sense that an academy is an institution that has a model. Greenberg laid down almost academic regulations for how certain kinds of painting could be conducted and why other paintings and other forms of painting were inferior. The inferiority of various genres is almost a Victorian obsession with the Ziggurat. There's also the Reinhardt joke about sculpture being something you back into, because of its physicality, and the sublime was the music of the spheres. I don't subscribe to any of that, because I don't find it particularly useful when you're teaching.

If one wanted to study in London, why would one choose the Royal College over Goldsmiths or Chelsea?

You're asking the right and the wrong person that question. If you're asking me why people still apply here in their droves it's because the Royal College is perceived and has been perceived as a place to go and study painting, and I can only talk about painting. At the Royal Academy, people tend to go end-on from undergraduate courses because the Royal Academy can pay them maintenance and stuff. So they regard that as years four, five and six. If anybody comes up here and makes out they think this is years four and five of their undergraduate experience they're riding for a real fall. First and foremost, there is a very diverse programme here. In fact, if you were to go to Howley Street, even in the first year group of, say, 15 people down there, I don't think you'll see two people who share a common practical methodology. The style of their work isn't common. It's very diverse, and that means we teach through empathy. So if you go back to John-the-student; if this is the journey you want to go on, or the trip, or the path you want your work to take, and you're conscious of the historical precedents and the contemporary discourse and all the rest of it, then this is the route I would take. You don't actually look for my approval or disapproval, because, quite frankly, why the hell would you do that if you're a postgraduate student? Approval or disapproval has to be withdrawn at a certain point. Because how can you make independent learners when they are waiting for your approval? It's a contradiction in terms.

There's something quite particular in the discrete disciplines you still have at the Royal College, and I'm interested in what you think that brings to ….

I'll tell you straight away what it brings. As professor of painting at the Royal College of Art, I've noticed a decline in the quality of education in British undergraduate courses, particularly at places like the University of the Arts. It's not the people, it's the education; they're not getting a good enough education. Two tutorials a year, no dedicated work space … that is no way to resource or to run a course of any kind in my opinion, particularly a fine art course. Goldsmiths was right in 1972 or '73, when Goldsmiths, and several others went into fine art. At the time when they made those decisions, Goldsmiths drew on, and still do to some extent, an extraordinary high quality of staff and students. I'm not going to give you their names, but you know full well who was there at the time, and whatever project Goldsmiths engaged in, because of their ability and the quality of the students, there was the confidence to make it fly. And it did, it really worked. But across the board and in a contemporary climate, 30 years later they're doing it out of cost effectiveness, they're doing it for resources. In a fine art discourse there is only that discourse, but we actually run four different ones; the painting discourse is not the same as the discourse around architecture, or any other activity, and I make no bones about it. The Slade is very strong in terms of its area disciplines or its discourse, and it's currently producing some of the strongest students that apply to do painting in the postgraduate sector, in my opinion. Although it's the Slade School of Fine Art, when you actually examine how it's constructed in the studio space, on the shop floor, you actually find that there's lots of sharing. Talk to Phyllida Barlow, that's who you should talk to about this, but I think they've got the balance about right. The University of the Arts haven't, because when you put painters into a fine art discourse, particularly when you're trying to do it on the cheap, as the University of the Arts blatantly are, you become media blind. There is the discourse, as it was called, particularly the post-Marxist one that developed in the late 1970s, early 1980s, which became depoliticised during the Thatcher period; it had to be apolitical, because HEFCE [Higher Education Funding Council for England] and all the government agencies wouldn't tolerate it. All the clearly Marxist discourses about class, and things like that, have been pushed aside, so the discourse would be about the body, identity, you know, sexual orientation, race and so on. We've changed the whole landscape of discourse. But in that change, the generalised, prescriptive nature of those series of discourses or options actually meant that all work was talked about as work; it was not significant that it was photography, or painting, or performance, or anything. This was the beginning of a political correctness at the time, to see all media as equally valid. When I was a student in the 1960s, all the smart students wanted to do video and performance, it was an emergent and changing landscape then. Of course now, 35 to 40 years down the road, it's got its own departments, it's part of the orthodoxy and people feel they can complain about video the way they used to complain about painting. The point I'm trying to make is that the depth of discourse, particularly in the kinds of students we get – going back to the profile of the 30-somethings who are practising, who are ducking and diving, who hit a glass ceiling – they're realising that their career prospects, if you like, are somehow blunted. They can't see their way through that mid to early career thicket of survival and the complexity and the confusion and the politicking that is the art world. So to put it bluntly, they come here to up the ante. This is postgraduate study if you want to be a professional painter, and we can not only sharpen up your wits, but give you a critical methodology that fits your aspirations, your desire, your agenda, d'you get it? Not the one that Greenberg, or Lawrence Gowing, or Peter de Francia, or Graham Crowley, or anybody in particular utilises for their own practice. It just doesn't fly these days, to come in and to say the same damn thing to every student; even undergraduates turn around and say, 'yeah, did he talk about Carla to you? Yeah, that's all he talks about.' Do you see what I'm getting at? Here we listen and we look at the work and we interrogate the student's engagement with their work. That's the first thing that we inspect.

And what are the dangers of opening up the field?

I'll tell you point blank what's happened. Painting and sculpture in the 1970s were independent, classic, belle-arte sort of traditions. They were the independent schools, the two great strands, historically. Then there was photography, which had not only a separate technology, but also a separate discourse and history. Then came the moving image and the performative, and so on. You have to recognise these different discourses. You can skate over it on foundation and maybe in the early undergraduate years, but when we're talking about years five, six, seven of study – as well as what I regard as the interregnum of practice that there should be, ideally, some form of life experience between undergraduate and postgraduate. I feel very strongly about that – that should be within the chosen area of practice. One thing I haven't said yet is that a lot of people come here knowing that the quality of staff are pretty damn wired. You talk about it like an art school, like going to the University of the West of England or something, and no disrespect to them, but when you come to the Royal College and you meet people like Dawn Mellor, John Strutton, David Rayson, Rose Finn-Kelcey, Jonathan Rae, Dr Jim Mooney … I can go on and on and on with all these wonderful staff. That's got to be one of the selling points from most peoples' points of view. Getting back to the question, the other one is the reputation at present. It is not about being a celebrity, it's not about the old celebrity culture, which the College and most institutions still trade on; the idea that because we who write the books and run art schools have never heard of anybody but Tracey Emin and Chris Ofili having been here … are the only names we hook onto. My alumni for next year will be people like Jamie Shovlin, Lali Chetwynd, Chris Orr – our Chris Orr, not Chris Orr the printmaker – Matt Weir, Eleanor Evans, Ian Kiaer … This is what we're doing. The students who've been through this department have not only learned to have confidence in their own voice. This is what pluralism is; it's permission to intelligently undertake, with historical cognisance, your own project. And not to look for critical approval from any quarter – because quite frankly there is no consensus in that respect – and to look for or to look towards critical consent or approval is to listen to a cacophony that will only confuse you. So we're trying to make people, give people, encourage people to think of a very long game, help them get to terms with the confusion and the red herring that is celebrity in the art world. The aberrant culture of celebrity in the late 1980s in particular, it's all gone out of the system now. No students are waiting for x, y or z collector to come round and open his or her cheque book, they just don't do that. They get on and create projects for themselves. The one lesson of that period is the fact that the project *Freeze* was a self-curated, artist-generated project and it's this that people have taken on in this new generation. Artist-run spaces like 39, for instance, is run through a member of my staff here in collaboration with Alan Miller and John Strutton. Alan Miller's son Jake runs it. We are wired, and people are coming into this department, not because of the simple … I'll be honest with you, this is the best team I've ever put together. I've worked in loads of institutions, I now know through the depth of experience, that this is the most diverse group of teachers I've put together. The three members of staff within their areas of practice do not overlap that much; Dawn is this kind of a painter, David is this kind of an artist, and John Strutton has what's called by anybody's imagination an extended practice, but within the historical discourse that is painting.

If I go back a little bit to the problems you suggested that Goldsmiths might have now …

I don't know how political you want to get John, but that could be a contributing factor. I'll be blunt with you; the fact that Sam Fisher is in charge of their undergraduate project has meant that people like Gary Stevens, *et al*, have jumped ship – that's all you need to know. There's no point in being soft about this. If, for instance, x or y had still been there and things had been different historically ... when it comes to the nuancing of fine art now, and the changes and the discretion we once had which we no longer have – we're increasingly told what to do by people who have no engagement with this area of discourse and this area of social activity. The thing that's lying behind Goldsmiths and all the rest ... I was there the same time as Jon Thompson. I'll be honest with you though: it was Jon who did the hard leg-work and the theory, but when it came to articulating the situation, Michael Craig-Martin was the guy most people called upon, because, let's face it, he was always good in front of a camera. He's very good, he's very telegenic, or whatever the term is. But Jon, the very few times I've ever seen him on telly, he doesn't impress. He's probably the most impressive intellect I've met in a British art school in my life, and it was Jon's sense of the historic, Jon's sense of the longer game. Credit to Jon when it actually came to articulating where we all were, and what the weather was going to be like. It was a bulletin from someone pretty far-sighted with a great sense of the historical, who'd been involved and engaged in Pop Art in the very early days. You get any of those lovely old Thames & Hudson histories and there's some of Jon's *Painting by Numbers* pictures and all the rest of it.

I think Michael would concede anyway ...

Oh, he does.

His best teaching was done he said when he was coming in one day a week.

Yes, that was later on when he got the fellowship.

He's talked about his anxiety over what he described as the insidious growth of academicism in art education.

I concur with that.

You share his anxiety?

I do absolutely, because when we talk to our students, we're not asking them to follow. I just made the point earlier on, that this is not an academy; you can't actually engage in academic discourse if you, like I have, have the description of the academy as something prescriptive and monotheistic. This is something I acquired partly from my experience of teaching at Goldsmiths and my experience of being a student here with Peter de Francia and John Golding, who were two of the most extraordinary minds teaching in the early 1970s in any institution.

But is that also embedded in your practice? That the practice provides a space to be able to withstand the demands of the institution? What keeps the teaching alive, in some way is embedded in your practice?

Yes it is. I've got a good answer for that; memory teachers, where students used to be able to spot memory teachers. This is 40 years ago, when you were able to typify the orthodoxies of high modernism and institutionalism in post-war British art schools. It was developing tropes, modes, or whatever. It was developing academic orthodoxy of that late high-modernist kind; 'keep it open', 'keep it free', 'yes, I think in order to make those better, you should make them bigger', 'oh! I do like that!' The old sort of thing about taste, and approval being a matter of enthusiasm; wonderfully kind of limited, lame sort of ways of going about endorsing things. By the way, I was threatened with expulsion from the painting department by Carol Waite; Frayling had me in his study but he knew he couldn't kick me out because I had an impeccable academic record. Most people who create issues and make demands upon their department are normally conscientious. The slackers actually want to do it horizontally; they don't want to stand up and be counted, do they?

What's this memory teacher you mentioned?

Those are people who've been in the system far too long. Even when I was a student you had people who had wonderful collections of boats or clocks or, you know, early Picasso etchings and engravings, and lived the life of Reilly. They were amateur artists – how much they got in or out, depended upon where the art school was. I met a few of them when I was a student. I had the privilege at Saint Martins before it turned into the current aberration that it is. We had visiting artists, people who came in, whose practice was fresh. I'll tell you, this is where it gets really interesting, when I can't stop enthusing about my work to my students and talking to them like peers, d'you get what I mean? Drop the 'please, sir, can I go now' or 'is it alright, professor, what I'm doing?' 'Is this meeting with your approval, Graham?' Students wouldn't even ask whether I like things or not. They'll ask me candid questions about 'so what do you think of that? Do you think that's better than that?' I'll give them a damn straight answer; of course I will! But I'll give them a reason for why that is a better piece of work. In some sense, because I know what they're wangling after, they're not asking whether I like it or not. They're asking me to say whether this, in some semi-objective standard, in some public sense outside or beyond my sensibility, whether there are structural reasons that can be articulated for this being more ambitious, more insightful. Do you see what I mean? I talk in a very different register, as you've probably noticed.

And what about today, when teaching has almost become a professional career choice for artists?

To be honest with you, that's why I'm doing what I'm doing. I have to make a career choice to pursue my career. I made a career choice eight or nine, almost 10 years ago when Michael Kenny asked me if I'd be interested in helping him at City & Guilds. That was only two or three days a week, but it did start to impinge upon my practice, because of the responsibility and the thought and the reflection to get this as right as you can. My project here is basically to make sure that in 20 or 30 years' time, everybody who's been through here, I stand a chance to meet them later in life and they speak well of the place, that they feel … I mean you go and speak to all the students and the ones who have just completed, and it has, nine times out of 10, far exceeded their expectations. And, quite frankly, maybe that's because people's expectations, if they've been to some of the London art schools or, sorry, University of the Arts recently, are not very high. In fact, something else is embedded in the system: because of this lack of expectation, people are not applying and not going on to do postgraduates. Numbers are declining. Ours are holding up, the Academy's are moving up because everybody has heard about their financial inducements. I think Slade's stacking up, and Goldsmiths, from what I understand. But we're not getting students applying here from Central Saint Martins, from Camberwell, we haven't for years, because they have these joint honours and that sets them back structurally. After having completed their degree they've had a year and a half of painting, just to put it in a simplistic sense, rather than three years of painting, like a student from Winchester, or from the Slade, or Ruskin. Do you know what I'm saying?

Yes ...

Central Saint Martins, one just feels for the people there.

Why?

Hold on. Just let me finish. If you look at the HEFCE report on student satisfaction and dissatisfaction, you'll probably know the University of the Arts came bottom. The key reason is the lack of engagement. They don't want approval or disapproval; people just want to feed their heads. They want their work to grow and grow, they want to feel they're growing as human beings. And to be perfectly blunt, that's not about marking or about approval or disapproval. It's about support, it's about empathy, it's about listening, it's about a very different set of human values, or human skills more correctly, than those with which I think most people think that we conduct ourselves – like atelier loonies, or something, from the 1890s, or the 1950s in New York. Do you see what I'm getting at?

It's not friendship, it's still within the rigour and discipline ...

 I'm sorry, I'm not friends ... I don't hang out, I don't drink with ...

... of an art college, and what you can give them in terms of cultural cachet. It is the Royal College after all ...

Yes, that's very well put. Hold on, you've touched on another point as well, don't forget there is such a thing as a network, whether you call it 'old boys', 'RCA approved', 'painting department approved', whatever ... students are applying these days, and they take that on board because they want a network. They're realistic about their career prospects. There are people who leave here 10 or 20 grand in debt.

You're not going to spend that money unless ...

Exactly! They don't want to be dicked-around. They don't want art therapy; they don't want a displacement activity for three years. Our job is to weed out the ones who we

think have not only got the ability and the desire, but who've got the resourcefulness, the savvy and the stamina. OK, we're interested in students who will survive coming here, and go on and survive the art market and the world. People who come to the Royal College because they want to come here to gain brownie points implode, because their agenda and their desire was to simply come here. They falter, and you can see it in them. Now, getting back to Camberwell and to University of the Arts: given there's consensus in the sector about the problematic quality of education, who in their right mind would want to sign up for years four and five of the same crap. We're actually losing a wonderful part of our national heritage. The art school is not uniquely British, but there's something about what it has come to represent in British society. It's increasingly PC – we can't have this or that event, because we can't actually have people skateboarding down the stairs here, or snowboarding down the stairs and videoing it, which happened one year. When the health and safety officer saw the video he, of course, wanted me to be told off and disciplined for allowing such a thing to go on. Quite rightly, of course.
Take that either way …

Can I shift the conversation slightly?

Is this of some use, John?

This is a lot of use, thanks Graham …

OK, because listen, this is straight off the top of my head stuff and I'm forgetting a lot of things and I know I ramble a bit and I understand why you interject and ask the questions, but that thing about networking … Student are savvier now and they're also a damn sight more broke so they won't come. As I've said once you've been to university, why would you want to go on and do postgraduate study if your experience, or model, is based upon that which is closest to you, in your, what shall we say, your host institution, whether it be Camberwell or Central Saint Martins, or whatever? There's not the motivation because the experience is a negative one predominantly.

Can you say a little bit about what you consider to be good teaching today, and can you link that to the current state of art education in the UK?

[Loud laughter.]

It's like handing me three matchboxes and asking me to build … Listen, I'm going to have to break that down into bits. Come again with the first bit, there was one bit I got my head round.

OK, what do you consider to be good teaching?

[Susan, Graham's secretary, comes in and reminds him of another appointment.]

Hold on, what do I consider to be good teaching? I can only answer these questions about things like love and art and teaching and desire in a forensic sense; you don't look for them, you look for evidence that they've touched something, or that they have been moving forces. Now what does it mean when students come up to me and say, 'I think so and so is a brilliant teacher', and you say, 'well, why do you think that's the case?' And they say 'because they were so insightful'. Now that's not exactly a twenty-first century attribute but it's one that within a certain area of discourse, particularly the academic, has not actually been acknowledged. And how is that insight generated? It's generated through looking and listening to the student's presentation, so a certain generosity. In fact the big word here is generosity, and that sometimes means being blunt and going off the PC agenda. This is why the painting discourse is so important; in order to know what the academic is, you have to actually be introduced to all the academic discourses as models of practice. Then what we encourage our students to do is regard them as buses that have just left the central bus station. And what they should be doing is actually looking for a job driving the next bus out, not getting on the last one out. You see what I'm getting at? Normally, good teaching is something that is supportive without being invasive, without playing parent-child sort of stuff – Transaction Analysis and that sort of nonsense. Supportive without being invasive, being rigorous with oneself, self-scrutiny. Showing students the difference between what is beating yourself up, being down on yourself, and analysis through description. As a culture we don't spend enough time looking and describing, articulating what we see, because there is so much ambiguity now. What we do when there is ambiguity, we differentiate it from vaguery. That's a really important intellectual proposition, is it not? I can see the look on your face! It is, isn't it? And once you get there, you then ask the student 'so what's the ambiguity?' When people are being a bit woolly and talking and looking and waving their arms around like windmills and stuff, and you stop them by saying 'well that's 16 different propositions and I'm sure you subscribe to all of them and that's absolutely fascinating, but that's just what makes it feel vague. Are there two primary propositions or two major propositions that seem to be intentional? Or is there something significant about this? It's for you to articulate and tell me this'. Then there is this whole discourse around the idea of the signifier and signification, which has been absorbed through late phenomenology and Merleau-Ponty, 30-odd years ago. But a lot of people now are getting interested in the discourse surrounding phenomenology – very big in the late 1960s and early 1970s – rediscovering people like Bachelard and stuff like that. Which I find really heart-warming, because I think Bachelard is not only very poetic, but actually a marvellously creative and reflective writer. So the experience of engaging with art or work like that – they illustrate the creative mind at work. When you engage with, say, *View of Toledo*, it's not just another landscape painting; the whole genre is problematised through this one painting. Whether everybody from the year after it was painted took that on board, or whether it only became noticed by the more specialist painters and the art historians over the next 10 or 20 or 30 or 100 or 200 years is another matter, OK?

OK, and …

No, hold on! I've got one … I've just got to …

OK …

Before you go any further; good teaching is when you've actually had a tutorial with a student and you've listened and you've looked and you've asked them questions. There is a little bit of the Socratic method here, and this goes back to Peter de Francia's methodology, where you unearth contradictions through a genteel form of interrogation. A generation ago it was about how you were going to square them, nowadays people don't even expect you to resolve them exactly, but to acknowledge them. Because the one thing that really generates when you get to this point is the notion of hybridity, the synthesis, in culture. The synthesis I'm talking about is alive and well in more of people's work. The methodology is out there now, and you can see it in projects of groups like *Rockwell*, for instance; in the quality of work that's going on there, the diversity and the accessibility of some of the work. There has been a change of tenor again, in fact. It was a great mistake when people put critical theory ahead of, or instead of art history. Because if art history doesn't reflect or cannot embrace some form of critical theory, what kind of history is it? It would be a list, or a timetable. That's been a massive mistake on the theoretical side, and a lot of people are realising it. That started 30 years ago as well and Goldsmiths led the way there. But, of course those innovations have been misappropriated, and taken by HEFCE and others as models of practice and stuff. They've used them across the board, irrespective of the standard of student teaching and the context in which this discourse took place, to become models of management. I don't think they intended to make people more stupid, or to make the education worse. It worked at Goldsmiths and places that were exemplars – not so much these days, but definitely were when this was going on in the 1980s and 1990s. People looked at this model and it was credible. But now, for reasons that you probably know as well as I do, it is no longer sustainable and, from what I can work out, Goldsmiths is in search of a new model. And if it's not in search of one, then it's probably in need of one. But what do I know! Finally, in terms of this good teaching; it's making sure you work on people's self-esteem and self-analysis. I'm not a shrink, I've got no training in stuff like that, but I'm a painter and I know when I'm beating myself up and I know when I'm contextualising and critically dismantling and analysing my work.

What do you think about the introduction of PhDs and how do you rate the current state of art education in the UK?

Oh!

[Loud laughter.]

Listen, I'll tell you one thing, this is really complicated. I went into fine art because I actually thought that this was research into the human psyche, which was the 1960s rhetoric. Fine art is a discursive, speculative, reflective form of collective and individual scrutiny. The way that we reflect that scrutiny is through these objects that are manifest to that scrutiny. I don't care about the medium, it doesn't really interest me at all. I happen to be a painter, but that's where I came from and what I did. Both of my boys are a generation later; one is trained to be a film-maker, and the other is an animator and designer. I don't want to get into film as the dominant discourse of the twentieth century

– that was just beginning to be articulated when I left art college. I could have been a bit brighter and realised that before, but I did want to engage in what was presented as the dominant model at the time ... hold on, I'm going off the script again ...

PhDs ...

Yes, PhD's ... I went into the business thinking – clearly I was wrong – that this was about research of some form, research into the human condition, in some oblique or undisciplined and wonderfully indulgent and reflective sort of way. Nothing to this day gives me the same delight as that reflection, making the objects through that reflection, irrespective of whether you like them or not – I don't give a rat's arse about that, to be perfectly blunt. It's about value. This is really difficult stuff, particularly in the climate at present, because people like me are gradually being pushed, we're being forced out. We have a body of knowledge and a particular cultural position that threatens the rather thin and rather tenuous circle of authority of HEFCE, and people like that. The people that have now stepped up, if you like, to absorb and embrace the research culture – I'm not going to name names because I'd be invidious – people for whom the world of art has no esteem. There is no reflection. So what we've done is we've created a virtual sort of model of research in fine art. For instance, take this one simple proposition: most institutions, when it comes to research in fine art, do not credit the practical element. There's text and practice, with a thetic or theoretical element. It all lies on small bits of A4 paper; it cannot and does not reside elsewhere, because the model – first scientific, or pseudo-scientific through the sociology model, then adopted broadly in a cack-handed and half-arsed way into the humanities, which is now cobbled together for fine art – doesn't fit. We've got some great research students in this department and there's some great research staff and there's some great stuff going on. But I don't think that there's more writing going on by those people in any kind of real sense, that they're firing on six cylinders instead of four. I don't get that.

So what use is a PhD?

You'd have to ask some of the people who come to do it. Personally I see no reason for me to do one at this time of my life. I have no desire to do one. That's not to say I do not have a desire to constantly research and read voraciously about painting, art history, theory ...

How would you counsel a student who asked your advice?

I'd ask them why they wanted to do it first, and then there are people here – I can only talk about the department – who are making an extraordinary contribution at a very high level. If the powers that be can stop making us carry so much lead all the time, because the bureaucracy surrounding this means that … There's an assumption that people like me aren't fit to run such things and at the same time they want us to run these things. Does that make sense?

People like you?

Educationalists, people who are seen as education managers. Basically, I don't see the project as anything more than a cynical attempt on the part of the government to take a tighter control over fiscal matters when it comes to higher education. It's as simple as that. There's going to be first rate and second rate. There's too many bloody smart people around. Look what happened in Germany 30 years ago.

What happened?

I mean Baader-Meinhof and all the rest of the Symbionese Liberation Army, the Red Army Faction. The smart money is on not raising expectations too high, because they cannot be, and they will not be met by civic and social society any longer. We're talking about turning the clock back, all sorts of revisionist things waiting in the wings now and my gut sort of feeling about it is that it's a bit … I'm a motorcyclist and people spend so much time debating the noise motorcycles make and all that sort of crap, but quite frankly noisy motorcycles save lives because they can hear you coming. Don't forget, most people who run art schools now have never been to art school and don't know what they're talking about. They know what they've got to do, because HEFCE tells them what to do. What I'm saying is that the vision has gone out of these institutions and I think its time to start again. But I can't see the right political climate in the public sector to actually embrace art schools, in the way I would like to see them constituted.

And it would be artists running them?

Yes, of course. The reason I'm leaving, is a very straight-forward equation: I love what I do. All of my teaching, I feel has been an absolutely brilliant achievement. It's been a great eight years. But I have to leave because I cannot continue to be a painter, and do this job properly. And by being a painter, I mean keeping my representation through the gallery in the West End. Once I do this, I'm out there; I'm a player. I'm not a clever academic bloke who occasionally writes an essay or two in *Art Monthly* about painting, or about the condition of contemporary art. I steer clear of conferences on art education like the plague. I really do! I steer clear of conferences per se, because most people there are using them to construct cvs, so they keep asking silly questions from the 1970s, and you think 'Jesus Christ!' Where have you been? And then, of course, they tell you where they work and you think, 'oh well, that's why'.

Graham Crowley taught at the Royal College of Art, London and is now retired from teaching.

Walter Dahn — a Sunday afternoon —
his studio in Cologne — loud music playing
throughout the interview.

Going back to what you said before I turned this on, why are you considered one of the best teachers in Germany?

Not best, maybe most successful.

How is this success measured?

In the first place very superficially, in a weird way. 12 to 15 of the students I've had over the years are now showing their work, and making a living from it, which is the dream that you start out with. They all seem to have found a place where they feel comfortable. Some are showing with Christian Nagel or with Michael Janssen here in Cologne, some are with The Modern Institute in Glasgow, some are with Andrea Rosen in New York, and so on. It's not so spectacular sometimes. It's not such a loud crowd, one could say maybe, but they are well received. Another student of mine, Antje Schiffers, just finished a show in the Wiener Secession, for instance. She's a great artist with a more conceptual background.

Are they great artists when they come to you? What do you do for them?

Sometimes somebody comes and you can already say 'this is going to work', and sometimes you have to have an ongoing discourse over five, six, seven years. I'm not interested in creating a school and they don't have to believe what I say; they don't have to work the way I do, it's the opposite; I've always said if someone starts to work like me, he better leave the class and find some other teacher. I'm interested in working with individuals, putting my focus on the individual. That creates maybe a little more work than the usual way the studies go. But they say I'm quite good at it, I'm trained and prepared. I started in January 1995. Most of the time new students who come approach me even before they join the class. It's also because some of their friends are there, maybe. When they finish their first two semesters, their Probejahr – or foundation year – we look at the work and most of the time *now* I approach them and ask if they want to work with me. It's the other way round: they're not invading the class, I go and ask them. I see someone working from a position which is not represented in the class, or in the collective I would rather say, that could enrich this, and I would ask if they want to join the collective. Most of the time it works and they answer, 'I wanted to ask you already, but I didn't dare', or something like that. It's funny.

Tell me a little more about the difference you make between the class and collective?

Actually it's the same … it's just two words.

But you seem to put emphasis on the collective …

Class is a German word. 'Die Klasse', which also means the space, the studio, or whatever you might call it we're working in; the classroom, so to speak. Then also something like the working class, the ruling class, etc. If I talk about a collective, I'm talking about something where I feel more part of the whole thing, as opposed to being a teacher who is in a sort of elevated position. Talking *down* to somebody …

It's about authority?

Yes, yes. And I tend to question that.

Is it also about your own experience? You studied under Beuys from the age of 17, 18 …

Yes, yes, yes!

And how did that affect you?

Oh, in every way. He was so great. I try to include some of the experience I had with him into my approach and *to do it my way*, like Frank Sinatra. I did it my way. There's no other. I can't continue where he stopped, that's impossible.

What characterises your class or collective?

It's 17 to 25 individuals. There isn't a superficial style, super-imposed. I still try to learn from them, that's the main thing! I try to learn from these young people, which affects my work now. It's going back and forth, it's an oscillating process. You should ask *some of them*. I'm not dreaming this. It's something completely real, it's completely realistic, and not idealistic. It's my idea. I'm about ideas and not idealism …

And when you say teaching is your practice now, what happens at that moment?

A lot of very precise talking and discourse over years. I want to get more and more precise and I want to find the right balance between a close involvement and a good distance, one could say. You always work on that, every minute you're there. In a minute things might change …

But are they very separate activities for you?

No, no, no, it's all one thing. I'm working on different levels as an artist. I do my work now, which is completely revitalised after a couple of years when I stopped – sort of stopped. I always made drawings and photographs and kept doing exhibitions and so on. But for a couple of years teaching became the main thing for me, *as an artistic activity.* Not separate, like 'I have to do this because I get money from the state and I'm now quite secure, blah, blah, blah'. Or I have to do it, and then I go home and do my main work. I could never make this superficial and arrogant separation.

Why not?

I always quote the Fluxus artist Robert Filliou, who said: 'Lehren und Lernen als Aufführungs Künste!' (Teaching and being taught as performing Art!). He wrote a text about it. Teaching and being taught as performing art, as acts of performance. Fantastic! I would subscribe to that. It's a 13-year long, ongoing performance. The best work of art I've ever done. I could never separate myself – teach, and afterwards go home and work on something for a show. Most of the work I do, which will maybe later be on show in a gallery, or a museum, I do there at the school. Most of the work of the last four or five years, 10 years, I've done there, because we have incredible people, we have incredible workshops, I have a wonderful studio here, and people who help me out. And so on …

Tell me if I'm completely wrong here, but to me, the way you describe your teaching, or what you've been doing for the past 10 years or so, has a very strong echo of your time in "Mühlheimer Freiheit"; there's this collective, this kind of group …

Well, I'm still part of a group, but now Rock 'n' Roll gets really serious!

… and it's as much about the relationships between people and the work being produced in this way as it is about anything else …

You're absolutely right. I think in Mühlheimer Freiheit times, even before, in Düsseldorf with Beuys, I was working a lot with friends, I was doing collaborations and so on. I was trained. When I came to Braunschweig I did a year in Düsseldorf, between 1983 and 1984, so one could say I had some sort of training of working with young students, as part of a collective. You're right. "Mühlheimer Freiheit" was important, because we were just six guys constantly working together. We had to because nobody had enough money for a single studio. So we shared this big one. Six guys, and everybody was talking to everybody, constantly. There was no fussing or fighting, nothing. It was just everybody looking at and caring about the other guy's work, to develop the discourse, to get better …

In his essay *Blood of the poets: the tribal '80s*, Tom Holert says that this moment was broken when Paul Maenz hosted a landmark exhibition of the group in November– December 1980 at his Schaafenstrasse gallery.

No, not at all.

What Holert claims was that once Maenz wanted to commercialise Mühlheimer Freiheit, to package and kind of institutionalise Mühlheimer Freiheit, that is where it began to fall apart.

We gave in very late. First he offered a show and we said, 'no we're not going to do this, we'd rather show in some sort of shitty environment. Or do a show in Rosemarie Trockel's living room.

She was living above Monica Sprüth at the time?

It doesn't matter now. Paul approached us. He saw a show we did in a very shitty environment here in Cologne, at the so-called BBK, Berufsverband Bildender Künstler. It was a completely no-go place, the Berufsverband Bildender Künstler. Terrible art was shown there, completely mainstream. So we said 'Fuck 'em, that's the right place to go'. And we did this show with the materials we found there. Working directly on the wall. There were drawings, texts, found objects, and so on. After that we got a good response from Paul, also from Jean-Christophe Ammann from the Kunsthalle Basel, who saw the show and wrote us a postcard which said that after seeing the show, he couldn't get to sleep. Paul offered us a show and Georg (Jiri Dokoupil) instantly said 'no, we'd rather show in an apartment, or a bookshop, or wherever'. But Paul came back and supported us; he gave us a little money for the tiny studio we had at the time in the South of the city. And money to buy materials. The relationship got a little bit closer. We always discussed everything between the six of us. Finally we said 'OK let's try and do it, but if we do let's force him to include people we like, so it's not just us.' So we said, 'we have some friends in Hamburg, one guy is called Albert Oehlen, there's this other guy Georg Herold.' Nobody was known at the time, it just started. 'The third guy is Werner Büttner, we want those three in the show. And two people from Berlin, Thomas Wachweger and Ina Barfuss, we like their work too, they should be in the show.' Paul called the show *Mühlheimer Freiheit und Interessante Bilder aus Deutschland* [Mühlheimer Freiheit and interesting paintings from Germany]. It was 11 people, the gallery was completely crowded. That was our impulse; not to try and start a career with an already super-successful gallerist. Our impulse was to open the door for people like Albert and Georg and Thomas and so on. We were completely aware of the fact that this thing could go down the drain instantly. Or be a smash success! We were not sure. Paul turned on the public relations machine, because he came from public relations. I mean he was very, very agile. But it was not an instant success. All the pictures were very, very cheap, and the installation was kind of rough. It was not about making an adjustment to the mainstream. More like the Times Square show which happened a little before in New York City. I was friends with Diego Cortez and Fab 5 Freddy, who later became very famous with his MTV Hip Hop Show. We felt connected to people like Francesco Clemente, who was just starting out. And Sandro Chia's paintings. Paul had already shown these people. And then the first important Jonathan Borofsky show at Paula Cooper, where he painted on the walls and we thought, 'wow, this is what we're doing, this is incredible!' We felt support from that, some self-confidence, maybe we were on the right track. But it was not safe at all. I don't know. Tom Holert is not completely right. He should have talked to me. So here's my invitation to Tom Holert: contact me to get the facts right, and nothing but right! There's so much bullshit going on about this time, the early 1980s, there's so much misinformation, especially from people who were not there at the time ... I don't know. It's not only my fault but I'm not going to write a book about how things really happened.

Holert goes onto say in *Blood of the poets: the tribal '80s*: 'their [Mühlheimer Freiheit's] lifespan was limited from the moment Maenz ...

Oh I feel what's coming, I don't need that again!

... took over and pushed Mühlheimer Freiheit into the art institutions and collectors' networks ...

Yes, thank you very much Tom Holert. I completely forgot! Now, here's a quote by the late William Burroughs: When You're Young, (this is about youth). Young people in general are so concerned and always in a hurry to go to bed with somebody, (that was our main interest). *You grab around you like in a haze, aiming for everything that would be an excuse for what seems to be the pleasure. As a matter of fact, the result is that you don't look exactly, or long enough; they or you are always under pressure. The main thing it seems is that you have those little two or three things to spice up the talk before you fuck, all of a sudden you seem completely happy. When you're young, you are most of the time easy to satisfy, but youth ends at that beautiful beach at the ocean shore, where women look as if they'd be finally free, where they are so beautiful that they don't even need the lie of our dreams ...*

Let me just throw this at you.

Yes, let's just throw things at each other, I like that.

Can you teach art?

No ... I don't want to get esoteric at all, but you still have to have a sort of sensorium, of feeling for a person, like a football coach. I think there is something like talent or no talent. Even if it's not in fashion, this term, I don't care! So, if I sense something like that, smell something like that, or look at a person. Certain people bring out the football trainer, or coach, in me and I try to find the right position for them to play. Because sometimes you see people doing things, like they are the goalkeeper but over a couple of weeks or months you find they shouldn't be the goalkeeper, they should be centre forward. You have to find the place, or position, where this person would be enabled – through an ongoing discourse, of course – to be in the right place to play the game.

Can anybody teach this?

Teach? I don't know. But I can talk about it. Maybe there were three or four people in 13 years, who left the class to work with somebody else. The rest stayed because we found a way to work together.

What happened to the others? Why couldn't you find the right position for them?

It's just like any other relationship. We have to make mistakes. There's always something that's missing. We have to be able to talk about that, and if we're not, if I'm not, and the other person is not willing to talk, well … Talking is much more important here than just standing in the corner with a loaded brush and making painting after painting; we're much more about talking together, we're much more about "the philosophy of art". We watch one or two films, I try to find a connection to the history of movies, because that's the form where all the arts come together. You can't teach. You can point out certain things, make proposals. I say to someone 'maybe it's the right time now for you to go to the Bibliothek and find out about Neil Jenney and look at his work'. I have a student, she's working in wood in a way that reminds me of the very early wooden works of Carl Andre. So I brought her a catalogue of the early work of Carl Andre. I point at certain things. I point at Blinky Palermo, I point at early work by Carl Andre. In another case I had to point to the 1960s and early 1970s work of Per Kirkeby, which are incredible "Nordic Popism". And, of course, I point to Joseph Beuys, Alighiero Boetti. Paul Thek is very important now … artists like Bas Jan Ader might become important for some of the students in the course of their studies … and so on …

When I asked you whether anyone can teach art you said 'I can' and I can't'. What makes you able to teach?

I don't know. It's a certain need I already felt as a child.

To do what?

Work within a group, find the right words at the right time.

Do you have to be an artist to teach other artists?

Yes, absolutely!

Why?

Because everything is art now. Also teaching is art, or should become art again, and not just a thing to make a living. We have to dig a little deeper.

But if you're not sure if you can teach art then why is it the responsibility of artists to do that work?

Who else should do this?

I don't know …

Maybe days and nights. Living life, real life as we encounter it. I don't know. Administration has nothing to do with art. Art is not about administration. Art is not about imposing or projecting your ideas on somebody else who is not in a position to resist. Art is about finding out from a 19, or 20, or 21 year-old person what he or she is about, what their abilities are, what their maybe pathetic or romantic obsessions are. You have to sense these things in a long, ongoing process, while resisting our constant demand to project our own needs onto other people. Put those things in the background and find something out about the individual person who's sitting right in front of you, I've found this out over those 13 years. I may be completely wrong, but then I need somebody to correct me and say 'no, Walter is completely wrong about this.' Though I don't think that there is just one way; it can only work like this. I meet with Albert Oehlen sometimes, and we discuss everything; from his involvement with music, with Red Krayola. And then he asks me a question like 'if a student comes to you and tells you this or that, what do you do?' I just tell him very openly and briefly. It's interesting to have this going on again, after all the so-called fights, or so-called distance in the 1980s and 1990s. Now that we're both teaching, we can talk again. Funny!

There's something I've been thinking about when you were talking about …

Sorry for interrupting … Maybe it has to do …

Go on …

Maybe it also has to do with the simple fact that we're just getting older and have no need to fight like in the 1980s and 1990s. Everybody has a position, everybody is "doing it" in his own manner.

Is this a good or a bad thing; that there's no fight anymore?

Well, of course there's a fight, but it's a fight of thoughts. It's not talking behind your back anymore … I hope …

Do your students provide the fight now? Provide that kind of energy?

Sort of, but every fight, or war, has to be a war of ideas now. If we can turn the real existing wars into a war of ideas, then there's no need for a war with weapons, or atomic bombs … The war of Ideas is also much more powerful!

But that's pure idealism …

It sounds idealistic, I know. I'm completely aware of the fact. But let me insert another fold-in, or cut-up, because I was talking about getting older …

When Winter has come, you don't like to go back, you don't want to admit to yourself that it's really over, you really want to stay, even in the cold, even at that age you still tend to hope. Understandable. People aren't so honest. We always wish to be, but you don't blame anybody. Sex and happiness über alles, that's how I see it. If you start hiding from others, that's only a sign of the fear of getting really involved, right? That's the real disease. We should ask ourselves, why we're so intensely not trying to recover from loneliness. Thinking of my past, it might occur that you thought of, seem to grab, or get hold of words that certain people once said. Or better, you want to grab and hold them, and also the people who spoke them. Just to ask them, why did you say that? But they're really, really gone. You were not smart enough to understand they have changed their minds meanwhile. But it's too late, over and done. You really have to leave all alone and continue to continue, all of your mates get lost, you couldn't even ask them the right question when there was time for it. Being right next to them, you just didn't know better. You lose, nothing but lose. You're always too late, always. But these are also complaints that lead nowhere. Though, as they say, age ain't nothing but a number, you still tend to think more and more about it. After leaving 50 behind me, they dissolve, they melt into my past. There is no use in turning round and just looking back, like Bob Dylan said. He was right; what am I longing for, I ask you? For youth? I tend to think that if you're not a real big-time success, like I never was, you tend, as you grow older, to become younger inside. But you must try and get rid of all the lies and the fears, all the smooth behaviour, all that useless boot-licking, ass kickin' that is implanted into you by the people in charge. The money, the terrible lie that money equals success in the art field. Not only there. I can only hope to be a little less disgusting at the end of the day, the end of it all. Everything else is not for me, doesn't bother me at all now. My aim is to get rid of all the conventions, to throw them up and spit them out. If I come close before I die, my fucking life wasn't so useless after all.

What brought you into teaching?

When I was 30 years old I was doing this one year in Düsseldorf. During the holidays, behind the scenes, they approached me and said something like, 'that year you did so well and your class is already something, blah, blah, blah ... Interesting people ... you work hard, blah, blah. Don't you want to stay?' And I answered them, 'fuck you. I want a rock and roll band right now, so call me again in 10 years.' Actually, almost to the day, 10 years later, I got a fax from Braunschweig, and they said 'we would like to have you, because somebody died, some teacher died, but you have to start instantly, like early January (1995). I said, 'of course, I'll be there'. So it started ...

Why did you say 'of course' at that point?

Because I thought around 40, I should ... I wanted to become a teacher. In my mother's house there's still a letter that I wrote when they tried to draft me for the army in 1973, I wrote some things, why I would never do it and so on; because my father was anti-fascist and so was my whole family. But I also gave them some reasons, that I didn't just want to do *nothing* for society, or the environment. At the end of this letter I wrote, 'at a certain point in my life I will become a teacher'. I knew it when I was 17. I just knew it. Maybe because every day at that time an incredibly good teacher was there right in front of me. Joseph Beuys!

Do you think that influenced you a lot?

More than anything else. There are also a lot of other influences when you're so young. I felt an urgent need to change my life and work with people again. After having incredible years in the 1980s, and early 1990s, I did my biggest show so far in 1997 when I was already teaching. The Stedelijk Museum in Amsterdam (together with Gabriel Orozco). He had the left part downstairs and I had 12 rooms to fill. So big-time success was not Mühlheimer Freiheit, or the 1990s, it came much, much later. It came after I became a teacher. That's when I had my most important shows, the ones I felt happier with ...

I was thinking about what Georges Bataille calls a secondary community in relation to you as an artist and how you've worked over the years. According to Bataille 'the secondary community needs a commitment and some form of creative effervescence if it's to endure, because belonging to a community of fact, as he calls it, cannot satisfy us and we become complete only if, as we gather together, we do so in a way that responds to our intimate demands, to the extent, as he says, that we no longer want to be disfigured and ridiculous in our own eyes'. I was wondering whether for you the teaching again provides the kind of community, creative effervescence, and commitment that Mühlheimer Freiheit once had…

Someone wrote that I'll be the Larry Clark of the German art scene. (Well, I don't know.) I am always involved with "youth culture" and so on. Also in the work I'm doing now. [Pointing to a photograph.] This kid is a 17-year-old photographer from Berlin, and he was lying there drunk and drugged out after an opening I recently had in Hamburg. I couldn't sleep, so I watched him sleep and then I photographed him. They compared us, and of course I like that. "Tulsa, Oklahoma" was a big influence on the photographs I do. On everybody's photographs … Excuse me, I want to put on another record. Did you see the show I did at Sprüth, Magers with Richard Prince last year, by the way?

I didn't see it but I know about it.

Anyhow so … Oh, this is wonderful. This is Glenn Gould talking about artists. It's from a DVD that's out now on Glenn Gould. Check it out:
People that I need around me, for the most part, are not artists. I think of artists as being like the apes that congregate on the Rock of Gibraltar; they tend to go for higher and higher niches and more and more stratified ones. They're very stratification-conscious people and they're very limiting people to be around, they use their own [egos] to such an extent. The most interesting people to have around one are people who are in a position to make synoptic judgements, diplomats, I DON'T KNOW, *and foreign service people, people in communications. Journalists sometimes,* YES, *if one doesn't get too caught up in clichés of journalism. But definitely not artists, they're all a bunch of Gibraltarians.*

[Walter puts on a new album.]

This is a great song from the Eels. I like the Eels. These are rock hard times. It's all about rock, this mixed CD. Anyhow, let's continue. I'll do another cut-up, fold-in here, if you have no specific question right now …

I have a couple …

OK. Maybe I can …
I'm getting a little bit excited here, but I want to make clear that being really young means that you love the world, just like that. You make no differences, that's the only truth, that's what being young is about. That's the news. Do we know people who are like that? I don't know any, maybe a few students in my class. Everywhere else there's only grey dumb darkness for my taste right now, breathing in more or less old bodies, and the more this dump-shit is breathing the more it really tortures youth. So you pretend and lie about how fabulous everything is, but it's lies, just lies, superficial blah, blah, blah. I know I'm disgusting talking like this; I can focus on something else easily, but it's not always easy not talking about something like this, something that follows you for so long and as soon as you live alone, like I'm doing right now, and nothing but alone, these questions about life torture you, they can drive you mad. So, to get it out of yourself, you splash it upon other people, everybody who visits you. You get on their nerves. Being alone means rehearsing how to die. The greatest joy on earth would be if we could finally enjoy dying, a joyful death. Everything else doesn't matter, means nothing, it's only fear that we admit, it's art. So, maybe, maybe I'm completely wrong here, I know that these things I want to talk about are pathetic and disgusting for a lot of people, in the art world especially, and the art schools.

Do you have regrets?

No regrets, like Scott Walker sang, the old Tom Rush song: 'no regrets, no tears goodbye. I don't want it back.' No, but I try to see things as they appear, as clearly as they appear to me, and I try to get rid of every kind of idealism right now for another understanding, a clear idea. 'I'm about ideas and not idealism.'

But how you talk is so full of idealism.

Yes, and I sometimes hate that. That's why I wrote this down! I wrote how disgusting talk can be. I told you how terrible this is, but it's a process, it's an ongoing process. I try to use the work to get rid of these pathetic idealistic roads that lead to nowhere. That's my own personal thing. I'm not trying to convince anybody. Maybe it has to do with these "rock hard times". If you walk the streets … I don't know. I want to make it very clear that I'm not … I try not to be optimistic or pessimistic at all. What I try to be is realistic. I'm aiming for a good realism, so we can get rid of optimism and pessimism …

Is it a good time to be teaching in Germany?

It's never a good time and it's always a good time. Hard to answer this … Of course it's a good time. I enjoy it and it's become such a big part of my everyday life that I can't think of myself not doing it any more. I can't judge other people, what they are doing now. An artist I really like is Michael Krebber who is teaching in Frankfurt. I can't and won't judge things they do or how they approach teaching.

Is teaching something temporary for you?

No, no, no. I'll do it until I fall down and die.

Will you?

Yes, absolutely. Because where else can you find young people who are so concerned, and who are so willingly giving up any safety. If you study Wirtschaft/ Wissenschaft – (economics) – or certain sciences, you're quite safe. After the sixth semester you can sign a contract with Bayer. But these people who come to art schools, they're now in a complete minority, they are risking something; they have to fight it out with their families. Or they're looked at by people who study these safe subjects as nerds. It's not in fashion anymore, it's not the 1980s.

How will you keep yourself interested if you plan to do this until you fall down and die, and how do you keep yourself interesting for students?

Through them. If they come to me and ask me, 'can I study with you?' When they give me the feeling that they need me. I'm getting so much back right now. It's not that I'm a sucking vampire, sitting on them, it's just refreshing. How can I make myself clear? Only through the work. This ongoing process of taking and giving. As a collective, or class, we try to be as autonomous as possible, and I find the niches beyond rules and regulations where more things are still possible. Most of the time, I try to be with the students, as autonomous as possible. And it goes so far that we don't go to the so-called Mensa (canteen) anymore to consume the food that doesn't make you feel good, it only makes you sick. We have big cooking sessions in the class, in the studio, for instance. For many years – 10 years or so – and I show these movies to give an understanding of the history of cinematography. Movies you *have* to know as an artist. Sometimes books, sometimes music. There's a lot of exchange going on; a lot of new music I get back from them. I am just involved. This keeps me going.

Do you work or play with the students outside the academy?

Yes, always. They come to my studio, and we sit and talk and work. Or listen to music. I now never say something like, 'we must', or 'let's go', like Mühlheimer Freiheit times, I rather ask ...

Can I take your photograph?

Yes. Of course. I'll read you some more. Cut-ups.

The final chapter ...

The final chapter, OK:
Our so-called hits and misses, trying to be a little happy, at least, are ugly and disgusting, so out of sight that it can make you sick. I'd go instantly mad if I hadn't the ability to forget. And then all the work, all the pain to become what we are now, to make our high hopes a little bit more interesting. Or our degenerated understanding of what might be real luck, all our incredible involvement and our lies, as well. So what's missing is not the intensity of our aims, no; we're just not on the right track, the one that leads to a calm death, all the illness and sickness eating up our lives, hour by hour, day by day. Lack of sleep rules my days and weeks. Meanwhile, you're getting even more sick, and never ever have as much time as you think you have.

I think that's the end of it!

Walter Dahn teaches at the Hochschule für Bildende Künste, Braunschweig.

Rainer Ganahl — Klasse Ganahl — in front
of the students at the Staatliche Akademie der
Bildenden Künste, Stuttgart, Germany.

How long have you been teaching in general, and how long have you been in your current post?

It's a good question. Administratively speaking this is my second year in Stuttgart, but 10 years ago I was also an associate professor at the École des Beaux-Arts in Geneva. Teaching has been part of my artwork, so to a certain degree the artwork is teaching – quote-unquote. I started doing this work in about 1993 or 1994.

Why do you put it in quotes?

Because its not institutionally framed the way my job is. There's not an academy that invites me. I have been doing my reading seminars and work I basically call linguistic services, where I teach a person, let's say, some language ... that is a kind of teaching.

Is that the *S/L* series?

No, it's separate from the *Seminars/ Lectures* works. In the *Seminars/Lectures* series I don't teach, I go there and I audit, or I listen.

What's the distinction you make between teaching in quotes and teaching administratively?

The differences are quite clear. The teaching that is institutionally framed comes with a salary, with students, with a curriculum and also a time frame. When I do it by myself I don't get paid, I can do it any time I want, and I have to look for students. I usually start with friends, and I say, 'let's do a reading seminar'. Interestingly enough we were supposed to read Foucault here today, this afternoon. That would have been a slight overlapping of doing the strand of work that I call a reading seminar – which is usually institutionally independent – while having it run through the institutionalised framework here as part of this professorship in sculpture. I'm teaching sculpture, by the way.

That's OK, isn't it?

I love it.

Is the reading seminar work meant to run counter to something?

It's not running counter, I'd say they cross.

What crosses?

The reading seminar work …

[Phone rings.]

OK, the reading seminar work that is institutionally independent but not contrary …

[A slight break for the phone call.]

… to any institution.

OK, let me go on and I'll get back to the thread of what I was thinking …

Do you want to first finish with the previous question?

About this crossover?

Yes, the crossover, yes.

OK.

So again … and you can always edit this … I look at the institutional framework and I look at my practice and they are completely different. But I can do something within an institutional framework and outside of an institutional framework. That's what I've been doing. I do not make a difference in terms of performing, in terms of teaching. I always love to talk about teaching with a 'quote-unquote'. You asked me earlier, why quote unquote? That's something I would like to come back to. I cannot ignore the fact that in one context you have an institution, and in another context you don't have an institution, that framework is important to keep in mind. With regards to your authority in relation to the people you're dealing with, with regards to payments, with regards to the fact that you know the selection process that goes along with it. If I'm invited to teach in Vienna, for example, I know that students there pay a lot of money. Here they pay 200 Euros, or not even that, and that's already difficult because we're used to not paying anything here. But in the West, people pay over 40,000 US dollars, and those are issues that to a certain degree I have to keep in the back of my mind.

Does this practice get rarefied or commodified, like the images in Venice, or was it *Documenta*?

Venice, Venice … The images you saw in Venice are from the series called *Seminars/ Lectures*. These are not my own seminars.

These are looking at somebody else's seminars?

In the Seville Biennale I had a reading seminar series, of reading Frantz Fanon, done over a couple of years; those are my own seminars. Even so, the images look similar because you're dealing with photos. What you don't have in my own reading seminars is the speaker. Sometimes a camera sits on the table and people photograph me too, so I can appear in those – I normally, at one point, appear in those photographs. It doesn't really matter who takes the photographs.

Are you recording all of these as well?

I don't record the *Seminars/ Lectures*; I just listen to them. The reading seminars I usually record, yes. When you're teaching – again, quote-unquote – regularly, it comes with a certain kind of distribution of authority and power and there's a certain notion of implied mastery. The person who teaches knows that, and the people who don't teach don't know that. With the reading seminar that is not necessarily the case; you can't take it for granted. Quite often what can happen is that the people who are in the seminars know more than I do.

It's mastery in the sense of you convening and authoring the event. It's not necessarily about somebody knowing more than you do in the seminar. The same as the way you talk about learning languages; it's not necessarily the competence you have in each language, it's to do with the act of studying. So the mastery is in you convening and to some extent choreographing the event.

I haven't yet addressed the issue of studying and teaching languages. I think teaching languages is more like teaching, because if I'm in Russia I teach English, or in Japan I teach French, or in America I teach German. Obviously it's clear the way it goes. But when it comes to the reading seminar, you cannot automatically assume the position of somebody who knows, because (a) I do not necessarily know my subject very well and (b) because that's one of the reasons I started doing these seminars. Today we were meant to read *Las Meninas*. I've read that text only once in my life and that was many years ago, but I would like to read it a second time. And the same with Lenin. I hadn't read anything before when I decided to start reading Lenin, I just had an intuition, a certain kind of idea. I knew he wrote interesting things about colonialism, and that was why I wanted to read Lenin. Not necessarily because of all the political aspects.

When you speak of mastery I don't think that's where the mastery resides; it's not a mastery over the text, it's in the convening of the event. That's where I think the mastery resides.

I'm not sure whether I understand you. We're still talking about teaching, teaching versus teaching …

[Phone rings, Rainer answers it, phone call finishes.]

What I wanted to say about mastery is that usually in a classical teaching situation the teacher is the *supposé savoir* – the one who knows. In my reading seminars I try not to occupy that position. Even though I push the situation.

But let me ask you then; are the reading seminars different to the Foucault reading seminar planned for today?

That would have been the same thing.

But the authority is reinvested at that point, isn't it? Your students are here with you, otherwise there wouldn't be a class.

That's why I said that it can sometimes overlap. Here I have two types of authority (1) is the natural quote-unquote authority that results from knowing, or not knowing something, and (2) the institutional authority, which I undermine all by myself, by my behaviour, by how the place looks and by the kind of easy going atmosphere here. Sometimes I allow students to insult me.

Do they insult you?

Yes, I kind of joke about it. For example I say, 'this is the professor-cup so please give me that cup'. 'This is the professor-chair', but I play with it. So this is the kind of authority you don't have, or that doesn't come with it, when you do it on your own, when you do it with friends, or you do it in situations that are outside of the institution.

But I would still say it's of a different order. I don't think they're equivalent modes of behaviour, I think there's a different order of things when you do a reading seminar outside the institution and circulate that as image or video. Otherwise it just becomes about reading a text like anyone else reading a text, and who cares?

The way you rarefy things by recycling; by-products such as photographs, and the tapes, the recordings, that's another question. I agree with you. That's why I wanted to put the teaching in quote-unquote. Basically, if I teach here I maybe put single quotation marks, if I teach outside I put double quotation marks. Obviously I would question the very notion of teaching, but not necessarily by throwing it out of the window, but maybe by trying to redefine it.

Because you're not in the business of rejecting it, you're very interested in teaching …

I'm very interested in it, absolutely.

So while you might be playing with the institution, it's not about undermining your own authority in any way.

In these questions, yes, and …

You don't want them to throw you out, do you?

Yes, but this stands even apart from art. It also depends on what you teach. If I would just teach language skills for money, that'd be one thing. You can do it well, or you can do it badly, but it's a basic straightforward business. But when it comes to quote-unquote teaching art, we have larger issues beyond the pedagogical at stake. There are pedagogical issues, but also issues about what you can teach in the first place when it comes to art.

Let me ask you the question then: can you teach art?

Exactly, here we are.

Well, here we are.

I opened up the box with the worms myself. It's an interesting question that I could throw back at you in a nice manner.

You can't, because I'm the interviewer and I'm asking the questions.

I know ... It depends what you mean by art ... what you mean by this? I would say, of course! Everybody most likely answers you in this way. There are some famous artists who don't necessarily want to be reminded of it, but they are the results of their social networks outside the academy. Obviously a kind of teaching has gone on. One in particular was a rich lady – a woman of society. To a certain degree she was just like an accessory; everyone looked at her as one half of this artists-couple, they paraded at art fairs and in their best years were beautiful to look at. Behind their backs people said, 'wow, they're so rich, and all they do is shop.' So it's not an accident that this artist's work became all about shopping. Basically, she threw it back in their faces. And she did a very smart thing. She took this semi-negative comment as an affirmative gesture, and started to shop and made an entire career out of an exuberant consumption. The reason I mention her is as another way of quote-unquote teaching; someone becoming an artist outside the institution. Now I'm going to talk about teaching, about art, within this institution, within a specified context.

You're going to tell me if you can teach art?

Yes, if you can teach art, exactly. Within the academy, that's the question, since we've already talked about teaching art outside the academy. A lot of people actually become artists outside of the academy through social networking. So what do you actually teach when you teach art? You provide a platform where social networks can incubate, so it's a nurturing ground for networking, for knowledge transfer, for certain kinds of practices. I come from a university context, so we really had to study and do homework, and I always made fun of art students, that all they learn is posing. Whether you're cool or not, in university, it's not about this – its not about how you pose and who you hang out with; your authority and the way you are looked at is established through the way you master the subjects you're supposed to master. I could argue in class, and I got respect for that. But when I came to art school and I didn't have that kind of habitus at all. I was not acquainted with being a cool artist, I was like a complete outcast there in that respect, and they hated me. I didn't get along, and they basically chased me out of town; I left Vienna within six months.

So can you teach art?

Again, what is art? We can provide a context in which artists can develop, in which a group of people can assemble and call themselves artists and act like artists and produce stuff that we consider, or don't consider, or discuss, or don't discuss, as art. It's a kind of game in a Wittgensteinian sense, in the sense of a Wittgensteinian *Sprachespiel*, or language game. When you're an artist you have to assert yourself with whatever you do; gestures, objects, dance steps, lovemaking, which you define as art. This is what then becomes, or is supposed to become art. You need a community for that and I would say the university, or the art school, is like a springboard for a lot of people. The reality today in the West is that art schools do play a role in the affirmation of young talent. There are certain academies that are considered very hot, while others are considered as less hot. I went to the Whitney Programme in New York and was shocked when I learned that when they looked through new applications, they would just scan them – even Ron Clark, people who are supposed to be beyond all this – all they did was look at university associations. So obviously all the people from the Art Institute in Chicago and CalArts – at that time the art school at Columbia University didn't exist yet – would get interviews. But if you came from Ohio or Kentucky …

What if you came from Stuttgart?

Stuttgart is a wonderful place. Stuttgart is a very strange city, because in a weird way it is almost like an unrecognised capital. You have the best industries in the city like Mercedes, and Porsche, which controls Volkswagen. So you basically have the main German car industries here. You also have Puma, Adidas and Hugo Boss, three major fashion companies and nobody knows that. And the same goes for the academy; it's a quite wonderful place, but we don't have people applying here. Other schools have 500 applicants between 20 professors, and we have 20 applicants between five professors. It's perverse. We don't have enough applicants for sculpture. This year we had 12 applicants for sculpture, between five professors, can you imagine?

How many did you take?

There are two more here.

You refused 10 of them?

We refused a couple of people … it's not that everyone shows up here. But we didn't take everybody.

When you look at students' work, do you know quite quickly which one is the 'artist'? And I'll put that in single quotation marks.

These are very interesting, sensitive, challenging questions. No, of course I do not know.

So on what basis do you choose?

I try to look at the person and I try to look at whether the person is interesting to a certain degree, and whether there's a link between the person and the work. Obviously I like people who have idiosyncrasies, particularities, or have some kind of obsession or question, some kind of intrigue or secret that is not obvious. And of course you have people who come from the street, without any prior art school training as well as people who come from other schools, who transfer. I prefer people who come with questions.

Can only artists do this … teach art?

I am an artist and I mean it's …

Well institutionally you're here right now as an artist.

Exactly, that's how they define me … I mean that question is interesting because when I gained my core identity in the first half of my twenties – when most people really get formed, between 20 and 25 – I was in a university context. I had no intention of becoming an artist. I didn't identify with being an artist. So when I actually entered an art academy, more or less by accident – I followed Peter Weibel, I followed the teacher – I got in through a theoretical door. I didn't qualify through doing what these people – namely artists – are supposed to do. I'm not able to do a drawing, I'm not able to do anything, basically.

Can you draw now?

I do draw but there are certain kinds of drawings that would qualify as regular drawings.

You seem to disclaim and say a lot about what you're not. You have always been interested in languages, from the age of 10.

But I'm not a linguist.

You draw, but you're not really trained to draw.

Maybe I could call myself a professional dilettante in nearly everything I do; I'm a fake academic, I'm a fake everything.

No, you're actually a real academic and a real artist; there's nothing fake about it, but there seems to be an idea of fakeness that you're interested in.

It's absolutely true what you say, and when I use the 'f' word for fake I play with the so-called – quote-unquote – traditional notions of the artist. What I'm actually doing is not necessarily disclaiming being this or that, but I am trying to problematise and question that very notion. I keep myself at a certain distance, yet still having to identify with being an artist. There are situations in which I speak of being an artist in an affirmative way and defend that role. I'm not someone who hates art or artists. But when it comes to those contexts in which artists become rarefied and commodified, and are part of this *Bildungsbürgertum*, this German notion of the petty bourgeois artist, I hate that and I talk against it.

I wonder when the amateur turns professional, and whether yours is a temporary visit to the academy?

It's a six-year contract. But there are two views; there is how you see yourself, and then there is how students see you. Students, at least when they're not dealing with me, just see me as a professor; there's never any ambiguity. When it comes to the students who work with me, they sometimes forget since I do not necessarily occupy that position and play it in the traditional way. And it's the same with me; I also partially struggle with keeping the distance to make it work properly. So again, it's not me who decides that;

institutionally speaking, it had been decided already for me, and I knew that when I applied for and when I accepted the job.

There's no doubt about …

There's no doubt about the function of the job, so there's no imposition in that sense.

Let me ask you another question.

Teaching art … did I answer you anything about that?

No, you didn't.

I started to answer it by saying that you provide a social context where people can develop, where people can learn habitus, where they can network, where they get to know people and learn how to self-organise and start an exchange. In the end it's a big exchange market, it's a *Börse*, like a stock market. In German you can say *Börse* and it doesn't necessarily imply the stock market, whereas when you say stock market in English it's just financial. It's a place for the exchange of information, of people, of affections, of affinities, of ideas. Not necessarily even a physical place that's bound to a city because for some of these programmes – the Erasmus programme – the academy is a travel agency. One of our next projects is that we go to New York and we'll do some work there. We've also started on a project to travel around the world. I like to make fun, to comment on these travel activities. Jankowski's class moved over to San Francisco. Today's successful art students are just on aeroplanes; they already have the same lifestyle as artists. The confrontation with people is important for students; the professors for example, and you coming by, or other visitors. But it's never straightforward, teaching; I teach by having you teach for me.

What you're talking about is becoming a conventional way of teaching. There is the ghost of the master who instructs from above, but the more vibrant challenge is coming from what you're describing.

I hope so, but I'm not completely sure that's the case. One of the modernist legacies is to de-skill; in the twentieth century, art has gone through a massive deskilling operation, which also deskilled the professors. In terms of art making, there's a re-skilling on the way. People like me are fine to a certain degree, but if everybody were like that then we'd have a problem. Students would rightfully ask for people who know how to do something technically.

It's not yet at saturation point by any means, the position you work from. I think it will take a while for that to reach saturation point. I'm not meaning to generalise your practice.

You think there could be more Ganahl's, is that what you're saying?

I wouldn't say more Ganahl's …

… or more people who work like this.

I would say people who are working within the institution yet seeing it as embedded, or immersed in the world rather than apart from it.

Yeah, yeah.

In an interview with Anna Sansom you say that universities are very important interfaces, where society produces and reproduces itself. Can you talk about this and particularly in relation to how socially useful an art academy like Stuttgart is?

I'm convinced that the university and the art academy are a subgenre, and are an important medium for society to reproduce. The art academy selects people to become artists, and whatever their role is – they do play a role. I want my students to first of all know what's going on in the world and to have a relation with the world that is self-sustaining, that is productive, that is useful in every sense of the word. I want them to be able to survive, to have a voice, to become critical, or not. I was once in an art school where I was 'accused' of being critical. In Los Angeles they said, 'oh, this is so passé, this is critical'. And I asked them, 'well, what do you want to do? What interests you?' And they said, 'shopping' – that was in 1995 or so. We then spent over three months reading books about shopping, which was quite interesting. So depending on the time, even the word criticality can become suspicious. To a certain degree I understand why, but if the school quote-unquote produces … if it enables people to become successful in whatever way – I don't even expect them to become artists, but if they don't, I want them to be successful in what they do – then I think the school does very well. That doesn't necessarily mean they'll start a revolution, but it means that they are able to resist forces that turn things negative. I want them to have a successful life, whatever success defines. What art really does, is it redevelops notions of success. I'm suspicious of commercial success. If people are able to withstand current, dominating notions of traditional success, for me that's successful. It doesn't mean I don't want them to have success, of course I want them to make money and to get along with each another and to be productive, and to change things for the better. But I don't want them to suffer, because a lot of people who enter art school enter an ideological framework that makes them crazy. When you subscribe to a given notion of success – showing in big galleries, getting written about, being famous and making money. The issue is not that you should reject it. What I'm trying to teach people – and it applies to me too – is to basically withstand that. It's destructive when people want something too much, because then everything they do becomes extrinsically motivated, extrinsically conditioned, in that sense.

You're talking about a certain kind of focus?

Yes.

So is that what you're teaching when you teach art?

I teach a lot of things. What I'm teaching is to read texts, and I hope I teach people how to think and to look at things and develop a relation to objects, a relation to their surroundings, to the symbolic world that we live in. We have the privilege, or we're expected to intervene in the symbolic world. When you are just a reader, you don't necessarily directly intervene, but if you're an artist, or a writer, you intervene; you create. That is what I teach people first. But in a naïve way I can imagine that there are many paths, and some paths are very seductive and you want to follow them. I want everybody to just succeed. But most people don't. Sometimes artists fail, and they then become bankers. I have a friend in London, for example. She's an artist, but she's also one of the most successful British bankers. She makes tons of money, but she is not happy. She thinks all the time that she has be an artist and she suffers. Obviously she can't stop it because once you're in that machine you have the costs of houses and mortgages and expenditures. It never ends. She supports a family and she supports some other people who are doing the creative thing.

Are you always working?

I could also say I never work. I don't necessarily work. It's difficult to say when I work and when I don't work. Is it working when I answer my emails, which pile up? I don't really consider the work I do as work. I was a ski instructor and I instructed very interesting people and obviously there were no restrictions to what to do with them afterwards, so it was a lot of fun. I really love teaching and I don't think it's work. Duchamp, for example, he sustained a myth of not doing anything, but he was a chess player.

He was also an art dealer, he edited catalogues and he taught French …

He sold all the Brancusi's to Philadelphia. He did a lot of things. I don't think you would meet many people who would say in an interview, 'yes, I work all the time.' It looks much better when you say, 'I never work.'

What I'm curious about is when things become other things; when you're working, when you're not working. Does everything fold into everything else?

I have more the problem the other way round. Once someone said, 'Rainer, we are making a book about recipes, show us what you eat.' You can find that one on my website. There are few domains that cannot be recuperated as art. I started my studies very early on and they were very tied to pleasure; studying languages were a way to get out, they were a way to speak, or a way to love, a way to get around the world. Reading is a pleasure. And now even the bicycle … I've always used the bicycle, simply for transportation reasons, but at one point I started to play around with it. I had this little disaster with some girlfriend and I used that too. And then I made this work about dreams, so even sleeping is involved. There's very little that is exempt from art. I could say that teaching is exempt to a certain degree, now you're making it public. I never tell anyone I teach, but now more and more people seem to know it.

I think it's pretty public.

Yes, but that's recent. A lot of people say, 'what? You're teaching?' I don't put it on my website, because I still feel too embarrassed about it. If you talk to Lawrence Weiner about teaching he'll be very negative about it.

It seems to me to be consistent with your art practice that you would teach.

It's consistent, but it's very funny; for nearly 10 years no one invited me. I'm here because of Christian Jankowski; I owe him a lot. He's the person who decided – there were actually 20 people who decided it – but he was the one that told me to go for it. He didn't just tell me, he told other people too. Five more people from his gallery also applied. But he was definitely the one who motivated me to do it. I wasn't actively looking for a job. I never applied in the West to anything. Though my life changed. I would say it fundamentally changed due to a teaching situation. The first time it happened and I taught in Geneva I really had no money; I was living on 100 dollars a month in a storage space. I don't come from a moneyed background and when I was in Geneva I was so used to not having money that I didn't touch the salary. I kept all the salary in the bank for two years and that allowed me to purchase an apartment in New York. I bought it 10 years ago in Harlem, when it cost nothing. It changed my life; I can afford to live in New York today due to that appointment and that gives me the freedom to just sit at home and do nothing. I mean do nothing quote-unquote, do my work and not have to care about savings or doing commercial work. It really changed my life.

If you're offered a further contract after six years, will you take it?

It used to be that you got the teaching post forever; Christian has his forever. After two years a committee gave him the OK. In my case, it seems that they want to do it for six years and then have a look again. It can be prolonged. I think they'll do it forever, but I don't know.

I was wondering about the kind of emphasis you put on teaching as it seems to be doing two things: teaching as a platform for producing work, and teaching as a means to have a transformative influence on education … in Stuttgart at least.

I hope I also change the life of my students, but this job changed my life. I'll give you two examples: I've been here for one year and due to the fact that I'm here I got this exhibition in the museum in Stuttgart. That was for me a major thing, because the work started to go in a certain direction; I did everything on the bicycle and began developing something I wouldn't have done otherwise. Next door here, we have the ceramic workshop, and the bronze workshop and all these other workshops, which I've started to use. I also learned a lot from the students. I got connected to Mercedes too and now I'm trying to develop a prototype of a bicycle, a car, a machine. So on that level, it's phenomenal for me. And it brings me to Europe. I didn't come to Europe that often, now I come over every other month and it reconnects me. I get to speak German and it doubles my life, to a certain degree. And look at this studio. I wouldn't have that otherwise. I'm not even talking about the financial aspect; it pays well but I'm not even talking about that kind of security. Its just very funny, it really did open things up. Even the fact that you're sitting here, I think is interesting. I didn't know you, we get to know each other, and then it becomes this book. It's a great book, I already like it a lot. It's this concatenation of anticipated events that can end up in amazing situations. I got the job in Geneva because I was invited to a lecture at the Pompidou, where a person who saw me invited me to Geneva. It's very funny how things can happen sometimes. Talking about success; you do an exhibition and nothing happens. Now I have all these major group shows. I'm currently in one Biennale after another; Moscow, Seville, Istanbul, Venice. I always have the feeling nothing happens. But things can have an effect. I'm sure they will have an effect. Maybe you're just here because you saw my name on these lists, who knows? I would get desperate – and obviously every artist has a tendency to just be desperate – if I were to compare myself to the really successful artist, who makes the real money, which sometimes they don't even make, then you become desperate and that's something I'd advise people not to become, and I try myself not to become. When I do an exhibition I now define success as being able to do a new work. Being able to learn something. Opening something up. I'm working on a show at Le Laboratoire in Paris, for example which already defines itself as completely different from a regular exhibition platform, because they do not ask you for an exhibition; they literally ask you to develop a work. The emphasis is all on research. I know exactly what I want, but I don't know how to do it and it's a big challenge. I want to do a play; I'm working on Alfred Jarry and the bicycle stuff. I want to do a film; I want to do a bunch of things.

Is this connected to Lenin and the Cabaret Voltaire?

Yes. It is because of Lenin I got there. I learned something there, and that for me is interesting. Lenin happened because I was invited to Bucharest and you don't expect dealers there. But the curator from the Cabaret Voltaire was there and he invited me to come to Zurich and that's when I started to develop that kind of work. These little events can become a highway into another direction and that's enriching for me. That is something we could also define as success.

Rainer Ganahl teaches at the Staatliche Akademie der Bildenden Künste, Stuttgart.

Liam Gillick — late June — Amsterdam central station — outside a nearby café.

I want to start with where you studied and what you think has influenced you as an artist and teacher?

I studied at Goldsmiths, but that was very much a big shift, to go to art school, because I'd always intended to work in politics. It's a funny thing, because you find more and more artists talk about their relationship to, say, activism, for example, or actions. But I definitely had this idea that my obligation was to look at – in a way it sounds odd – my family history, and my obligation as the educated one would be to go into organised politics. I found a course that you could study at Warwick University, which was philosophy and politics – a double degree – but they cancelled it. So I decided to go to art school instead. At least initially for a year, because I thought I could go back to politics later.

How did you make the leap from that to art school?

Because I'd always done art, and been interested in it. It had been something that had been encouraged; my mother had studied art in the 1950s when people used to go to technical schools. So I was always given encouragement as a young kid. Of course, it's a totally different idea of art, but at school I was given encouragement with my work and I've always found it a terrain that was interesting, and I find this a fascinating thing to talk about. In a retrospective of my work that started in Rotterdam and then went to Zurich etc. and on to Munich and Chicago, one of the things I turned to in the end, because I was a bit stuck structurally, was what I call my pre-art aesthetic sensibility. Partly because it was a way out of some of the problems I was having with the show. But it was also a reminder to me that without thinking about being an artist, or without going to art school, people can be very sophisticated, or at least have a level of critical aesthetic sensibility that's quite precise. I got interested in contemporary art by going to places like the ICA to see films or going to art centres. Art centres were the thing for me. I would go to see a concert or a film and I would walk through an exhibition on the way there, and that's what gave me the sense that there was a meaningful, functional role in the world of contemporary art. So when I went to art school, I already had a very precise idea of where I wanted to go. There was no doubt the only place I wanted to go was Goldsmiths, because it had a conceptual legacy – that was the word on the street in the late 1970s and early 80s – it had this conceptual thing going on and maybe some of those people were still around.

What did you find?

To a certain extent what you found was that there was a battle taking place between a group of tutors who, at that point, were probably my current age, in their early to mid-40s, who were fundamentally opposed to each other, yet could still have a discussion. So you entered into this world of heated discussion between these people, and I found that extremely interesting. Of course it was a moment of an emergent, quite useable discussion about postmodernism. So there were people there like Ian Jeffrey, the photography theorist, and a few others, who were trying to talk about contemporary ideas, but not in the way that they now teach critical theory; it was still called art history, but you felt they were very free and unchecked as theorists to do what they wanted to do. In fact, the discussions were quite freewheeling and quite obscure in a strange way; they probably wouldn't get past the assessment committees nowadays. One of the most memorable aspects of it – one of the most significant discussions that took place was around Althusser. When I say discussion, I'm not suggesting there was a really articulate discussion about Althusser, but there were these moments, these fragments that stuck with you that I think were very important and definitely effected something.

Do you think this is more policed now?

Yes, absolutely. It's become formalised and I'm not against that. I'm actually all in favour of the teaching of the theory of ideas; it's absolutely crucial, but it's changed, that's all. If you look at, say, Columbia in the last 10 years, could you really argue in any objective way that the fundamental disagreement about how to function and how to behave as an artist has been between one studio-practice teacher and another? Or has it been the battle over who possesses the ideas and the theory? It's been the battle over theory that's been the one. I don't mean necessarily that everyone is a kind of activated agent in that battle, I just mean that that's where it's been, that's where the ideological fight is; between the people who want it out, or want it suppressed, and the people who believe you'll just be a victim of existing frameworks if you don't at least address it.

I want to talk about the 'transfer of responsibility model' you address in *Selected Transcription from Talk at UN Plaza, Berlin, 2006*. You write about different models of collective behaviour and in the case of the fifth model, which is the transfer of

responsibility model, you say: 'You will not start from any basic assumptions, but instead we would actually start again, every year, and redefine the "school" from scratch. We would also severely challenge the notion that teachers, or artists are the best people to teach. I actually do a simple poll every year at Columbia, asking "do you think it's an automatic assumption that artists are the best to people to teach artists?" Surprisingly the answers are not straightforward. Quite a lot of the graduate students don't automatically assume that artists are the best people to teach artists'.

You have to look at cultural production as not the exclusive territory of artists, but rather in terms of how ideas are formulated and put out in the world, and how they get discussed and analysed – the production of ideas, as it were. It's not necessarily limited to artists. What's interesting about that quote, and about asking this to the people at Columbia is that a lot of those people are, you could say in a superficial way, quite conservative, or clearly recognisable as artists. I'm talking about people who make paintings of old jackets, or some kind of intuitive, self-conscious, self-representation. I'm not just talking about a lot of earnest people making documentary films about abandoned former Soviet buildings. This is an interesting phenomenon, and it's where I think they also realise that what they want is a degree of access to the way art is talked about. It's not so simple any more to find one location for the production of meaning, or significance, or collectivity, or coming together-ness. They feel that what you need is multiple input, and they're really the ones who are there on a daily basis. That you have special moments when they want that person who comes to talk about Deleuze and cinema to be around in the morning, at 10 o'clock with a stick and a slide projector. Like a lot of these things, it's not necessarily completely logical, it's not necessarily operating with complete self-interest, it's not even necessarily about a belief in intellectual pursuits. It's more about this feeling of getting to something that's a bit out of reach, or of continuing the discussion ...

How do you institutionalise that? How do you allow for it?

You have to find a way. In real university situations the problem is that departments jealously guard their own fiefdom, and their own people. There's a fear of dispersal and breakdown of departmental autonomy and, therefore, it's difficult. Unfortunately, the only easy places to do it are often the schools that are more free-form, or they're more like … I'm not sure if I know the answer actually … I'm always worried, because then you start to think about private schools, or independent schools, and then you're really fucked, because I don't believe in that either. There has to be a rethink of university structure, in order to make it easier and to make it possible for people to have that time to devote to maybe a less-specific sense of engagement between the person and the student. The thinking is that the artist has time. Artists have time, they have all the time in the world. One way to upset people if you go and do a lecture in an art school as an artist, is if you turn down the chance to do studio visits. Because there's always the unspoken assumption when they invite you for the lecture and say to you as an aside 'of course we were hoping you'd stay for a day to do some studio visits.' It can be as simple as that, shifting that kind of thinking to the other person, and maybe it's about rearranging some of these things.

But in the university you need the institutional structures in order to be able to shift them around …

Yes, I would say so. But what tends to happen a lot in the US, for example, is that the people who are best placed to defend the semi-autonomous status of the art department within a big institution are not the ones who are the most interested in backing up a flexible way of addressing these relationships. They'll say things like 'we've reached out to the art history department, but they're not interested'. This is a way of defending their own belief in the idea of an artist. The artist as a kind of person who is not subject to the same mini-behaviours and laws, or whatever they are, of how things get done within an educational environment. I can see the problem, because a lot of those freedoms were hard-won; the idea that you break down the studio system, that you break down this or you break down that. The idea that you could sustain the amount of territory that an art school usually needs within a bigger framework, yet still claim that you shouldn't be subject to too many checks, is quite political. So I can see why those people end up running those places.

In *Curating for Pleasure and Profit*, you write 'irresponsible people in responsible positions can provoke quite important developments'. What would irresponsibility be within the context of where you teach?

Jesus ... I think that when I was a student there was clearly still the legacy of trying to retain the feeling that teaching was a student-centred enterprise. Basically the idea is that you have these people who go somewhere and you try and bring out the best of what's already within them, which is very much an idea about recognising differences. It's a sophisticated thing, in a way, but also a very patrician and indulgent thing. What's happened over time is, as one gets further and further away from the political dynamic that changed those hierarchies, and changed those power structures, that the staff themselves have become less proactive and offer less. So you have a student-centred and student-orientated system that still exists, yet the structuring of the way it operates doesn't put enough obligation – and I'm not talking in terms of administration – put enough obligation on the people teaching, or being involved on that side of it. So my thing is to be radically inconsistent, and to change every year the way I approach it. I always try and set up a discussion between the students and myself about the nature of the school itself. That is the only consistent thing I've ever done; to try and have a real discussion about the nature of the school itself, and to have an awareness of the environment within which one operates, in what that produces, and how that impacts on the work produced.

If you set that up and that's the responsibility you take on, what, in turn, is the student's responsibility?

Good question. Actually I don't even think they have one. It's more about recognising that for a brief period, they're in a high-end educational environment, and to make use of that while they can. But a lot of things get 'angsted' about in art schools, especially when the art world seems very dynamic or seems to be moving along. It can appear to be heavily populated and hard to get 'in'. Strangely enough, I strongly believe that that's not the thing to worry about. For me the difficulty isn't to sustain an identity as an artist – obviously if you have no ideas, or you don't have anything to do, or you find it uninteresting to do exhibitions, or whatever, then of course it's going to be difficult. For me the real difficultly is to actually retain some critical self-consciousness, or some other kind of sensibility. What I'm often trying to do with people is to get them to understand that this is a really unique moment, at which time they don't need to worry about being artists so much. That sounds a bit old-fashioned, like people who say you should unlearn, I don't mean it like that. I just want them to develop other discursive models, at least for that brief period, because it 's an interesting and fairly unique time and it's my job to remind them of that.

Your *5 models of collective behaviour* – the rogue individual model, trial or process model, updating model, suspension of decision-making model, and transfer of responsibility model – do they all co-exist in art education? Because the trial or process model, for example, seemed to fit the kind of group seminar teaching that exists in many art schools, particularly in the UK, while the suspension of decision making model might be the kind of model that existed prior to what you describe as 'the increasing provision of parallel structures alongside that of studio practice', and 'where proximity of artist to artist could ensure a suppression of the critical cultural processes taking place between them'. Could you say something about the forms of refusal that are still possible within an art educational environment, where 'it is no longer possible for someone to teach "artist to artist"'?

It's very hard, because a lot of it has so much to do with the way these things are structured. It's actually more to do with the engagement with the physical facts of the institution, the way it works, the way it's built, and the way it operates, and certain spaces that are there or not there, certain zones which you can occupy and can't occupy, these kinds of things. It's actually very prosaic and quite straightforward in individual practice. Of course the ability to assess collective practice is continually difficult and hard to do. I think this refusal thing really becomes a question of trying to find whether there can be a discussion with people who are only within this environment for a very short time, which they'll then leave and not have to worry about anymore. Of course that's why change is difficult, because you know they're not going to be there very long. I'm not sure who should be doing this remodelling of the site of refusal, but I feel it has to happen.

That's what I wanted to ask you, or is there a model that currently exists?

No, not that I know of. There are temporary schools and there are these events that use this site of refusal as a kind of umbrella under which to do something else. They appear and disappear … and reading groups, and so on. I've just been reading Susan Kelly. She's an example of somebody who's deeply committed to a very specific radicalised idea of coming together and coming up with hyper-critical eternal critique built into every self-conscious structure, where really the refusal element goes into the activist terrain, where the only logical way to function is to really get together with a community and do activist work. I am interested in the idea of a high cultural practice, I'm interested in the autonomy, some idea of artists being a special community within society that isn't completely dispersed into the activist terrain, nor completely absorbed within a kind of quality market idea either. I'm not sure that there are any really good current models of rethought educational systems, and I'm not sure how it would happen. I think the unitednationsplaza thing was quite interesting because, funnily enough, it was very old-fashioned. It was generally people sitting down and listening to older people telling them something, so in that way it was the absolute extreme, the pure extreme of my definition earlier of changing the responsibility. A lot of young people came, young artists, art historians, and so on, and it was almost like they wanted to know what someone's position was. They felt that they'd been denied access to some more intimate, extended explanation of what you think you're up to. This, in itself, was very interesting. But if you really put that into action you'd just have rooms full of older people telling younger people what they think. You know that's why I've been saying to Anton (Anton Vidokle), you have to stop; we have to ... it can't carry on, or certainly not by someone like me.

I was wondering if this alternative is what you're describing in your essay *Outsiding*; an alternative based, you could say, on a transfer of responsibility model. You're describing Rirkrit Tiravanija's *Places* and the converted garage in Oslo, where, you explain, Rirkrit is 'officially employed as a teacher. He is like a visiting professor. It is hard to know when the "moment of art" starts or ends. While most of the people inside the converted garage are students, some are older artists and friends. They've been around for a while, yet this is not an open-ended exercise. It is a deliberate sequencing of moments and interactions with constantly tested limits.' Is this the kind of idea, the kind of involvement or moment you're trying to describe?

In a way, because what happens is that there's an anxiety about the art object, or the moment of art, or whatever you'd call it. It's like these discussions I used to have. I remember when Hans Ulrich Obrist, Rebecca Gordon Nesbitt and Maria Lind started Salon 3, down in South London, and it was supposed to be this other type of place where things could happen. On the day of the opening Hans Ulrich actually asked me what I was going to do. And I said, 'well, I thought we were doing it'. But he meant as an artist there, he was waiting for the art moment. Now of course, I'm interested in the idea of this thing that can function culturally as an artwork, but in that case it seemed to undermine the potential of the place. This is why we were quite clear in unitednationsplaza that it was not a place of production, in terms of physical artwork. The focus of the attention of the discursive moment becomes about not being anxious about what they're going to produce, but to rely on the fact that if they want to engage in their own conception of what art might be, or cultural production might be, they will find a way. But the collective moment isn't the moment of asking, showing and analysing the thing; that's a kind of a secondary component of this main event.

But isn't it, nonetheless, a highly self-conscious moment? Something has got to get you there?

To being in a garage in Oslo? Yes, I would say so.

Isn't there a kind of equivalence here to the art moment?

It's a commitment to what I would call a discursive model of practice, where art is the result of a self-consciousness about others – about a broader kind of discussion, rather than the spontaneous production of a kind of intuitive genius. It's a kind of workman-like process of analysing and understanding the various venues for art, and finding where you fit into that system. Both of those processes I employ at some level. Everyone employs them on some level, otherwise you just disintegrate as an ego. The difficulty is actually sustaining the discursive model. The bit about everything else – that can be done. There's time for that and there are moments for that. So the focus in Columbia is on finding little homes for each artist to make sure they've got the right zones within which they can produce art, which will then become the subject of discussion and testing analysis, until you feel that the student and the work somehow have come to represent one another. If you read people like Lazarato, or you read about immaterial labour, or you read certain other writers on these questions of democracy and agency and culture – I'm not saying you have to read this in order to understand art. It's maybe about starting with an intuitive problem and realising through reading that you're not the only one with this problem.

People have problems about how you fit as a human in society in a broader sense than just art. But I'm very conscious of the fact that there are quite articulate critiques about exclusion and inclusion, insiderness and outsiderness, and all the rest of it. But I'm sticking to it. The refusal to take part in this would be an example of a mode of refusal. I'm not talking about some Habermasian sense in which everyone is equally participating in this discursive framework, I'm talking about a complicated one, where it isn't equal and it is fraught, and it is problematic. One of the biggest misrepresentations of, say, Rirkrit, especially by people who weren't at any of these things, is the sense that it was a smooth space that was provided. Where the assumption was that everyone was equal; that is really not the case, I can assure you. From the slightly drunken guy in Cologne who's pissed off with all the art people hanging around to the moments of fracturing and difficulty. But I'm not saying this can be a stable model. I'm not looking for a stable model.

Is this a little like Chantal Mouffe's agonistic model; you share the same symbolic space, but you differ over how it should be used …

I'm a big fan of her writing, and of course I also recognise that she's a good Marxist in the end. I think part of what she'd like to see, is a minor breakdown – the agonism would hopefully become antagonism. I think there's a Marxist logic that underscores her work, that tries to recharge a true Marxist revolution, so what you do is you recognise these ruptures that basically will hopefully lead to more articulated political positions in society, which will then genuinely lead to a breakdown. I'm very, very interested in this. I think it's also possible to view an artist as working in parallel to someone like her, rather than being a symptom, or a carrier of the actual thing itself, whereas Rirkrit occasionally trips up or, if you're positive about it, succeeds in that he actually tries to put these micro-communities into play. I'm much more interested in standing alongside someone like her, but without the rigour and without the education, and looking in my own way, with my own training, at the way things have appearances and how things find form in the world, where I can find traces of these new relationships, or these uncomfortable moments where you can describe new terrains to think about in terms of art. There's also this other guy I've been reading a little bit about, this Italian guy … in fact, I was just reading it on the plane … he's called… Danilo Zolo. Zolo's thing, like Chantal Mouffe, is about complexity. He's tried to look at where complexity and technology, and so on, really come into play in all of this. Of course, the danger is that this will then produce lots of new art that seems to just be about complexity. My position often seems evasive to people because I feel really quite close to some of the things that this guy has been talking about. In the last work I've been doing, for instance, I've been looking at this idea of what happens in a society where apparently there's no problem when you have the closure of a factory, but reading that filtered through Brazilian academic papers about post-Fordist working practices, that is the kind of territory this guy is interested in, which is much closer to the way I'm thinking. I can see why a thorough dogmatic adherence to the proper, correctly articulated theories of someone like Chantal is going to be hard, It seems to then limit some of the five potentials about how to behave, because at what point do you become the authentic within that sense of super-articulated differences? I don't think it means all people are included ...

I was wondering why a lot of artists seem to be taking up Chantal Mouffe in recent years?

Partly because she likes art, and she's quite smart about art. It does make a difference. It's the same with Rancière, in a different way, although she's actually much smarter than he is about art and seems genuinely engaged. If you talk to her she has something to say, for example, about Venezuela, or something that's actually happening in the world. She's not stuck in a completely disengaged academic world. And I think the effect of having worked outside of France and Francophone countries has also affected her thinking; she's been subjected to that kind of weird pragmatic, what can feel almost like an anti-intellectual environment. I'm not saying that France isn't partly anti-intellectual, but you know what I mean. On the other hand, I think it's partly to do with what I've been describing before about the educational system; that when you're confronted with what seems to be a void, something that's not being discussed ... There are two things in fact: one thing is the void, the desire to enter the territory that seems not to have been discussed, not properly addressed, and the other is the rise in the clarification of the teaching of critical theory, of critical issues within art schools that has provided a moment of clear argument where you wouldn't get that anymore, even between, say, Gregory Amenoff at Columbia and, say, Rirkrit, even though their practice's are totally at odds. Today doesn't seem to be the moment where those people want to battle that out, they're tolerant of each another. But where are you going to find a productive intolerance?

You're going to find it in the critical theory class, because you will get strong statements, you'll get a battle for territory, and you'll also get a feeling that this could be close to describing a role in the world that's actually meaningful. There's this kind of cultural void, and people under the umbrella of art can enter that and do all these different things. Which is extremely interesting to people, I think.

You see it as opportunity?

Absolutely.

You wrote about the relationship between teachers and students, which you think should be under constant review – this is part of the transfer of responsibility model. You say 'this would mean that the staff should present work alongside the students in order to create a true debate and shift the potential hierarchical nature of the students to critique …'. This assumes that staff actually have a practice they are willing to put before the students.

I was probably talking about those schools that tend to focus on trying to employ people who you could say are … practising artists is the wrong … they always say practising artists and it's the wrong term … people who are visible and seen to be taking part in the network of exhibitions, and so on. You know that moment when the person hasn't turned up to do the visiting lecture, and they might ask you. Because you work there and you're around. And you notice a fundamental difference in the way the whole thing works after that, for at least a year, because you've actually had to stand up there and explain yourself and talk about what you're doing. I mean in the old school, sort of Jean Luc Goddard … you show you're working, you show you're thinking, and you represent yourself, too. Of course it's easy to slip into being anecdotal and coming home with stories of what you did in Amsterdam, or you did in Nice in 1990 – it has to be in the recent past, and I found occasionally this has created genuine anxiety. There was a project at the Henry Moore Institute a few years ago and they asked me if I'd like to be involved by coming up with a series of talks. I said I wanted to arrange a series of quite specific discussions with people where they really talked about their last few days. And I think they found the whole thing too open-ended and too unclear to really commit to, the fact that this wouldn't really be a broader discussion about what the theme of the show was.

Now you could say that, when everything works fine, these things sort of naturally happen; you get this kind of easy engagement and ongoing processes of revealing. But what happens when you can't rely on that? When it's not naturally happening in the canteen, or in the bar? And what happens with those students who decide they're not the friendly, open talkative people – you know, who don't want to have a conversation all the time – the silent ones. You often hear this idea that work is a conversation. A conversation does imply a two-way relationship, at least. But, of course, we know that people are drawn to certain cultural forms because they don't readily converse, and they don't want to, they're uneasy. Even if you look at some theoretical writing about this, in the Lazarato sense, about the fact that contemporary work involves having to be a good team player, you have to be able to open up, you have to be able to describe yourself, you have to be able to redefine your job, you have to be able to even make some minor choices about it. Even in quite banal jobs that's the case. A lot of it is to do with trying to find a way to also encompass those who refuse to have a dialogue with anyone, who don't want to have a dialogue, as such, in a formal way.

This idea that 'staff should present work alongside the students …' is quite a radical idea, particularly in a system of education where often, for a member of staff, their work, or practice, is quite guarded, as if 'not showing' or 'not telling' is almost a way to preserve a certain kind of authority …

Well, there's a good reason for that, because it could become difficult; you could have a breakdown of authority, of moral authority. Or just authority in the loosest, weakest sense, meaning the authority of the person here to be able to get me to pay for my drink, or to feel that their opinions have any value, or are of any interest. Having said that, one of the most important artists for me, when I became conscious of real functional contemporary art, was James Coleman. I always had the feeling he didn't seem to produce very much. I think he actually produces a bit more than I thought he did, but it felt like he really didn't. I've always been interested in the idea of an artist who doesn't necessarily produce very much. I, unfortunately, am not that person. That's why I find this complexity-focused complexity-discussion very interesting.

Has teaching become a career choice for some artists?

For my generation, no it hasn't. Although there's a younger generation now – they could nearly be my kids, as it were, a generation of very young artists teaching. Maybe they're saying, 'yes, I want to do this deliberately, and I want to be in this environment to do something'. But what's interesting is that sometimes the model ... you know, for a few years at Columbia, the critical theory course was taught by two artists; Andrea Fraser and Coco Fusco. It wasn't taught by people you'd think of traditionally as theorists, and this was very inspiring for some people. It's very interesting, and this has caused quite a lot of anxiety in the school among the old guard, who maybe see teaching as a natural extension of their complete and total constant 'artness' – their visual and aesthetic awareness doesn't stop at any moment, it's there in the bar, it's there in the studio, it's there in their own studio. I don't know if a career is the right word ... There's a sort of skipped generation, in terms of power, that's for sure. The people of my generation, both curators and artists, decided that at a certain level – meaning people that I'm aware of, that I've worked with a lot -– all seem to refuse positions of authority in any art school environment. So, in fact, they're still run by people who are 10 or 15 years older.

Why is that?

There's a real difficulty in communication between artists who were born between 1955 and 1960, and artists who were born between 1965 and 1975. There's almost zero communication, and there's totally different models of understanding the world, understanding how to teach things. Part of it is because, even if those artists sometimes can appear careerist, or whatever, there's some part of them that's still aligned to that feeling that they remember – the kind of 1968 changes that were real and meaningful for them. They fundamentally believe in the autonomy of artists and that the role of the teacher is merely to share their way of viewing the world critically through signs, and objects, and things. I've been in the situation where we virtually can't talk. In a really fraught, real high-end seminar group crit environment, I virtually cannot communicate with some of the people there, because our value systems are so opposed – it's really difficult. There are some real old-school postmodernists; the work can be multiple and complex, but if it's carrying false trails, or false leads, then these things need to be corrected, or the falseness needs to become the total work, or something. The idea that there could be multiple, contradictory, concurrent interpretations of work, or that work itself may not carry the moment of significance, is totally offensive to some people. I can see why it would be, and I even tested it during one student's crit. The crit is modelled on the idea that the student has to sit quietly, while the other people talked about the work, or talked to the work – after which the student could talk. So I would try and filibuster my way through these things. In one case by going on a long and extended monologue, which I refused to stop, about the fact that this work was a protest against the war in Iraq. There was no specific rhetorical message in the work that was against the war in Iraq, but to me the work carried enough traces within it to suggest that it could only have been made under the conditions of an American total war, it carried enough signifiers to allow my argument to beat all others. If we're going to pretend that the work sits there, mute, or it sits there as a thing to speculate over, then I'm not going to speculate. I'm not going to. Strangely enough, we've got this weird contradiction here; you have a group of artists like Philippe Parreno, Rirkrit, myself, even Jorge Pardo, who seem to be, at one level, really committed to a sort of open framework in terms of the work. Yet, within the structural institutional system, Philippe for example cannot function in relation to some of these teaching models. Not the daily practice of going there and being a visitor, or something, but the idea of being in a position of authority. If he were, the entire thing would have to change, and maybe this is a failing on our part that we haven't all got together and done that. But there are other issues, around questions of curating, for example, that seemed a bit more urgent and dynamic though you could start to suck some of these pedagogical questions into the framework of the exhibition structure itself. Going back to a show like *Lost Paradise* in Vienna in 1993; I did a parallel information service alongside the exhibition, not in order to make straightforward points about revealing the institutional transparency of the place, but actually, genuinely, to start some new discussions about what might be taking place. A lot of the people I ended up talking to were young artists at art school. But frankly they felt that what they were being given wasn't sufficient, wasn't really talking about what's actually taking place in the world. That is just the way it goes sometimes.

When you mentioned how Andrea Fraser and Coco Fusco taught the critical theory course for a time at Columbia, could this be an example of the kind of irresponsibility we talked about? In the sense that one could be responsible to a certain discipline, or a set of ideas?

Yes, I think it could be, but it's partly because they were much more antagonistic towards the students than the normal artists/ teachers were. Partly because of their own political viewpoint, which was leading them towards feeling that things are a bit more urgent and desperate than they may appear to be, and that stepping into the art world is the moment at which you should clarify your commitments politically, and not the moment at which you just go on permanent semi-retirement from the world. So, of course, because they were in a presentational mode, they would be much more aggressive towards the students. So I don't know if you'd call it refusal, but it was definitely antagonistic, that's for sure. In a sense, it was a refusal to go along with the normal smoothness of the old kind of guild model of art, in which you mentored people and created these smooth transitions.

There seems to be a culture in art schools where it's almost obligatory to be at odds with the institution, with management, bureaucracy, etc. To be in so-called crisis in order to withstand, justify, or survive the system you're in.

I've tended to avoid becoming involved in the organisational structure of schools, partly because the last thing the world needed was more straight white middle-class men telling them how to behave. But I've also always been really conscious of the fact that I didn't want to slip into what you describe. I don't know, I really don't know. I'm really stuck, and I don't know how to behave, and I don't know what to do now. It's interesting that half of this has been about teaching – I'm really a very consistent, kind of monogamous teacher, as it were; I've been involved with one school for 11 years, which is quite a long time without any movement within the hierarchy – not applying to become a professor, or not trying to become more embedded. Having this kind of consistent, intensive moments, and then leaving, and then coming back for another intensive week, and then leaving. So I don't have the same anxious relationship to the structure that some of the other people do there, because I don't even know what people are talking about, so I can't engage with it and that's been deliberate. I've deliberately tried to avoid falling into that trap. You can do that for a long time if you ignore and take out of the equation all the meaningful daily work aspects of teaching, like paying the rent, getting by, all the rest of it. I've essentially become an extended guest and I've used that. I also have this idea, if you never take your jacket off, you won't be stopping, then you can avoid some of these more mind-numbing procedures. But the reason why I say this is difficult is because it has aspects of letting down the side from an old school solidarity thing; you're encouraging the permanent kind of temporariness of work-life and all the problems that come with that. I don't know what to do next. Should you then try and make that precise and bring that together, and with a few people actually really try and do something? Or recognise that you're reaching the point where your ability to just do this intuitively, and on the fly, runs out of steam. And it is about age. If you talk to some of the older artists from a Conceptual art generation about age, they don't like these discussions. Not because they're older but because they think that's not the point. But I do think that there might be a point at which you become too different, or too alienated from the people that you're working with to sustain this permanent guest status.

Going back to something we were talking about earlier; about change and the possibility of another kind of educational environment. Would getting involved more in the bureaucratic structure and taking the steps upwards allow you to physically and intellectually change things?

I think one couldn't happen without the other. I used to work quite a lot with this idea of deferment and suspension of things. This is something I was always interested in, in relation to the political, psychological terrain. When I was a child in the 1960s my grandad used to ask "What are you going to do with all the leisure you are going to have, what are you going to do with all the time you will have in the future?" As we know, this didn't become permanent leisure; it became a kind of fragmented temporariness and permanent insecurity punctuated with moments of benefit, which are interesting. The interest that my generation has is in this idea of suspension and trying to set up the conditions for it in relation to teaching something – the conditional circumstances rather than conclusive circumstances. It's one of those rare moments where you would have a change that would be so fundamental, like one of those big decisions in life. You can see it in the curators of my age as well; Maria Lind, Hans Ulrich Obrist, and a lot of these people – very few of them have actually started anything, if you see what I mean. Even someone like Klaus Biesenbach, who did start something. As soon as he did, he used it as an authentic base in order to then move into a more established museum. So this question is not unique to artists of around my age, the curators have done it too; they've wanted to keep this state of suspension going. It's connected to some cultural psychological anxiety that's not articulated, and I've tried to talk about it a little bit in this film I'm showing at the Stedelijk Museum [in Amsterdam], as part of the 2008 Vincent Award – to somehow keep in play the potential of some notional date such as 17th of June 1974, when new forms of revised post-Fordist work practice really seemed to be coming into play, and there still seemed to be post-war social democracy, and there seemed to be truly articulated anxieties that were going to have an answer just around the corner, like in Ireland and Palestine, and elsewhere. There were, of course, moments of trauma and difficulty and disaster, but they had some framework of projection. In a certain generation you get this feeling of 'if we try and pretend that we're still in this suspended moment, if we can stick to that kind of moment, then everything will be fine'. Like in a Buñuel film; if we can recreate those conditions, if we can get back to how the dinner table was at that point, then hopefully we'll be able to leave the party. But of course it doesn't work like that.

What do we need to think about today, in terms of art education? What's urgent?

I think of the site of art education as the site of production in a certain way, which doesn't just mean the artist producing work, but also the production of other things. This of course already happens to a certain extent, but a bit more than just doing it in order to get research points, or whatever. Viewing it again, or maybe for the first time, as a real machine for the production of all sorts of layered things. And, of course, one of the only ways that this can happen is by breaking down the degree show, or the thesis show as they call it in America, as the moment of assessment, or the moment of focus. Where the school itself is authoring and putting stuff out, not just the students, and that there's this kind of thing taking place. One way around it is to have years that work in clumps, rather than just a constant rolling admission process. But then you have to completely change the entire funding process, you have to change so many things to do that. That's really crucial; a complete rethink and redesign of the actual spaces within which people work, a total transfer of power to other people. And, potentially, not worrying about whether or not departments close. Certainly art schools in the UK often have this feeling that they've got to save the department.

Who would the power be transferred to?

Not me. It's really difficult to generalise about these things, but there is a new generation of people who studied art history, who are extremely interesting, and extremely interested in contemporary art. I can give you names, but you meet them constantly. Those people have to decide what they're going to do, because in the last 15 years they've become curators and that's been the dynamic model, that's been the place where they've found something to play out. I don't believe that that's where they all feel it is right now. I meet too many of them in too many interesting situations, like in unitednationsplaza, where there was this genuine community of people that weren't 100 per cent convinced that their trajectory was to do a project space, or run Cubitt, or do something like this. They're just not sure. So maybe they're the ones to somehow … I know they're already forming these kind of strange alliances and strange communication routes that are not clearly defined elsewhere. I think this new generation needs to decide what they're going to do, because, in fact, the field is quite open in various ways to actually step in and do something. But it means they have to be prepared to give up something; they have to give up their academic self-image, or their academic trajectory, because the spaces of dynamic contemporary art don't always just lend themselves to being a good academic, in the classical sense. I'm not against academics, but if you're going to have that career track, it's going to be quite difficult to run an interesting contemporary art school.

Liam Gillick teaches at Columbia University, New York.

Vanalyne Green — Leeds University —
after lunch — her office.

I'd like to begin by asking you how long you've been working here in the department, whether you continue to teach in you current role, what other colleges you've taught in?

I've been here for almost a year-and-a-half. I'm the head of the fine art division. The school is comprised of three divisions: history of art, cultural studies and fine art. And I've just got approval for a module on curatorial practices using Mary Douglas's ideas about purity and danger, to pose a different way of thinking about curating. I have taught professionally since 1990, although I taught before then in alternative feminist programmes, such as the Woman's Building in Los Angeles. My background is in feminist art education. Two really important teachers for me were Judy Chicago and Sheila Levrant de Bretteville, who is head of the Yale Design School; both of whom were children of communists, so-called 'red diaper babies' in the States. Their pedagogy was profoundly influenced by community organisation techniques. So that's had a major effect on what I think about teaching, in the sense of teaching not being separate from the rest of the world – teaching as a kind of looking for ways to make the connection between what students are doing in their work and what they're doing in the rest of their lives, and what's going on in the world.

How do you institutionalise that?

You look for places of equality between support staff and academic staff, so students see a different type of role model, or a different model for what happens in an academic institution. The boundaries, the hierarchies, are less distinct between support and academic staff. That's one way. I haven't taught here, I've been working with dissertation students, but when I taught at the Art Institute, I would sometimes meet students in their dorm rooms. If they were having a hard time getting up in the morning, I'd say, 'OK, I'll meet … we'll come to you.' And I took an active interest in their health and tried to find ways to help them with what they were struggling with in their work or their class assignments and that related to the rest of their lives, so that they weren't struggling to find a source of making art that seemed unique or original, compared with what else was going on in their lives. My teachers, Judy or Sheila were really … I can give you an example; one time I called in sick, and Judy said 'well, d'you need anything, like someone can come and pick you up if you need a ride, or someone can bring you food if you're sick.' That makes a huge impact, especially if a student is used to teachers who accept passivity and withdrawal.

I wasn't actually sick, I just didn't want to go. So there was a sense that it was really important to her, that students were accountable in the same way that teachers were accountable, and that there's a sort of back and forth quality to that.

How do you think this inflects on a student's practice?

In the short term it didn't because it was such a culture shock; it really freaked me out. In the long term it had a huge effect on my life, in the sense that it changed my values to ones that were more community-oriented, compared with individualistic. What effect it has on art students, I'm not really sure. I can think of groups I worked with when I was more actively teaching at the Art Institute. I'd been a faculty advisor, and sometimes I would have the idea that the classroom wouldn't end when the class was over, so we would pass on our phone numbers, so that people would have someone to talk to. The idea of what a classroom was could change, or be malleable, so there wasn't just the hierarchy of the classroom in the space.

Almost like social work …

A little bit, yes. Lauren Berlant said something really important to me that I sometimes use. She's a well-known writer, scholar and a former collaborator with Feel Tank Chicago, who teaches at the University of Chicago. Sometimes she asks students to figure out and to tell her where they think the *hymen* in the room is. Where the entry point is. To think architecturally about what happens, and to brainstorm about how architecture and the interior set affects the learning process.

Because you're still left with an institution, aren't you? You're still left with the bricks and mortar, and the so-called exclusivity of that – the students who are in there making the work, as opposed to the students that aren't. So you're still left with an exclusive space, which you're trying to open up to other kinds of conditions, to reach some kind of parity with other areas of a student's life, but it is a rather privileged activity …

It's both privileged and marginal.

Does it need to be privileged? Is that part of the potency of the practice, that privilege and marginality?

It doesn't have to be. What is important, which seems really difficult, is to introduce people to the idea that teaching is dialectical, it's paradoxical. I'm thinking of Theodor Adorno's *Minima Moralia* where he writes about paradox, saying one thing and contradicting it in the next sentence, which is necessary in the sense of not thinking in simple ways about something that's complex and complicated. There's a lot of work to be done about the politics of political art that doesn't get articulated, that's kind of under-theorised. John Hanhardt, formerly the senior curator of film, video and new media at the Guggenheim Museum wanted to have a show, *the politics of political art*. I don't think it happened, and I don't know if he's still thinking about that. There isn't an adequate discourse about what work might be considered bad social science, or bad social work. That's really complicated; I've seen students doing work thinking 'well, that's like bad social work'. One of the things that's excellent for students is trying to do work that's about social energy, from way back since *Block* magazine onwards. Working in a system and growing up in a system that privileges the studio model and the career model, they want to do socially-engaged work, or work that maybe plays on relational aesthetics. But at the same time they're working with unquestioned tropes about originality, and some very anachronistic ideas about the career trajectory of the 'artiste'. Because socially engaged art, or new genre public art, is still considered "political" by some tutors, they don't teach it or teach it in a regressive way – which is to say not insisting that the artist is responsible for the relationship between content and form – either content is "bad" or one can't critique the form adequately.

Are you proposing an alternative model to the kind of overly academic one, that some people feel is either creeping in, or has crept into our art schools, and that is not necessarily good for art?

I taught at a private art school in Chicago. I wanted to teach in a state university or a public university or government university, because I thought there was something perhaps too distilled, too condensed with just teaching in an institution where one doesn't have to negotiate how art is contested in wider cultural milieus. I wanted a broader range of both colleagues and students. But at the same time I knew, and I see it all the time, how difficult it is for scholars to understand art practice. It seems as if certain words have become incorporated in the language of art making, such as a student who says she's a practitioner. What's she saying? She's a surgeon? Practitioner: where does that word come from? Maybe that's cultural, maybe that's me being American, but I see the effect of the Research Assessment Exercise.

Is that having a corrosive effect?

Oh yes. Polytechnics were better for artists, and I'm referring to Jon Thompsons's observations about this.

I want to read something to you, something you say about your *Film and History of America*: 'Being a woman in a position of leadership, directing, funding and managing people for my own work at the moment remains the place where I experience what it means to be a feminist.' I was thinking about this and your place in the university, and was wondering whether you see your role here partly as an act of resistance. Is this a political project for you? You're not just a manager, you're not just what we might benignly call a teacher. So that to reconcile or consolidate these different desires requires you to teach as well.

No. I had a good job that paid the bills. It was much better for my art than what I'm doing now. But because of my teachers Judy and Sheila, I've always thought that teaching and thinking about pedagogy, and about how people learn, is part of citizenship. Which is difficult because some women artists will say to me, 'well, why do you teach?' And I think it's sad that they ask that question. I love it when people say to me 'I want to teach'. Or ' I like teaching', and when they take that on as integral to their artwork rather than as inimical or antagonistic. I do feel influenced by it, and I do see intensive failures, and I see myself failing, and I find the gender politics to be immensely confusing. So I don't feel like I'm a role model, but the project is an honourable project.

Does the practice pick up where this leaves off?

It does. I don't think I'm a good teacher unless I'm doing my own work, and I don't think I can do my own work well unless I'm being inspired by my students. There's a kind of back-and-forth. I'm humbled by a lot of work that my students do, and I learn a lot from what they do.

From what I understand about your practice, it's exploratory. While we could say that about all practices, I was thinking about yours in particular, in the sense that it contains collage plus found footage. It seems an exploratory way of working that could be conducive to teaching and pedagogy.

That's confusing for me though as a teacher, because I did not learn traditional art. I went straight from being a psychology major into modern art; that's what Judy was teaching us. Although I had introductory courses in art history with some great teachers, it was really only as an autodidact where I began to fill in the gaps of my knowledge. I did things backwards, so sometimes when I teach I'll think, 'well, I don't have to teach the canon', and then students will feel like they don't have a map, they don't know where they're going because they don't know where they're coming from. And then I think 'well, hey, I didn't either'. But I've had to take that on and really think about that. I taught myself a lot of stuff, and therefore I assume a lot of people will learn that way, but they don't necessarily.

How did you adapt?

To the teaching?

Yes.

I still am adapting. I have this inherent resistance to telling people what the rules are, either historically or ... I mean knowing ... it's really difficult for me to do that. It works better if I co-teach. The syllabus is like a narrative, it's like a story, so in a lot of ways it's like making time-based art, in the sense that you're plotting, you're trying to figure out what kind of effect you might have on an audience at this particular moment, so sometimes you make works-in-progress. The first class is plastic, and you hope – I hope – the students will get some of the excitement of a work-in-progress. But inevitably they'll also experience some of the gaps, or the problems with a work-in-progress. The first time I taught the history of video art, it wasn't brilliant. We learn by feedback, I suppose.

I cited earlier what you said about your work, and being a feminist. Can you explain in more detail what being a feminist might mean in relation to your role in the university and your role as an artist?

I use the resource of the Helen Chadwick archives housed at the Henry Moore Institute in Leeds, which I think is a really good teaching tool, a learning tool for students. If you go to the archive, she doesn't just document her work; she documents herself documenting her work. It's staggeringly interesting, amazing. It's possible for me to develop modules that give language to things, such as the curatorial module and the work with the Helen Chadwick archives. When I first started teaching, I thought, 'oh, this will be great, I'll be a great role model for women students'. And then I realised they didn't want the kind of role model I was going to be. It was too close to Second Wave feminism. It was too close to what they were struggling with with their mothers. So I stepped back and said, 'OK I won't do those things, I won't try to be a role model'. And then about five or 10 years later, women approached me and said, 'now I want this history'. It seemed like a different generation of women students. I'm despairing; a lot of the women who are doing dissertations with me are doing it about body dysphoria and anorexia and bulimia, and I think, 'my God, this is still full on, still really alive!' And they say, 'what's this about? What can we do?' Sometimes I get too close, and I give so much. Sometimes I've given so much that I then disappoint students, because at a certain point when the course is over I pull back. So I don't feel like I've ever really achieved the right balance, when I've had the inner resources to teach my heart out. I've certainly received the kind of feedback through which I've felt it's been positive, or it's the best class, or I've sensed that I've created a community and that I've given people some inner stuff to go on. But I wouldn't have a clue how to quantify that.

Do you think in certain people's practice there is a predisposition towards teaching in the way they'll practice, as, perhaps, in your case?

I don't think I had a predisposition toward teaching at all. It was my education. It was having these really great role models. And of course there were tough moments. But I was like a little duckling being imprinted. Sheila once had a party for the students in her programme and she and her husband went to bed. She just said, 'you can stay here as long as you want', and we stayed. I stayed with two other students and we got drunk, and we were there until around four in the morning. I mention this story because it suggests Sheila's trust and tolerance for her students. The two other women were Ann Noël and Bia Lowe. Along with my roommates I had a party to which the feminist art historian Arlene Raven came. She got so drunk that she passed out on the floor and when I woke up in the morning she was sitting there, propped up against the wall. There was just something right on, like 'this is a person!' Funny little moments, aren't they?

They're the ones you remember.

Yes.

Can you teach art?

Sure you can.

What are you teaching when you're teaching art?

You're teaching people how to think. I mean this was a big issue at the Art Institute; students would come in from the suburbs, especially as tuition got more and more expensive, and they would want to do what they thought were original paintings. And we'd say, 'the experience of you growing up in the suburbs and wanting to produce, or wanting to create a sublime moment for other people is not original. That idea of what you are, that's a construction.' Judy said her teaching was personality reconstruction; she was trying to transform us from socialised young girls to strong women. I'm not saying that that works, but there are moments when I internally flinch and say 'no'. I try to give them things to read that will maybe tip them in the direction of 'this story that I think is so unique, isn't so unique'. That's giving them a better intellectual repertoire than just being more open to what they do on their own. I had a class that was really going nowhere once, and I told them they bored me and that we were going to do something I wanted to do. So, unplanned we went out on a walk along buildings I liked in the centre of Chicago. I hustled my way into special parts of buildings that you normally can't get into, and ended up getting architects' guides, blueprints and books and stuff. And it was just fun. I do strive for those moments, if the class isn't working or the people are bored. I try to find ways to break it up, for my own sake, really ... The problems of teaching are endless, but they're such interesting problems, and I always feel that I can never figure them out. But that said, oh my god these are the problems. Every week there's another set of problems based on how the class is progressing, or a student is acting-out, or is in bad shape. I know I'm teaching well if the other students handle that well. If I have to handle it, I know that I'm doing something wrong.

How does this work when working with a group?

At the Art Institute I co-taught some classes, but that cost more money for the school. You had to work hard and had to apply for a grant to teach a class together. Mostly I taught by myself, which seems really lonely to me. Teaching can be really lonely. One time I wanted to teach the politics of narrative, and I got a copy of this famous film by Edwin S. Porter about the firemen that shows narrative from two points of view. It's from before they figured out how to do cross-cutting, *Life of an American Fireman.* So you see the narrative of the firemen going in to the building and they rescue everybody like from inside the building, and then they tell the whole story all over again from outside the building. So I went to all this trouble to get this film I'd read about and I put it on and it was cross-cut. And I just felt like a total failure. Later on I found out they'd gone back and cross-cut the film – to make it modern! – so it was actually really interesting, but it didn't do any of the things I thought it was going to do!

Can I ask you something about your experience of teaching in the US, as distinct from your experience of teaching in the UK? I know this is very general, but is there something particular that distinguishes these experiences, either in terms of students, in terms of the bureaucracy, the freedom you have, so to speak?

Students in the States tend to be less well educated. By the time they get to college they're still quite infantile – perhaps especially at an art school – in comparison to European students. People over here have had a better education and they're more mature in some ways. But I taught in an art school that attracted people who were pretty damaged by mainstream culture. The institutional milieu privileges staff here, where it tends to privilege students over there. The students who come from the States say that too. At times, I'm just shocked at how seldom people seem to think, 'well, is this good for the students?' And I know the critique of that is because America is a consumer culture society. And there are huge labour issues, which a lot of us were really unhappy about in the States. I mean the idea that a student … you've got a student who gets home deliveries and drives a BMW and who says, 'well, I'm paying for this class', £15,000 or the equivalent for a semester. And you think, 'I hate to tell you, but this is a labour issue, I'm not you're servant'. But with a little bit of tweaking, with just a little shift, students could feel a lot more cared for.

What would that shift be towards, or what would personify that shift?

Maybe some attention to studio hours and just walking through studios to see what people are doing. If the staff offices are closed at noon, it is possible to stagger that, so that when students are most available, someone could be there. It seems that a lot of the time the students are inconvenienced and that has an effect on how they feel about being here.

It's very interesting that you mention something as simple as access to studios. If there was 24-hour access it might go someway towards broaching that divide by giving students the freedom to come in after the pub or sleep late and come in …

Or just a sense of ownership or inclusion. When I was at CalArts, I'd spend the night there. The composer Charlemagne Palestine got permission to live in his studio because he said he needed to be near his equipment. It doesn't matter if any students show up. It matters that they can.

Vanalyne Green teaches at the University of Leeds.

John Hilliard — late morning — the busy
but elegant Senior Common Room —
The Slade School of Fine Art, Gower Street,
London.

You're currently director of studies, graduate programmes and graduate tutor at the Slade. Are you also teaching?

I've got two hats, really; I teach primarily graduate students. I'm head of the fine art media area, which comprises students who are working with photography, film and video, computers, sound, performance, and so on. But I also coordinate the whole graduate programme, along with my two colleagues Edward Allington and Bruce McLean. Bruce is head of painting, Ed is head of sculpture, and we work very, very closely together. The form of teaching is such that all three of us are engaging with students from the three separate areas; the course attempts to find a balance between subject specialism and a more general fine art discourse. Those are my two roles.

And you teach on a weekly basis?

I do. I'm foolish in the sense that it's teaching itself that interests me most – that is, engaging in discussion about the students' work. Anything by way of administration, management, etc., I tend to accommodate very poorly in my own weekly timetable and do probably rather too much at home. When I'm actually in the school it's most interesting for me to be on the shop floor, as it were, rather than be in an office doing administration. Bruce, Ed and I actually share an office, but none of us are ever in there, which gives you some sense of the proportion of administration work we do, and the proportion of teaching. It's loaded towards teaching.

Can you say something about how you think about teaching within the context of your own practice, and whether you understand these as discrete activities?

They're both discrete, and not. The culture in the UK is not one of teaching from your own practice, as such. In Germany, for example, if you're still adhering to the studio system where you elect to go and work with a particular artist, then you're probably within a group of like-minded individuals, and the artist is likely to be teaching primarily by example through their own practice. I don't think that's the culture here, and I certainly don't do that; I'm by no means exclusively teaching students who work with photography. I teach students who work with many different kinds of media, not all of which I have direct familiarity with myself, but that doesn't mean to say I don't have anything interesting to say about those things. Teaching in the UK at graduate level is certainly primarily led by the individual work programmes of the students themselves, which are then put under a kind of critical scrutiny, either in one-to-one tutorials, or in group tutorials, or in group seminars. In that sense, you could say that's distinct from my own work. The connecting things are inevitably that I'm contributing ideas and information that draw from my own practice. It's always interesting to engage with an ongoing discourse about contemporary art and to see how people introduce new ideas and new ways of working. You get that in any art school environment. So it's a very lively situation to be involved in, and that's a real positive. For me personally one of the most direct connections between my own work and my work in an art school, is that I do use the environment for producing my own work. I use my students as models, assistants, helpers, etc., and I use the locations … we happen to be sitting in the UCL Senior Common Room, and I have used this room to produce several of my own works with the assistance of the students. That is exactly the kind of thing I'm likely to do; I'm likely to be looking for a certain kind of location, and I'll find it either within the Slade itself, or within the larger confines of UCL.

And is the room chosen for it being within the institution, or it's more a generic space you're looking for, and this happens to suit your needs?

More than likely I'm looking for a place, which could be found outside such an institution if I knew where to look for it. But there certainly have been instances where I've deliberately used an art school environment, or, let's say, the photographic studio here, or some kind of workshop in the school, or the office, because I've actually had it as a subject, the art school environment. In the last two or three years, I've made a number of works which actually do take that as a subject. So, in that sense, there's a very, very particular connection. But, because of the way I work – quite frequently using models within my photographic work and very rarely ever using a professional model – I'm reliant on friends, colleagues and students. And the great thing about the student community, of course, is that it's quite large, and it's constantly changing. So, in a purely personal and rather self-interested way, it's a huge convenience, it's a fantastic resource.

Is teaching something you just found your way into, which in time became a career?

I've taught pretty much continuously since relatively soon after leaving art school, primarily a day a week, two days a week, with only one break – for three years – in the late 1970s. Two days a week is a very manageable balance, I think, between being a practising artist, and contributing something to teaching, and taking something from teaching in an economic sense. The good thing about having that economic safety net is that you have tremendous freedom as an artist. It's a kind of trade off; you're giving up maybe two days a week throughout the academic year, and in exchange for giving up that time, and giving your time to the students, you're being compensated. And that means you don't have to be concerned with basic living costs; you don't have to be overly concerned about buying materials, or producing work in a certain way. It seems to me to be a perfectly workable balance. About 10 years ago, I finally took up a full-time teaching job, which is my job here at the Slade. But, because of the conditions in a place like this – the academic year is not too long – the requirement for teaching is not that great, because one's also paid for research time and in any case, as I've said, at least part of my work benefits from being produced in the school, or in the larger university environment. I've just found a way of making it work quite well for me, and in exchange my contribution is quite committed, it's quite serious. I don't take it casually. So, yes, it's something that starts, as you suggest, as a part-time thing, maybe the odd day a week. If institutions feel you're a useful person to have around, and you have something useful to offer, then it's something that's likely to be extended to what is, for you, a workable limit. So, even though I'm technically full-time, I don't find it an inhibition in making my own work and there is this real bonus of giving you a considerable degree of economic freedom.

You took part in a seminar on teaching in Reykjavik in 2000, organised by the Association of Icelandic Art Teachers. One of the objectives was to 'contribute to the discussion of education and visual arts at the beginning of a new millennium, the age of image consumption'. What went on there?

You're probably going to be disappointed by the reality of what went on there, and the misleading word is the word 'seminar', because actually it was a week-long workshop. Different people were invited to do simultaneous workshops, two or three workshops going on at a time. As I recall, each of us kicked the week off by making a presentation and a talk to the entire group of art teachers, who were drawn from all the Nordic countries.

And then they split up into workshops run by the different presenters. What I was doing, which is all I ever do now if anybody does ask me to do a workshop – and by coincidence I was in Lugano last week doing precisely this – is that I will go to make a new piece of my own work, and that piece will be made in collaboration with the group running the workshop. It starts with discussion, but people have to have a willingness to help me; maybe by appearing in the work, maybe by lending a hand, maybe by giving me some technical help. They will, in turn, produce their own work, if you like, almost their own versions of that work, because we've hammered it out together. In reality, they're not literally mimicking me, they're doing something that is individualised, but it stems from a similar set of ideas, and maybe a similar set of procedures. At the end, there's a kind of summary; everybody makes evident what they've been doing, and there's a discussion about it. So, that's what went on there. It wasn't really a huge debate about the future of art education, I'm afraid. It obviously touched on the subject, because the people there were involved in teaching, mostly in secondary schools in Sweden, Norway, Iceland, Greenland, and the Faroe Islands, so it was great. I came away with a very interesting piece of work, I thought, and they did some great things as well. They went back to their schools, I hope, equipped with refreshed thinking on how they might go about teaching art, especially using photography, in this case.

Can you say something about what is particular about the teaching model the Slade employs?

I think it is different. It's interesting, because when students apply to one of the central London art schools, they're very often applying to the Slade, or Goldsmiths, or the Royal College, or possibly all three, and they may even get offered a place at more than one, and they have to make a choice. So when I talk to students here, I'm always clear that these are all very good places to go. I don't try and privilege the Slade, but I do try and explain the distinctions. One of the distinctions about the Slade is that it is subject specific, in the sense that it has departments of painting, sculpture, media, and the history and theory of art. But it also has a very integrated programme, which allows all those fine art areas to overlap and interface with each other. It really is trying to have the best of both worlds in that respect; somebody who really wants to concentrate on some very specific aspect of painting, let's say, or video, or working with the Internet, would be able to do that, and get some expert supervision. But somebody who wants their work to develop more flexibly, and more generally, within an ethos of a broad range of contemporary ideas and practices, can do that as well. And as their work develops, changes, they are likely to move around the school and take benefit from different sorts of workshops, and different studio staff, and so on. The other thing, or one other thing, that's particular about the Slade, is its convenient location at the very heart of UCL, and the University's policy of making available expertise from different departments, where it's appropriate. So we have students who are working, for example, with the neurosciences, or with engineering, or with computer science, or with anthropology, or whatever it is. The neurosciences are quite popular at the moment. And you get very good advice and assistance from those departments; access to facilities when necessary, access to interested people, to their staff and so on. I feel this is something that the Slade offers, which is not easily offered in many other places, and that connects to something else I'd say about the Slade; which is that there's not so much an emphasis on the marketplace. There's much more an emphasis on developing work in a genuine research environment. There's a real encouragement for people to experiment, to have a very investigative kind of approach, to be very research-minded. And that's a situation in which you're likely to develop really innovative work. Maybe it's not the most finely finished work at that stage, but it should be very strong on ideas, and on new ideas, and on new ways of working, new kinds of practices. There's plenty of evidence to show that this work then finds its own market, as it were. If you take as a barometer of achievement, for what it's worth, something like the Turner Prize, you find a huge number of Slade graduates who are either Turner Prize winners or nominees. So, clearly, if in the market place success in the art world is a measure of students' eventual achievement, then there's plenty of evidence to show that. All I'm saying is they get there by being involved in this – what I'm calling a very research-minded – establishment.

What do you understand of practice-based research?

Both Goldsmiths and the Slade for example run PhD programmes, and I suspect that, even though their PhD programmes may be quite academic, ours are even more so. Within fine art I understand there are PhD programmes where it's possible to do a PhD largely by project, which is through a form of practical research. Now, I certainly don't have any problem with artists doing research. Clearly they do so, in the sense that they come up with truly innovative original work, through original thought, and they contribute to the larger field of knowledge in that subject area. That's what I call research, and I have no hesitation that artists do that. Artists are capable of doing that and certainly, I think in most art schools in the UK, you'd have to say that, with the emphasis on individualised programmes of working, the environment is set up to encourage something which you might describe as personal research by students. When it comes to a PhD programme, I think one becomes more anxious, because for a PhD to have meaning it has to bear comparison with PhDs in other subjects. There has to be an academic side to it in order to establish that comparability. And the PhDs that we do can either be by thesis only, or they can be by thesis and practice. But there is a condition: they must parallel each other. The development of ideas must be in parallel; through dissertation, and through practical work. They must be different ways of expounding, of articulating the same kind of thought. But even with practical work, the minimum word count for the thesis is 60,000 words, with a maximum of 80,000. That's a considerable effort. So even though there's no actual proportion, I'd say the likely proportion would be something like 25 per cent studio work and 75 per cent theory. Personally, I feel quite comfortable with that. I wouldn't feel very comfortable about somebody doing a PhD purely by practice. You don't need to be Doctor Artist to have credibility in the art world, and, in fact I rather suspect, certainly in the UK, it would be counter-productive. If you announced yourself as artist Doctor-whoever, as a kind of seal of authenticity for your work, people would laugh! Because they would rightly be thinking 'well, we want to judge this person's work on the work itself, not on a piece of paper that seems to authorise its creativity'. The other thing to say, perhaps, is that because there's been so much theory produced which has had direct bearing on the visual arts, and which uses examples from the visual arts, certainly since let's say the 1960s, that it obviously is of interest to artists to have access to those ideas. However there's a distinction between having access to those ideas, and considering the work that you do in the light of those ideas, and using particular theoretical texts as a kind of users' manual. That's a very tricky position to take up, because the risk is that you end up illustrating a set of received ideas, and not necessarily having a very interesting work of art. In fact, perhaps the art somehow drops out of the equation.

Is this one of the dangers of PhDs?

As far as I know, most of the people who do the PhD at the Slade, even if they're coming from the direction of studio practice, tend to end up in a more theory-based and academic environment. In other words, their own working position seems to have shifted in consequence of that study. I think they drift more into an academic environment. There's nothing against that, but they then become more cultural theorists, or art theorists, than practising artists.

Has teaching become a professional career choice for artists? And, if so, is this necessarily good for art?

When I first started teaching I would have been teaching within art schools, which were quite independent of the larger academic, or educational, community, and were organised according to the dictates of their own subject. There'd be the academic side, which would probably be in art history, but, otherwise, everything would have been organised to serve the development of practical artwork. Then a lot of those art schools got merged into polytechnics, and I wouldn't say that at that point they became academicised; they became, perhaps, more bureaucratic, and had to fit an institutional mould. But they were still allowed their own identity as art departments, faculties of art and design, once the polytechnics became new universities. Within the old universities, like the Slade within UCL, they were probably for a long time also allowed to function rather independently and didn't actually award degrees; they awarded their own diplomas. Then they began to award first BAs, then MAs, and eventually to develop a PhD programme. So what's happened across the board is that all art departments have been made to fit a larger academic mould. The flipside to the benefit of the Slade being at University College, I suppose, is that of taking all the advantages of UCL, as a fully-fledged department at UCL, like other departments do, and interfacing with them. The trade off is to have had to adapt to that academic mould, and there are benefits to be derived from that. There's also a downside to it, because sometimes the requirements that are put upon us are not best suited to the subject.

Are we speaking about the Research Assessment Exercise?

Well, the RAE would be part of it, because it's largely predicated on a notion of people writing and delivering papers, having them published, writing books, having them published, and so on. Although the art and design panel has its own set of equivalents – exhibitions, retrospectives counting more than non-retrospectives, shows in museums counting for more than shows in commercial galleries, shows abroad generally counting for more than shows in the UK – it's still not such a good fit. And I'm sure there's a perception that it's an attempt to give credibility to art as a subject, but to academicise it is a little awkward.

What do you consider to be good teaching?

… a good teacher?

Good teaching?

Good teaching … I think … well as far as I'm concerned, it's no longer appropriate to have a model where a teacher is saying 'this is absolutely the way to do things – this and only this way'. At the Slade, for example, presumably it would have been like that when members of the Euston Road School were teaching here, and everybody would have been working from models, using the same style of depiction, and using the same methodologies. Then you could go around and say 'this is a good painting' and 'this is a bad painting' according to those criteria. There isn't a fixed model held in mind for somebody who's doing useful teaching now. It's much more a question of being capable of addressing some very fundamental ideas about the whole business of making art. One has to be able to address many different manners of working, both in terms of method and in terms of style. One has to be able to address many different sets of ideas that people bring to bear on their work. If you don't have this flexibility, then probably you're not such a good teacher, because you'd be too narrowly limited. You would have a very restricted usefulness in an art school environment. Beyond that, you're going to be useful to your students if you have very good information, both historical and about contemporary work, and I think you'd be a good teacher if you were capable of being properly enthusiastic about the subject in general, and about the work you find your students are doing.

Can you teach art?

It depends what you mean. You can certainly teach what I've just been talking about. You can communicate good information, you can communicate constructive ideas, you can show people how to do certain things technically. Art itself, it's almost like the soul, or something, isn't it? It's something that you can't actually physically put a handle on. I wouldn't say its innate, it's something that can be developed, but it's something that, in the end, individuals have to introduce themselves to their work. They have to make that contribution, and that you cannot make for them. You can speak around it, you can speak about existing examples etc., you can supply everything, but that ingredient – art itself, the thing that really fires, that animates the work in the end – is probably the very thing that is most difficult to talk about.

John Hilliard teaches at the Slade School of Fine Art, London.

Martin Honert — Haus A — Hochschule
für Bildende Künste — Dresden, Germany.

What do you think of the institution you teach at?

It's OK here, in Dresden. It wasn't necessarily the object of my desire. I had done interviews for different institutions at the time, so it was kind of by accident I came here. Nowadays I would say it was a good accident, and I'm really happy here. Maybe what I want to say is that I didn't really have an ambition to teach here, and only here. It happened. It happened in Dresden.

You studied under Fritz Schwegler?

Yes.

In Düsseldorf?

Yes.

I'm interested in how Fritz Schwegler influenced you as an artist, or as a teacher, or both.

I think both. He was a teacher who interacted with all of us students in a very personal, intimate way. The most important thing I learned from Fritz Schwegler was a general acceptance of what somebody wants to do. He was a very humorous man, but in relationship to us very serious with a precise look on what we did. When I started in his class, the artist Fritz Schwegler wasn't so important for me. I really only understood his work very late on, at the end of my own studies, so the decision to study under him wasn't a case of, 'oh, he makes wonderful things and I want to learn from him'. No, it was more the person and the way he interacted with us ... this was really special and really interesting. I learned this from Fritz Schwegler and use it today as a teacher.

... and the kind of relationship you have with your students?

Yes.

So what can you do for your students?

I can do a lot, but this is something I can't answer generally because I only react to what I see. The student has to start, and then I see something. I operate with this very individually and very exclusively. I have difficulties in making a general definition of teaching art.

Is this what Schwegler taught you?

This is old Schwegler School.

You accept everyone for what they do?

What they do, and that is the starting point of our journey together towards the question 'what is art?'

Can you teach art?

Can I teach art? Generally, I would say 'no, I can't teach art'. I can only teach students to make their own work and how to work with that. So I would say generally, I can't teach art, because the definition of art is so wide and complex. As wide and as complex as the people who make up the definition. I don't know how many artists there are in the world – perhaps 20 million? So we have 20 million definitions of art.

Can only artists teach art? Can only artists do this work?

I would say only artists can do this. But I would also say that what is more problematic is whether it's important that it's very well known artists who teach art. It's a false logic that a great artist should also be a great teacher. That is very important. However, I do think an art teacher should aspire to being a great artist. I studied in Düsseldorf and you know that the academy there is very famous, and all the German stars are teaching there and I think that's very good and I'm very happy I studied there. In this team of teachers in Düsseldorf I would say Fritz Schwegler was not the artist.

People like Katharina Fritsch, Thomas Huber, Thomas Schütte and Elke Dende came out of Schwegler's class.

Yes.

So there were quite a few artists who came out of this class. Gregor Schneider …

Gregor Schneider didn't study the whole time with Schwegler, but he did some years with him. Some interesting artists …

Was Fritz Schwegler so influential on these people?

Yes, but he wasn't influential in terms of how he believed something should be done. He was influential in a more general way, in terms of students doing their own work. It's also interesting that there were students who did performance, painting, video, everything really in the Schwegler Klasse, without a concentration on any one discipline.

The publicity around an exhibition in Dresden by four of your students talked about the Honert Schule.

This was the curator.

It was called Meister Klasse.

Yes, but it was the curator's title.

It made me think about what would characterise the work of the Honert Klasse.

Everyone would firstly say it's figurative. This is partly true, but I have to say this is a special thing here in Dresden at the HfBK. The teacher I replaced was a really old-school figurative artist, and he represented – like others of his generation – a special reputation in sculpture for the HfBK being a traditional figurative school. So I came here to a well-established reputation. It was a misunderstanding and I've put a lot of work into saying that this is not the way I think about, or understand, figurative art. This is not the figurative art that I have in mind. So it was not so much my thing as it was an already established area. But it is true even today that many students work figuratively, but for me it's very important they find their own way of doing that.

So that you break with …

Yes. It was really hard work to establish a completely new idea of figurative art. I hate the title that I am a figurative artist; I don't like it. I've made some figurative work, but it's not a real characteristic of my work. Here I'm a little bit a teacher in sculpture and figurative art and I have to live with that.

Do you have to build up a tradition of your own so the students are attracted to coming here?

Yes, and I can't avoid that some of the students are a little bit too close to my own work for example. I can't avoid it. I can't say 'I forbid you to make this'. I can say 'pay attention' or 'be aware – this is a very dangerous direction you're going in'. I'm sure that students of their age, between 20 and 30, really have a desire to make figures; you can't struggle against this force, against the desire of this generation. So I have to accept it, no more and no less. But my hope is that they'll find a way of working that is really their own. I don't think that someone deliberately says, 'Oh, I think I'll make the same thing as Martin Honert'. They want to make their own work, but this unconsciously drives into or near my work. But then I can help them with that.

The students who had their work in the Meister Klasse exhibition; was there something similar about their work?

That was a little bit of a problem, I was very proud of the show, it was good, but it was only five students who all made really figurative work, so it wasn't representative of the whole class.

Was this the curator's choice?

That was really the curator's thing. It was OK, but it was really … It's wrong if someone sees the exhibition and says, 'Ah, that was Martin Honert's class'. They were some of my best students, and I was really surprised by the work, as I'd not seen some of it before, because they'd made the work in Berlin. But in this concentration, in this choice, it wasn't really representative of my class … I hope not.

Maybe more the curator's perception of Klasse Honert?

Yes. And maybe he knew one of the students, and you know how it generally works …

Can you teach if you no longer have an art practice? Are the two positions bound up together or can you separate them?

I can separate these. When I'm teaching I'm not an artist. When I'm an artist I'm not a teacher. But generally I would say they are bound together, and I can only say what I say as a teacher because I'm an artist. But when I speak with students individually, then I speak more as an artist, because I have my art in mind, but not only my art, but art in general, and I'm really within the context of art. But there is a completely different way of thinking when I'm in the studio making my own work, it's a completely different thing, and for me this difference is very important. Both things have something to do with one another, or they influence one another, but the points of view are different and I like to attempt to balance these really different points of view. For a long, long time, maybe 10 to 15 years, I was a struggling artist in Düsseldorf and I had to really fight the stupid attitude of artists. I lived this stupid attitude too, so for me it was of great personal benefit to start teaching here in Dresden, because it really added new points of view. So it was not only my own work that was the central thing, but more the other's work; that was very important for me and also maybe for my work. I can't see it, but I'm sure it also influenced my work.

Do you think art education in the academies is in good condition right now?

The academies are really good. I really believe that. We have this discussion about the reformation of education, about the Batchelors and the Masters, and perhaps this is a really important reformation for universities in Germany in general, but not for the art schools I would say. Because the art schools are part of a very special tradition that works very, very well, and is of a very high quality. The international art world, the world of art, profits from good German education.

Martin Honert teaches at the Hochschule für Bildende Künste, Dresden.

Christian Jankowski — interview conducted
against the background of a very loud video
work during his solo show — Lisson Gallery,
London.

When did you start teaching?

I started teaching a year and a half ago at the art academy in Stuttgart. I heard from a friend, who is a professor there, about this open position and I just applied and thought it might be an interesting experience. I'd done a couple of workshops and a lot of studio visits in previous years. When you do exhibitions in different places, they also often ask you to do some crits, or to go to some artists' studios, or see art students, and I actually enjoyed doing it and looking at people's work. I did a workshop in Leipzig in the art academy …

Seminar (*Selbstpositionierungen im Kunstfeld*) and *Diploma*?

Yes, *Seminar*, you saw that one? That was one of these workshops, and from this I somehow thought that teaching was maybe something to experience, something I hadn't done before, so that's why I applied. But I didn't hear back from the school at all for a year, and then they called me and said, 'you can start in two months! Yes, come now.' I live in New York, so there's some extra travelling involved. The good thing about the institution is that they're very flexible with me, and they're very understanding about the fact that I have a lot of work and have to travel a lot. So I'm a bit free with my schedule and with when I come. I come over once a month.

In comparison to the expectation you had of teaching, what's it like?

It's funny; it's almost as if teaching had always been rolling in my direction. When this friend said to me, 'oh why don't you come?' At first I felt, 'oh, that's an honour to be asked', and then you think, 'Why not? Maybe it's an interesting thing, instead of just doing a lot of different very short crits', as sometimes I felt it was not really right for students I met. Art students, especially in the US, meet like thousands of people who give them crits in a very short time. You spend 15 to 20 minutes with them and maybe have two or three sentences to say to someone before going on to the next one. I thought that I'm more interested in developing a certain kind of dialogue between some people I see more regularly, as you can follow their work and really see how it develops. So I didn't have these big ideas or expectations as to how it would be to teach, I just thought maybe it's an experience I'd like to have.

And is it a good experience in Stuttgart?

It's hot and cold, it's both. The first two or three months I was there, I thought, 'oh, I've made a big mistake in agreeing to come.'

Why?

Because so much of it was new and I didn't know exactly what they expected from me. I took over a position where students didn't have a professor for two semesters, but I didn't want to take everybody in my class. So I said, 'no, everyone has to show their work – I'm not taking everybody in my class'. And students began thinking, 'oh, he's difficult'. And some professors even said to me 'oh, I heard you're not taking some of the students', and 'you're not taking students who want to become art teachers'. But it was actually because their work didn't convince me one bit. Now I also have student's who want to become art teachers, but I was really looking at the work, and I didn't want to fill my class with people I'm not really interested in. I just thought that I wanted to start a class in which I could have a choice of students to work with – especially at the beginning of a class it's even more important to establish a certain group that finds each other through their work and through their interests.

And is it good now?

Altogether it's good now. Yes.

How does it feel to work for someone?

I'm used to working for someone. It's a different kind of politics to gallery politics or museum politics, but in the end it all comes down to either meeting some nice people in a place or not. Another thing that's attractive to me about Stuttgart is that a lot of positions are opening up right now. We just got Rainer Ganahl, whom I recommended to become professor. So, I'm thinking in terms of not only having to build a class, but also having three other professors coming soon, I think something is possible in Stuttgart. It's basically a generation change. It's as simple as that; some people are retiring ... Of course, it's really important to get great people in.

How involved do you want to get in Stuttgart? How involved in the academy, the committees, the administration, in the whole institution?

[Long pause.]

I'm as involved as is necessary to make it a nice place. At the moment I know that I will do this for a couple of years, but if you were to ask me if I would still be doing it in five years, I don't know.

You're not exactly looking for a career in teaching?

I don't know. The main thing is that you are comfortable with it, and I already feel that over a year and a half it has got better than it was in the beginning. For some time I just thought, 'wow, it's extra stress I really can't deal with right now. I have so much other work to do … My career – I'm constantly travelling.' My girlfriend lives in New York and doesn't see me so often, so that is also something. Maybe in a year from now she'll say, 'hey, you have to decide'. And she's more important to me than this art school. It might not be forever, but the last years have been running very well financially which also means I'm paying 40 per cent in taxes in Germany, so the amount of extra money I make in Stuttgart right now is already halved. Plus I pay for the travel costs myself. I'm not really doing this for money.

So why do it?

I do it because I feel, after 10 years, or longer, working in this kind of triangle between museums, galleries, and producing my work, it's another form of discussion. In the long run, if this turns out to be something where I establish another context with a new generation of artists that's great as well … The thing that I like about it is that you also become friends with some of the students over time. When I'm in Stuttgart it doesn't feel like work for me; I'm just looking at and talking about art, which I like doing anyway. If I were just a teacher this would be a fantasy life. It's a luxurious job. I have a great big studio for myself in the academy. One could ask why I don't work in Stuttgart … but I have a different working practice, I'm travelling from project to project and for each project I need a new production team, and a new atelier.

Are teaching and practice, in your own mind, very separate activities?

Yes, I think so. I see each semester as a kind of project, or artwork – to come up with some stimulating ideas for the students and myself. It is like an art project, but I don't present it as such. In my first semester in Stuttgart, we ended up doing a show simultaneously in the Kunstmuseum and the art academy. It was actually based on an anecdote I heard about Joseph Kosuth; when he was teaching here, the students barricaded the studio with stones and bricks because he didn't show up that often. That's the first thing I heard about Stuttgart when I applied. I don't know how many people told me this story, and then I thought, 'wow, let's use this as the topic of an exhibition, and let's say I call the first show *Sculptures to Eliminate the Professor*, because it is a sculpture class I'm hired to teach in Stuttgart. So I said to my students 'this sculpture is the perfect sculpture, because it should make the student free from the professor'. Which is, in the end, what every art academy should do; to produce individual, independent characters and artistic ideas. That is why I thought the Kosuth wall was such a beautiful metaphor. So you develop your thoughts and work with this metaphor and by the end of the semester, we decided we should do an exhibition, and, as well as doing this at the art academy, we should also do our thing in the museum. This change of space distanced the students from the teaching context. So I talked to the museum director and said, 'OK, we need an exhibition space here in the museum for the students' work'. In the end, for the art school part of the exhibition, we just had a live cam showing the projection of the museum show *Sculptures to Eliminate the Professor.* In the classroom there was a big projection in which you saw museum visitors walking in and looking at our sculptures. The next room was just a big stack of invitation cards leading people down to the museum. So it was a whole installation. It was a whole concept for an exhibition. A lot of which resulted from mixing up ideas from the students, but also bringing them to a form. That was one project. I did three semesters and the third project was about working with the idea of collaboration. I wanted to do this matchmaking thing as I see myself as somebody who tries to find platforms for the students, to experiment, and to gain some experience, and maybe inspire them to do some work. My work is very film-based, so I made contact with this film school in Ludwigsburg, which is very close to Stuttgart. They're one of the best film schools in Germany. I met the director, who is also a very young guy and he was really up for collaborating with us. So they had a big 'pitching' event ... you know, film pitching; everybody has five or 10 minutes to show some slides, to show some storyboards, to pitch an idea for a film to other people. As a director this is a way to get support for your film project and find a camera crew, actors and so on. Everybody, the faculty and students from this film school attend this event. So I had seven or eight of my students pitch their ideas, among ideas pitched by the film people. Some of my students approached it from a performance background, describing a totally surreal project. Others were coming up with something in which they really needed help from the film side. Now there is a lot of dialogue happening between these film students and the art school. Many collaborations took place.

This whole process you go through, how do you reflect on this again with the students?

We videoed the performances and presentations, and we talked about everything. It's interesting that some projects are still in negotiation, while some of them have already been produced with the film students. The possibilities of how to do a film as an artist in a semi-professional team could be reflected on in this collaboration with Ludwigsburg. You could learn to split responsibilities like on a film production, instead of just asking your art student colleague who doesn't really know how to hold a camera … to hold a camera. Why not get somebody who studies how to be a cameraman at Ludwigsburg?

Did the film school get a lot out of it as well?

Yes, I think so. Marco Schmidt, the first performer, stole the show from the four film people who went before him. They were so boring, and we were so lucky when Marco did his performance. After that everybody said 'they're absolutely from the art school, let's see what the next one does'. They were not all so good, but Marco made such a good start; I was just sitting there feeling very happy, almost proud. I'm very happy at moments like this. It's great when you push someone in the right context, where he just shoots off and it goes. I think the film students were inspired by our presentations – I'm sure they can use something of this experience for their next pitching.

Can you teach art?

I think you can, yes … you can't … I mean it's not a guarantee that you become a good artist, but if I wouldn't have had the teachers I had, I would not have thought about art and not found this perspective in this amount of time. When you ask 'can you teach art', there's no guarantee that you can teach art that is going to make someone a great artist. Something I learned is that it's about finding the right words and learning vocabularies, to describe and validate and discuss work. There are so many strange words around art schools and art teaching, like something has 'presence', or something 'functions' … How can something have presence and something else have no presence? What does it mean? So in this regard, when teaching in a school, you have to find your own ways of talking about things. I'm learning a bit about that too, because I was not so super talkative about art as an artist.

Maybe that was a good thing …

Maybe that was a good thing! But you sit there with 10 or 15 people, and then somebody puts something there; you have to say something. I can already see after a year and a half, that sometimes I start repeating stuff. I can see how that could very easily happen more often over the next 10 years!

[Laughs.]

Fast-forward 10 years; you've just said the same thing for the 50th time. If you're to continue teaching, what do you think stops you becoming that person?

That's when you're not excited about art anymore. The great art teachers that I knew always got excited and they could really look. If you start repeating your sentences so often, you may also have developed a very structured view, a very one-dimensional view of something. You may have become too dogmatic about only one single viewpoint on things. Somehow it's about keeping your mind working, always questioning, and always reconsidering your position and other positions …

Is that about having your own practice? And if so, do you think that a good teacher has to be practising?

For me it's a must. That's the problem that I've seen many times in art schools. What was really important for me as a student was to see that I had a practising artist in front of me, and not just an art teacher. So when I had a hard time in my first year of teaching, I decided that maybe I had to change it somehow according to my needs, and that I didn't always have to look to the needs of others. And because I've now got so many projects to work on, I began discussing the work in class. And I got such great feedback from the students. This basically came out of my thinking, OK, architecture teachers have their whole class working on their buildings and their projects all the time, it's very normal. I opened a lot of this up ... my students sat in when a journalist wanted to interview me. Or my gallerist was there ... they could come and listen to us talking about new projects. Or I tell them about the unfinished ideas about a new piece of work. I let them be part of all aspects of that. Because it's so abstract as an art student, how all this somehow works. With an art teacher, who's only a teacher, you don't see their life; you don't have this vision of them as an artist. It was very stimulating for me to see my professor, Franz Erhard Walther, working with curators, publishing books ...

Living in New York as you do, does coming back here to teach in Stuttgart help you make a bond with your country, with its culture? Could you live in Stuttgart?

You are right, I like to keep in touch with my people. But I could not live in Stuttgart. When I'm in Stuttgart I almost live in the art academy. For me the good thing about Stuttgart is that it's a model city. Things are within reach. I know people in Berlin very well also, and I could maybe do student projects there too. But in Stuttgart I can go to the museum, meet the director and I can say 'my students want to do something in the museum'. It's not really a big city, everything is accessible, it's very comfortable. But living in New York is good, and it gives me an excuse to not be in Stuttgart constantly.

[Laughs.]

I can stop over on my travels to and from Europe. Sometimes I fly to Frankfurt and take the train from there. Stuttgart is only an hour from Frankfurt, it's not too bad.

That kind of space is a space to think as well.

Yes, Stuttgart is always like a framed time and it's a very intense time. Sometimes the students start working with me in the morning and then it's one-thirty at night, and I think, 'oh no, it's been long enough, and I'm still there talking and discussing'. I'm there at all different times of the day, when I'm in the art academy.

And you've got access to young, interesting, German artists who are excited and talking about things ...

You say it's so exciting to meet young artists? There are some students ... I sometimes lose my patience there. It's the luxury you have of working with galleries and with curators, really working with professionals. You have to learn to be a bit patient with some students when you're a professor, because you can't just take five or six students in your class.

I want to ask you about your teaching methods.

The only important thing is to really do something, to set yourself targets to get something done. That's why each semester leads to one event, for example, where everybody has to get to this point and find their position in relation to the task. It's only because of seeing this work, and seeing it in the long run, that you somehow understand yourself and your work better. In terms of pedagogical background or teaching methods, for me it's basically just helping them to get stuff out.

But it's not collaboration in the way you'll collaborate with other people, or is it?

[Pause.]

It is a collaboration. We work together. This is always the task; that one semester leads to one project, and I find that interesting at that moment. Last semester I saw some students' work and said to them that it looked like something out of the 1970s, and when I said that, I remembered when I was a student my professor said the same thing to me and, back then I never totally understood what he meant by that. And so I thought, 'OK, now we all go to the Staatsgalerie in Stuttgart, where they have this big video collection from the 1970s, and we'll look at all the video work they have in their archive, and each of us will make a video in relation to an artists video we find there.

You included?

I was not included, I was just organising it.

Does the collaboration continue outside the institution or is the boundary of the institution the limit of the collaboration?

I'm always bridging things. I realised that just now when you asked me. You already saw that the first show we did was putting the projection of the museum up in the art

school, and having the show in the museum. That was a clear bridge to the outside.
In a way, of course, that was possible because the museum director knows me, and
thinks it's partly my work. I'm presenting myself there, as well. It's similar with the
Staatsgalerie in Stuttgart. Now they want us to do something there in a few months,
after we did the exhibition with these new interpretations of the old videos. But
it makes total sense, because they want to contextualise their collection of 1970s
performance art. Of course, it's great having some art students come in and show
some new video work in relation to that.

Can you author some of that work? Are you willing to take that and make it you own again?

I have done it a couple of times. Earlier you were referring to the workshop in Leipzig,
for example. *Seminar* was a student workshop and my artwork at the same time. It
became a video you can buy in one of my galleries. A workshop situation is something
other than a class. For the moment, I don't necessarily need to do this, but there's
constantly the potential for doing it. When it's the right time and the right moment
it will be discussed with my class. It is important that it's a win-win situation and that
people don't feel used. I could maybe author the whole way I teach them and what
happens because of this?

What would you change about art education?

I don't know what I would change. Of course I don't like bureaucracy and, of course,
somebody has to do that. It's like doing your homework; you have to do some of it,
I also sometimes hate to be in conferences and spend so much time there.

Why did Stuttgart employ you? What do you think they were getting?

I did the presentation there and a lot of people liked the work, and in the end the work
brings you somewhere, and if people find that interesting ... That's also why I focus on the
work of the artist in the class. If you can manifest something through your work, that will
bring you into exhibitions, into art galleries. In the end it brings you back into art schools.

**The work includes the reputation of the artist because without reputation they might
not know about you.**

I don't even think that the reputation is important. We saw that recently by having some people in to present their work, when they applied for a professorship. If you have to do a presentation for 40 minutes, present your work, what you want, what you have to offer, you see how people can communicate, and how much it all links together. There's a buzz around certain people, quality is a hard thing to describe, but you see who fits well into a context. It's something to do with what is already on offer, and what characters are already in a school, etc., and how it all hangs together. You need a good team. I'm concentrating on getting some good professors here right now.

Who would you like?

Who would I like? I don't know if I can say that! I have some people in mind, yes. Rainer Ganahl is someone I'm very happy with. I think he'll be a great teacher. I also wanted Mike Bouchet and Olaf Nicolai.

Christian Jankowski teaches at the Staatliche Akademie der Bildenden Künste, Stuttgart.

Klaus Jung — late morning — mid-January — his office — Glasgow School of Art on Renfrew Street.

Let me begin by asking you what art school should train people for? And I say people, rather than artists.

A good starting point, although I find the word training difficult when it comes to art schools. I don't think there is so much training involved. I don't think there's so much difference in the way people, or artists, teach, or relate to the idea of teaching. The way art schools are organised and art schools are placed in the educational system might be different. While German art schools are very much focusing on the career of an individual artist that might come out of it, I learned here, and in Scandinavia before that, that art schools can do much more. By learning through art, and being connected to art so intensely, as it can be in an art school, you gain something that is relevant to many other areas in our society.

Such as …

For example social engagement, ways of managing yourself, and – that's what I find most important – ways of taking a critical distance from yourself, which is absolutely necessary for any kind of art thinking. You produce something, and you see it and you have to take a distance from it in order to judge it, or value it. That is absolutely valuable for other parts of society. I wouldn't go so far as saying it's a skill that automatically leads to a career in industry, it's more a preparation for a social role.

It almost suggests some way to behave.

It's probably an approach to learning, and if an approach to learning is a way to behave then I absolutely agree with that. This particular approach to learning is that you always have to base it on your own individual experience and decisions; it's not learning facts, it's actually learning by digestion, learning by dealing with things in a direct way. It's not accumulating knowledge to use it for something. There is no endpoint. Learning leads to further learning and a different social behaviour.

And is this particular to art schools?

I would not say that we are the only ones that do that. It's particular, probably, to higher education in general, or should be, if we look back at the old Humboldt model. But I think it's very explicit in art schools, because there is something visible, tangible all the time – the work of art – which requires further reflection, leading to a new visual result, and so on.

And can anybody teach this?

No. You probably would have to have an experience with this open ended learning.

But if you're suggesting that it's possible to find this form of behaviour in other forms of higher education, not only art schools, what is particular to an art school?

The open endedness probably goes even further: there is no final goal. The goalposts are not only shifting; the shift is determined by the learner, it's not determined by another given context. Of course there is a market and other elements framing what is happening. But it often seems that the only way to get into the art system, or art market, is to criticise the art market. And that's different. You don't get into medicine just by criticising medicine, you have to learn the details to be a practicing doctor, and I would expect that my doctor knows how to treat me and not just be critical about me. Or that an architect knows how a building stands up, but I would not necessarily expect that from an artist.

What would you expect from an artist, if we're talking about certain kinds of skills that a doctor or architect might have?

I would probably say a clear critical distance from yourself, and being able to review and renew yourself all the time. The other skill is about looking, or better still: perceiving. It's having a chance to perceive out of your own judgement and not out of a given judgement, not through mediation. When I get a mediated piece of knowledge, I still have to use my own judgement and experience to understand what's going on. You have to base everything on your own decisions, you cannot do things because they are done like that, and that is a particular skill.

And can you teach art?

That question again!

Again?

How old is that? And how often have you heard you cannot teach art? Coming out of the German system of the 1970s: any professor would have said that.

Who was your professor?

I was a student in Düsseldorf with Klaus Rinke. All of them said, 'you can't teach art'. And they also said, 'good art just sells itself.' If you believe it, that's fine, but better not to believe it because it's much easier for you if you don't. At some point I turned around and thought 'if you understand teaching just as a technique to learn, if it's about learning, then art and pedagogy are very closely related, because making art is a great way to learn; about your surroundings, about your world. I can help people to learn, which is close to teaching, but it's not teaching in a traditional sense that sets achievable skills right at the beginning. A good pedagogue would always say 'it's about you learning, it's not about me teaching,'

Do you need to be an artist to do this?

In an art school I think you do.

Can you say something about the advantages and disadvantages in terms of approach and outcome between the British and German systems?

The German professor system focuses on bringing in big international names, which creates a certain kind of trust in students; there's somebody who knows what she or he is talking about. You can see it outside, they get money for what they're doing, and it is a very tempting role model. If it all works well it can lead to something very powerful for that particular student, to really see this professionalism in somebody else. We have probably all heard the typical anecdotes, about some German art professors only being with students for just a brief visit in an airport lounge. However, it's strange to still see, for instance, that a student of a big name professor has an easier access to the gallery world than somebody who has been a student of a lesser known name. That could be very dangerous; that would be education by selection. Because I have been selected by artist 'x' into her/his class, gallerist 'y' might say, it must be interesting what I make. This can turn into a strange reproduction mechanism. It is not reproducing style, technique, or form; it's reproducing attitudes. I'm worried about that. I would prefer the idea of students being exposed to many more influences, which I think we try to provide at least here in the Glasgow School of

Art, and in many other UK art schools as well. It's not only your professor you're dealing with; you have different influences all the time. It gives students a wider sense of professionalism, which is different than selection. I also think that there are far more students in art schools in the UK than in Germany. I spoke to a collector the other day and he complained that there is so much rubbish coming out of art schools today, and that there might be far too many art students. I tried to explain, if you leave behind the assumption that art schools should only produce successful artists, you might find that learning through art might be of relevance for many, and a very valuable function of art schools as well.

I was reading Stephan Dillemuth's *The Academy and the Corporate Public*. How much do you think these things can be separated – the world of the academy and the world of the market place?

Not at all, they should not be separated. They are part of the bigger picture, the world of culture, or art. I had a discussion with somebody a couple of weeks ago about opera productions. Opera productions can now only be done as co-productions, you can no longer, as one opera house, produce big productions. The effect is that you see the same set up in Tokyo, New York or Paris. It's very similar in the art market, with all the festivals and Biennales; you travel around, but you actually see mostly the same artists in Istanbul, in Venice, or in Los Angeles. But there is something beyond that: a rich culture of artists with a strong sense of self-organisation. There is the curatorial level with exhibitions curated around and towards the big market scene, but there is also – and Glasgow is quite typical of this – another level at which artists organise themselves, and sometimes that is much more influential. Normally it will become part of the market at some point. It will always be absorbed. But up to that point it is powerful in refreshing culture.

I would say it is part of the market.

The market needs this, it's not making the money, but it is part of the full economic model, which drives everything. I was sitting with our MFA students in Berlin a while ago. They were having a show there, and we were talking about all these new galleries in Berlin, hundreds of them just popping up, and one of the students asked, 'are they sustainable?' And I thought, 'no', they might not be sustainable. But the big galleries need the small galleries, because it's the activities in the smaller galleries that actually attract the collectors to come to Berlin in the first place, although they would go to the big gallery to buy a piece of work. There is a symbiosis there. As students, when we had just finished the academy in Düsseldorf, we started a studio house, Hildebrandtstrasse, that was the address – and produced exhibitions there. We started in early 1980. We thought we'd just open our doors for a day or two, just for a weekend. In the beginning we didn't even advertise anything, but to our surprise it was packed full of people. We didn't know where they came from, including Konrad Fischer with Richard Serra, because he had Serra visiting. Serra hated what he saw there, but that's another thing. But then I understood that there is a link; they need each other, we need each other. And that's something we probably have to be even clearer about with students; it's not just the drive into the direct market, the address-book pedagogy: 'can I have the phone number of your gallerist, or would you make an appointment for me?' That might help sometimes – but you have to make sure that there are other activities running parallel to it.

I'm interested in how you talk about it being difficult to judge an artist's practice on the basis of a single piece of work, and that you must look at it in terms of an overview. I was wondering if persistence is at the core of this – that one persists with one's practice – if so, how do you teach persistence?

How do you teach persistence? In two weeks' time we're going to have a guest here for one of our talks. Nan Hoover, she is in her late 70s now. She's an artist who has been teaching in parallel to Nam June Paik in Düsseldorf, and I'm actually very proud to know her. Even after a period of 50 years of practice she still has the persistence *to continue working*. Many people know her and many people value her work highly, but she's not necessarily making big money out of it. I think she continues working, because it is the only way of life that she wants to have. Then creativity is not a trick anymore that you switch on or off to make a product; then creativity becomes an attitude, becomes a way of life.

Can I turn to a question of architecture and ask you what are the physical conditions that either encourage, or limit creative learning?

Physical conditions … I used to use the term 'complete flexibility', now I use the term 'complete adaptability'. That means that any kind of space could be used for any kind of purpose. What is a video studio today might be a studio for environmentally friendly painting tomorrow. If you can plan that way, you can change the use of space all the time, constantly. Many art schools around the world, including Glasgow, are thinking about new buildings. Resources are never enough to do what you want to do but you can be much more efficient with new buildings. One argument that you get back all the time is that the best thing for artists is to move into abandoned industrial buildings and just make new use of them. I'm actually not sure about this anymore. I think it's probably a romanticism from the 1970s. We all did it as artists, used these industrial spaces. Now it actually limits exactly this kind of flexibility and adaptability. If we could find the right architects, to think with art school people how you can build something that remains flexible for at least the next 50 or 60 years … When we started thinking about a new building in Bergen, I thought 'we don't need a new building, we just need building material and an open site, and students build their own studios on it. At the end of the year the rector would come with a bulldozer and tear it all down, to make space for the next generation of students.' But you also have to provide some infrastructure. And I also think increasingly – and other art schools might think differently about this – you need a certain amount of openness for the public. The art school should not be a hidden place. We need the retreat where students can be left alone for a while, but, at the same time, we need to be as open as possible. When I arrived here and I saw the first guided tour coming through, I thought, 'my God we have to stop that!' And now I really love it. The tourists come in and don't disturb anyone, they don't go into studios – that's very, very clear – but they just have this kind of curiosity for the Mackintosh building and some for what is happening in it. They are all friendly people. Why should I lock them out? If one thinks about art schools, one probably should also curate a public.

You seem to suggest the art school should have a particular attitude/politics, or place in the public domain. What should that be?

All art schools should be rooted locally. That doesn't make them provincial places. There is a lot of influence coming in all the time. If I compare Bergen to Glasgow again: in Bergen we struggled to convince, or persuade students to remain in the city, to build up something like an art scene, because Oslo appeared to be so much more attractive. It's starting now, but it really was a long, long, long struggle. Glasgow is the opposite; many of the students, also international students, who came specifically through the Masters programme, remain for a few years in Glasgow, and they actually do something to the city. The city is not giving money out for that, but it is embracing it, which makes a cultural scene within the city. All these artists in the city can sometimes be quite disturbing, but they are also necessary to break down the fatty deposits of continuous creative over-production, when the term creativity gets misused and everything has to be creative. At some point you have to get down to the ground again. I'm not necessarily giving an argument here for the Richard Florida thinking, that creativity is defining a new class and it's attracting people. There is something in it, of course, but I think you can also be lulled into something there, which is not real anymore – when creativity is regarded just as a trick. Let's think about the political function again, or at least a critical function. One thing I thought about recently – and I don't know when we will start yet – is to introduce a programme element that is literally about economy. To bring in people who can talk about how economy works, and listen to them, and the different kinds of schools and views on that. This could be the background to start thinking whether there are alternative economic models that will not only support art, but will support culture, and life in a city like this. I do believe that there are roles for artists in society that, at the moment, we don't know of, that we still have to develop, and I have no idea what they might be. Our students will develop them. I don't want to sound too vague and Beuys-like. Of course, there's a little bit of that in it. I would wish everybody to have success, also commercial success, but, at the same time, we also need to be realistic about it and start thinking about economically viable alternatives.

What was the outcome of the research initiative in Bergen?

You mean the research on building art schools? It never actually even started. We had quite a few conversations with a lot of people, but we did not find time or resources for deeper research. The situation in Bergen is that the site is there, and the building has already been designed by a very good group of architects. Then the financial plug was pulled. So now they're at square one again, having to raise money to make sure that the building can happen. How much of the discussion that we had before will, in the end, feed into the building, I don't know. You have to be realistic about what is do-able, and then, as Kasper König always says, live with your own frustration.

How much do you immerse yourself in the Bergen initiative and eventually risk losing any kind of creative input?

No, no, no, I don't … Yes it's utterly frustrating, but I am here now. There's always a
 lot of frustration in any kind of organisational structure. And in political realities, and
in funding realities … But, again, it's persistence. Even if I'm frustrated, it doesn't stop
my engagement and it's still worth it. There is an equivalence to this process in any kind
of artist's studio; I just recently visited the enormous studio of a sculptor full of little
maquettes, and models, and I realised how much is destroyed, how much isn't good
enough. You try something, it doesn't work out, and you have to throw it away. But it's the
basis for doing something that works in the end. So you learn this kind of frustration right
from the beginning. The idea of the studio, and specifically the studio in an art school is
important: all the mistakes you make, you actually make in public. It's a limited public –
it's your fellow students – but there's a group of people who see your mistakes that you
would usually hide. You would normally only present the final result. In the studio you learn
that it is more important that everybody can see where you're going wrong. That creates a
strength to live with the frustration. In Bergen, in Norway, when I started there, I discussed
with a friend that trying to manage an art school could be seen as a sculptural process. It
has the same elements in it; how you try to shape it. Maybe it is not such a big step from
being an artist to being a teacher, to being an art school manager, because you're still
involved in the process of shaping. OK, sometimes this can also be self-deception as how
much influence do you really have over it, even if you're managing it, or leading it? Because
there's so many other factors that are determining it.

**At a certain level administration becomes a form of management where you have some
influence over what actually happens on the ground. Do you understand teaching to
include these kinds of management skills?**

Absolutely. It doesn't manage itself. That's just an illusion. You need a certain element of
organisation, and some people are better at that than others. Some people enjoy providing
the frame for others to do their teaching, to get the time for their teaching. Teaching is
the individual contact with a student, or contact with a group of students, when you give
a lecture, or a seminar, or a tutorial. But teaching is also being behind the whole kind of
thing, providing the frame. Yes, I agree with that.

Do you have the Research Assessment Exercise here?

Yes, sure.

Do you think this is a useful exercise?

We had a very intense process and tried to be as inclusive as possible. At some point I found myself on a flight back to Germany to meet some friends and, all of a sudden, I heard myself saying, for the first time, 'I really understand why German colleagues in art schools don't want to be involved in that *at all*.' The reconciliation between research and practice still needs some work. There should not be a value distinction, that research is better than practice. The exercise itself could make that gap bigger, rather than bridging it and bringing it together again. For an artist, there would not be any research without practice; it wouldn't really make sense, probably for many others either. One of the experiences I have of the UK system that really surprised me is that it is far more an audited, controlling system than I had experienced in art schools elsewhere. I always thought the German Higher Education system would be world leader in bureaucracy, but that might have been challenged now. Of course a level of quality assurance is important. In the end it is about spending public money. In Scotland, quality assurance is based upon enhancement, not just about judging what is good and what is bad. But trying to find out where things could go wrong, and if you know where things could go wrong, what will you do about it? When a reviewing team came to visit us in 2003, it had been made very clear that none of them would be a subject specialist, so it could be somebody from agriculture, somebody from chemistry, somebody from engineering. First, I thought, 'this is mad'! In the end, I realised it was the best thing that could happen to us. The reviewers came with great curiosity: how actually are *you* dealing with the issues in Higher Education? It's good to listen to the reflections of others and there I think German art schools make a mistake in isolating themselves too much, in isolating art education in itself. Glasgow, although validated by Glasgow University, is a small specialist institution, an independent art school, not part of Glasgow University. But we are part of the higher education system. Back in Bergen, at some point a new law for higher education was developed. My director colleague, the head of administration, used his political weight to make sure that it's a law for universities *and* art schools, as a special category. It was a very important step to claim open, public responsibility for art schools as a special entity of their own. Of course it came with responsibilities to be fully accepted as part of the good society. But it also fostered the curiosity of the other universities: 'hold on, there are art schools as well in our club. How are *they* dealing with things?'

So what is the art school's relationship to the university?

The university is validating our degrees. We send an annual report to the university, and they have an annual meeting with us to make sure we're not deviating too far from any kind of educational rules. They don't have any influence on the content; we have our director, we have our own board of governors, we have our own management. At the moment, the relationship works very well. It can also be different. I remember other art schools being absorbed into universities. The first moment was kind of a golden marriage, the university saying, 'oh, we'll give you a new gallery, we'll give you new material.' But that can wear off when the president, or chancellor, or vice chancellor changes interest. Then you're just at the mercy of another bigger managerial structure. It also has disadvantages to be small, because we have to do all of the same things that a university has to do, but with much fewer people. So there's quite a workload on the managerial group in Glasgow School of Art.

We've spoken a little about the relationship between teaching and management and this being, let's say, an extension of a kind of teaching practice. What about the relationship between your practice and teaching?

It's a little difficult to answer, because there is fairly little teaching for me at the moment. Just a little anecdote ... at some point in Bergen, a student came to me and wanted a tutorial, and I said, 'of course I can do that.' I spoke to her about the work, and what she had tried to do, and the typical stuff you do in a tutorial, and we had an intense conversation. All of a sudden, she said, 'you know what I actually really wanted to ask you was, do you know about somebody else that's done that already?' I couldn't stop laughing! I had become the guarantor of innovation because I might have seen a bit more than the student. The attitude to teaching, the attitude to management and the attitude to my own work is based on the same attitude to creativity; creativity as a guiding principle. The constant shift between overview and detail, which surfaces a lot in my own work, is also typical in a managerial context and in a teaching context. What have you done there in this corner of that piece, or in this part of your concept?

And how does that sit in a larger context? How does it sit in contemporary history? How does it relate to society? What has been happening in the world at the moment? That constant shifting in focus is the same.

Is there only one way you can teach? Is the way you teach somehow determined by your practice if you're an artist?

I don't think there's only one way to teach. Even if you just take your own individual experience; teaching only works well if you adjust constantly to the individual intentions of a student. This automatically asks for different ways of teaching. Does that need practice? It needs experience, as a practitioner in the arts or from the field surrounding it. We have quite a few curators and theory people in many art schools now, and they're also doing an excellent job as teachers.

But is there only one way you can teach as an artist, which is predicated on the kind of practice you have? It's absolutely what everything is built on and refers back to. Your practice lays out a certain kind of framework and limitations for you as an artist and or teacher.

I think you're right, if you describe this as a position. You can only teach what is your own experience. But an artist's experience normally would go far beyond the materials and methods one is using. If you focus on painting red paintings, that does not mean you can only teach how to paint red paintings. That's ridiculous. You can talk to, or work with painting students, sculpture, photography, film students, whatever they are. Behind that is the same approach in how it relates to art, life, the world, whatever form it takes. However, I think it's crucial to be exposed to different kinds of teachers and forms of teaching. Students should have the chance to see different ways of dealing with things, and then make up their own mind ... for Christ's sake, that's the whole point! If we just briefly touch on one aspect of the Bologna Declaration follow-up thinking – to divide studies up into two, or probably three cycles – with a possible PhD on top. German art schools are completely opposed, saying you cannot divide it. I actually feel they're wrong in this decision; a student can, maybe should, go somewhere else after a BA to continue, because it's so important to add a different kind of experience. You pack your cultural baggage in a different way. That means that you can decide to do a BA in Cologne and an MA in Reykjavik, or Istanbul, or even in-between. It's more than exchange. Spending time somewhere else helps to build up a new and individual view. I finished at the academy in Düsseldorf after I'd been there for six years; quite a long time; at that time there was no end to it – *you* said when you wanted to leave. Then I went for another year to London, to the Royal College. It was a very important year for me, because it was taking what I had learned and having it tested and challenged somewhere else, and it was fantastic. I regret that I didn't take the second year and really make a Masters out of it, to really deepen that experience further, but gone is gone so ...

What you say turns on an idea that difference is always good, exposure to something new is always good. You might also say that six years in the German system is about consolidating something?

The consolidating happens anyway; do you consolidate just with one influence? Or do you consolidate as *you* consolidate, as the student yourself? And I think this is the point where art teachers have to let go. I have difficulty with the term 'my students'. I don't own any students and it's them who study, it's not about me who teaches them. I was quite lucky as a student, at the time Klaus Rinke had just started. The most important thing he did was create a social atmosphere for a group of people to learn from each other. He came in and had his rants on and off and shouted about something that he'd experienced outside. It was very important that he was there and facilitated our learning, but it was even more important that we were enabled through him to have our own conflicts, and our own discussions, and our own way of thinking. There were other groups, there was Richter's group and there was the Bechers' group, and there was a very intense dialogue between these three classes. In that sense it was already a different kind of experience than the normal academy student would have at the time. Take Beuys for example; his teaching was always centred around Beuys. At some point he tried to accept 350 students into just his group, which was a little bit irresponsible and it didn't work out. So they had to take matters into their own hands. Consolidating is your job as a student and not my job as a professor.

Was Fritz Schwegler ...

Fritz Schwegler was actually teaching me in my first year.

What was that like?

I was 17 and a half when I started. For Germany this was quite young. I always enjoyed talking to Fritz Schwegler and he was a very friendly and supportive person. We went out with him and helped make some of those film productions he did using his sculptures. The first time I heard him sing on stage I was so embarrassed! I thought, 'my God, what is this man doing?' Later on I learned to love it as something very special. At that time, he was responsible for the first year; that was the first time ever that the academy in Düsseldorf had a first year. It was just after Beuys, something they called Orientierungsbereich; you didn't have your professor, you were in a group of people, a bit like a foundation year. Fritz Schwegler, however, really developed being Fritz Schwegler the professor, when he had his own class. I don't think he enjoyed being in the Orientierungsbereich. He really wanted to get out of it and have his own group, and then, of course, he had his influence on people.

What I think is interesting about Schwegler is that he was teaching amongst some very renowned artists, like Richter and so on, but according to Martin Honert, his student, he really didn't know much about Schwegler's work.

Oh?

Until his last year …

Oh, really?

He said he was much more interested in him as a professor, as a teacher. He felt he had a profound influence on him …

I could imagine that. I think Fritz started at the academy in Düsseldorf when I started as a student in the Orientierungsbereich. He talked a lot about what he was doing. We were involved in his work, which was also the case with Klaus Rinke, but on a different kind of level. Rinke gave us jobs. We had to earn money, so when he went to install a piece at the Documenta or in a gallery we travelled to do the work with him. It was a fantastic experience to see how this kind of context worked, how he dealt with a gallerist, or a curator. Not that it would then create an opening for us into that gallery, nothing like that happened, because we were the workers, paid for our labour. We were artists working there. It was a very interesting and important experience for that time. Now I see that sometimes being exploited: professors gathering a group of cheap assistants around them.

Do you think this is something that we don't do as much here? Karin Sander for example will take her students to Italy for two weeks and they'll work, eat and drink together. I was wondering if this is something we're lacking in the UK?

It's getting more and more difficult to do that in our system, isn't it? How to fund it? And then there is the endless loop of health and safety regulations and risk management before you take a group of students to Italy. That nearly kills it already. However, I think it can also be done locally. When it comes to the individual professional experience, what we started to do here in Glasgow, is to think about placements for art students. Placements could be with a gallery, but also with an individual artist. I'm not totally sure it worked out, but when Simon Starling was doing his project for Cove Park we managed to have two students work with him and that, I think, was a good experience for them. On the other hand, if we talk about our Masters programme again – the MFA, which is fairly small, with about 55 to 58 students over two years – one thing that attracts students is that it still has a sense of intimacy, that they create their own community. Of course, with the help of their tutors, but its their initiative, and that's taken onwards and outwards, and it's creating networks that hopefully will be sustained. We did that in Hildebrandtstrasse, the studio house in Düsseldorf that I mentioned. Somehow we are back again at this bordered culture that we experience quite strongly here; people became too frightened of what they can do, and what they cannot do. We recently talked to artists, architects and designers outside the school to think about how the Glasgow School of Art should develop. They all came back with 'be more anarchic.'

Did they tell you what they meant by that?

Of course not! But I often wonder, 'could we be more daring?' But what would that mean, being more daring?

Klaus Jung teaches at the Glasgow School of Art.

Simon Lewandowski — during a delivery
of wood to his studio — London.

Can you say why you teach?

It's become more important because I have become more interested in it while doing it. It's very important for my mental health, because it gives me contact with a lot of other people, it maintains a work contact, and it maintains contact with a constant stream of young, mostly intelligent people and a range of ideas. So, in contrast to sitting in a place like this, or in my office where I edit, it's quite important. I teach what I do, in the sense that whatever I'm enthusiastic about, or what I'm interested in, comes into the teaching. I use that as an input in a lot of subtle ways. I'd redesigned my website historicising the practice, as well as advertising and documenting it, and a couple of people said to me, 'oh, it's quite a pedagogical site.' The website is about things I'm very interested in; about things and making things, but also about talking about these things, and sparking off some kind of discussion about the things I make.

When I looked at your work I was thinking that you must have to reconcile this somehow with the business of teaching in an art school. I say this because there seems to be a question around the connectedness or disconnectedness of your work from the world, which might conflict with the curricular, disciplinary and bureaucratic demands of a college …

To some extent I see the way I teach as being subversive, or counter to the curriculum and to the vagaries of the art world. I'm absolutely happy that I tell students things that, in a sense, run counter to a lot of orthodoxies in current education and practice.

What would you think as running counter to these dominant practices and discourses?

[We're interrupted by a delivery of wood for a case for shipping a piece of Simon's work to Italy in two weeks' time.]

OK, sorry.

I negotiate the art school with a certain helping of cynicism, or scepticism. My work is, in fact my stance on a lot of things, is sceptical, I wouldn't say cynical. I'm sceptical of a lot of things to do with the way people think about art, with critical theory, with a lot of attitudes to art, and I always have been. My work came out of quite a community-based practice a long time ago, and out of performance theatre and punk and stuff. And to some extent that continues. So I always encourage students to question any verities that might fit a bit badly with the kind of customer-based models of university education that are prevalent. But then that's because I think they're wrong and I'm right, so why should I stop doing it because it doesn't fit? In the end the consumers vote with their feet and the students seem to respond well to what I do, and I think that I've consistently helped, or been part of a team that have produced very high quality student work.

So what do you think you offer that would run counter to the more dominant model, if indeed there is a dominant model?

In some ways that's really hard to define, really hard to verbalise. Often what I'm saying to students, what I'm stressing are aspects of practice, and particularly what you might call professional practice. How you survive and how things work in the world – that can often sound quite old-fashioned and commercially-based and object-based – has to do with the fact that results matter, that process in some ways isn't interesting, that theoretical grounding of things doesn't really matter. All theory is ... ultimately, you're not dealing with anything other than fiction; it is just telling stories about your work and one story is as good as another, it's only as good as it is interesting. No critical theory or art history is true, it's only interesting, or boring, and there are certain things about giving people value for money and producing something that people want, or that they relate to in certain ways. I like to demystify things in some ways, and I'm quite interested in ways of speaking about work that are unburdened by jargon. I really try very hard to render things in ways that are clear. But I also like things to be re-mystified, because it is just entertainment, it is just pleasure, it is just things. There is no underlying truth or reality that you're getting at objectively in the sense of science, or something. Stories can be entertaining, and you don't have to understand them to be entertained. These strands are quite important for me. I enjoy materials and processes a lot and I enjoy research and looking at new things and areas of knowledge. In some ways there are a lot of things I don't like about the Leeds course, which has this reputation as being 50 per cent theory, a lot of which is art history and cultural studies. While I like the idea that students study a lot of things, and it does make them read a lot and they're very erudite in some ways, in other ways they're not. If they're going to do 50 per cent non-studio work, they should do anything else except art. I always say to them, 'for God's sake, don't do another art history elective.' Go and do Russian, or astrophysics, or something. In that sense I'd like to see the course change a lot, and I do come into conflict with other people about that. But not in an unpleasant way; where I am there's a very good dynamic.

I'm curious about something – it's kind of an aside. The Steve Bell exhibition in the foyer – were you given the job of curating it, or is there more to it than that?

There's a bit more to it than that, it's a thing called Leeds Fine Art Projects. A guy called Pete Morton, who's actually the senior technician involved with exhibitions, does all the stuff to do with that and a lot of other things. He's from a fine art and photography background. He'd been trying to do some shows in the building, which is crap for showing because it's really just foyer space, and I said, 'well, what about working up a thing that looked at other parts of the building and outside?' So we dreamed up this thing called Leeds Fine Art Projects, which was a kind of gallery-less curating initiative with me, Pete, Chris Taylor and Runa Islam. So we had this idea of art that's not in a gallery. In the case of Steve Bell – which was an idea Peter had, because Steve's an ex-student of Leeds – we thought, 'what about stuff that shouldn't be in a gallery?' So we have cartoons in a gallery and we have sculptures on the outside wall. It's nothing earth-shatteringly original. It was also because we wanted to work with Steve. He's done a whole lot of historical pastiches, a whole series of art historical pastiches of great paintings. One of the essential things was to use all those relating back to the art historical training he'd had. The other one was this choice of 'if' cartoons. He gave me the whole archive on disc, which was like the dark evil twin of *March of the Penguins*. It was the entire Steve Bell wildlife thing, which is the entire story of the penguins and a lot of other animals. It didn't quite work out how I wanted because I'd been on sabbatical; I'd been down here. [In London.] Had I been up there working, I think I'd have done quite a few things different, but it was a nice show and it was good fun. We're working on another one with a guy called Ben Woodeson, who's a friend of mine. He's an artist, but he's not teaching. In fact, he's working at the ICA. We're doing a sound piece in the school itself. It's a surveillance piece which includes microphones; we're going to have these planted in some of the public spaces and then this feeds into one low-fi channel, which you'll listen to on headphones, and all of it'll be web-cast live. We're having legal problems with that, but we're hoping to just lie our way through it. There's also a few other things coming up.

The other thing I do at Leeds is organise the visiting lecturer programme. I've been doing that since I started. I was doing that at Nottingham for a couple of years as well, and that partly involves just booking people to come up and give a talk in slots once a week during teaching weeks. But I've kind of expanded it to look at other ways in which you can get people in and get artists in the school, and it's been quite good.

What other ways have you explored in terms of bringing artists in?

Those have been the main ones. We've worked quite a lot with local groups, because Leeds is having a bit of a renaissance of a certain kind of work. There's a certain, quite socially-based and very diffuse model of working with things, like the Situation Leeds Project Festival every year, and Vitrine, and Artists' House, East Street Arts. We've worked with the Festivals that they've done, having artists come in and our students doing stuff outside a lot. I've gradually pushed to allow for the student degree shows to take place off-site, as we used to do at Nottingham. Part of the students' job is to find a place to show in and to mount a show in a space for real, rather than just white-washing the studios and doing it in there. But this year they're all showing in an old office block somewhere down by the station. That's kind of getting the work out, and because I run the fourth year that's one of my jobs, as well as the visiting artists. Whenever we get artists coming up for things, I try and get them in to do something in some way with students. Sometimes it's just to do a talk, but sometimes I try and match them up with small groups of students, or the right people. Or if there's a crit, or something going on for a particular project, I can time it for someone. Maybe I'll show the students their work at the beginning of the project block, and when that person's around at the end, they can give a talk in the afternoon and they'll come a bit earlier and we'll pay them a bit more just to sit in on the review, that sort of stuff really.

When you talked earlier about challenging or countering orthodoxies in current practice, or in art education, do you think one of these orthodoxies is a current and creeping kind of academicism in art education?

Yes, I do. I don't think it's actually even the nature of what those orthodoxies are, it's the very fact that they just happen, because I think it's to do with a lot of factors. Other countries have different situations, but I think the relationship between the art market, how art is funded generally in all its multiple ways, and the numbers of students and the nature of education now, all those factors do encourage a formulisation. The fact that certain people end up in art schools as teachers; people who, unlike me, were possibly quite good at art school and liked it, which makes them want to go back to it? I hated it and I was crap and they threw me out, which is a real weird thing for me. I was thrown out of my degree course. I went back and I did an MA quite late in life – about 10 years ago – and actually I didn't like it that much in a way. I don't think I responded very well to it, looking back at it, which was a bit of a waste. It was the digital arts one at Middlesex, and a couple of the best people who taught there had left by the time I arrived.

So why put yourself through all that?

I'm quite interested in students. Obviously there are the ones who are just really good and do the right things and follow ideas through and do their research and all that stuff. I try and distract them and get them to do different things and throw them off the scent. And then there are other ones who are often dismissed. I'm probably quite sympathetic to them in some ways, though I'm actually harder on them in other ways. There's a lad here at the moment who nearly got thrown out last year and he's awful; he's lazy, he's a total waste of space, but he's got some little ideas in there he could make something of. In many ways people say, 'he's useless, he's not going to do much'. And I say, 'well, he might if you give him a lot of encouragement'. And they say, 'well, yes, but he doesn't know what he's doing, he doesn't understand what he's doing'. And I say, 'well it doesn't matter whether he understands it, or not; I think the first thing that matters is that he does it.' That's one of the absolute creative constipations of students in art schools now; this feeling that they have to justify doing something. Or, 'I've got this idea but I think it's a really bad idea, so I haven't really got any ideas', or that they have to sort of understand what they're doing before they do it. In some ways, I probably dumb down a lot, when I say, 'well, it doesn't matter, just do it anyway and figure out what it means later, or let someone else figure out what it means, because what you say about it will not be any truer, or falser than what anybody else says.'

What is it that creates the kind of environment where there is, as you say, a need to justify the work in advance of making it?

You could go right back to post-Coldstream, you go back to the 1960s and say, 'ah, it was actually the shift of the art colleges from the diploma into a degree, and the requirement to make it into a degree.' For all the frustrations I find with the over-intellectualised, over-read children I teach at Leeds, in some ways at least it's more honest; at least they can say their degree is equivalent to someone who's got say, for example, a philosophy degree, like my daughter who did philosophy at Leeds. She wrote hundreds of thousands of words and read an immense amount of stuff and had to deal with very, very difficult concepts and sweated her arse off to get a high 2:1. At least our best students do come close to that in terms of what they've had to do, and that's great. But I could say, 'well, just go and do fucking philosophy and do an MA in art'. But I don't like teaching on MAs curiously enough, because I find the people who come on those already think they're artists and are already poisoned. Whereas at least on a degree you get people who haven't been filtered out yet.

What's happened to them by the time they get to the MA? In other words, how are they poisoned?

They've learned to do what works within an academic environment, I could jokingly say 'they're swots'. A lot of art is made by swots, people who do massive amounts of research and everything is really right. I think the Arts and Humanities Research Council and research funding, and the Research Assessment Exercise are encouraging practice-based PhDs because of grade inflation. You now need a PhD, instead of an MA. PhDs encourage the art of a project, there's a lot of project-based thinking. You have to have a project and it has to be quite big, and it has to be ongoing, and everything seems to have to do with the process of that project. It's quite hard for someone to make something because it actually doesn't fit in with this big pattern of everything else, or it does because they made it. If you look at artists who don't really have a great connection with academia, they often work like that, because they have different pressures – galleries pressure you to produce objects that are similar, because they want to be able to sell the same thing and people want to buy those objects.

As an active member of research staff you have the RAE, which may be another way of demanding a certain coherence and consistency to you practice?

That's hideous and poisonous – oh God! As an active member of research staff, it's really nice they give me money to make work; it adds to my meagre salary. I'm very happy about that. But I find myself thinking up projects that fit in with the RAE kind of thinking, rather than being the right thing to do, because it will benefit me. Unfortunately, I don't have a gallery. If I had some gallery owner to say, 'hey, do a few more of those and we can sell them', in some ways I'd rather do that. But I've never moved in that world since I stopped making prints and pictures. At least it's a bit clearer: 'we want those, we sell them, people like them'. Fine, OK. And at other times I think, 'well, God, why should I complain?' People are giving me money. All I need to do is … but it makes you cynical, it makes you lie about your practice. And instead of telling the stories that I think are amusing, I'm telling stories that I think will please someone else – not the ones that please me. It does make me think harder about the work I do, which is fine, but I think that's a very insidious influence. I don't like practice-based PhDs. I supervise a couple of them at the moment, because I got suckered into it a couple of years ago. It seemed like a good idea because it was a while ago when I joined the staff at Leeds. But I wish there were other models for how artists come into the school, which is what we were talking about. At the moment what they do is they come in, they give up being artists and become academics. So how can they do the opposite? How can they come out as artists? A few years ago some French theorist was writing about the new medievalism, that in the twenty-first century we'd return to the model of the medieval in which corporations and governments would become like feudal Lords. And rather than there being fealty to the state, you are protected by being part of an organisation. To some extent, to be part of the career structure at a university gives you some protection; it gives you an income, it gives you a framework, which is quite important when you've lived like me, leading a professional life of total insecurity.

When you spoke earlier about connecting the students up with what's outside the university – is this something you feel is incumbent on art schools to deal with today; that sort of connection with the wider world in one form or another?

It's incumbent on human beings. There's a bit of 'do as I say, not as I do', a kind of guilt thing, in the sense that my work, in some ways, is quite hermetic. It's not particularly socially engaged – one or two things here or there have made reference. What I do has other political dimensions, in the sense that I try and make it accessible and site it differently. But there is a social commitment, or a sense that if I'm not doing that, then certainly someone should be. And maybe 20 years ago I was involved with that and I did my time. The young middle classes of this country are often vapid consumerists and if you can at least suggest that they should maybe think slightly outside that and do things that somehow question what's around them and engage with the rest of the world in some way, then that's probably a good thing. But there's also the aspect that it's a good education for them, because it's good for them to go out and get involved with other people. It's good for your sanity to be rooted and engaged socially and to meet lots of people who are not just people like you, not just middle-class intellectual art students, or their tutors, or your pals who are doing French and went to public school as well. I try and point my students that way, and say, 'well, even though I might not have quite lived up to some of my own ideals of the past 30 years, or whatever, that doesn't mean I don't think that they're important.' The other side of the Steve Bell show was that we wanted a Trojan Horse thing. It was all very amusing and had these art historical references, and *March of the Penguins* jokes, but actually there was a lot of very hard-hitting and very important social commentary in there. He's a man of the hard left, and we wanted people to come into the university art gallery and students – who probably are Thatcher's children's-children by now – to come in and see what I described in the catalogue as 'his respectful and moving tribute to Lady Thatcher'. Because he also included a film of his that's not been seen on television, a thing he did with Bob Godfrey, *The Thatcher Years*. It was this sort of Thatcher biopic cartoon. Steve said he did it with Bob Godfrey because he was the only person he'd ever met who hated Thatcher more than he did. They couldn't get it screened, Channel 4 didn't show it, but it's great, it's really funny.

What do you consider to be good teaching?

I was trying to explain to Vanalyne [Green] earlier this year, about how I did the final year; she was saying she was trying to get someone to sub for me while I was on study leave, and I said, 'well, it's like swimming, it's like taking your kids to swimming lessons, and you hold them up and say, that's right, I've got you, I've got you, just kick.' And they say, 'you've got me?' 'Yes, I've got you'. And gradually with some time, you move your arms and you say, 'yes, I've got you, it's alright, I'm still holding you', and you're not, and you walk off, and then they realise they're swimming. That's perhaps a rather flippant metaphor for it. I'm old enough and grizzled enough to not expect them to say, 'oh, you're right, wow, that's true', any more than my own daughter does. Good teaching is introducing them; in some ways, all you can do is just point them to lots of things, throw lots of things at them ... and if they catch some of them, then they've got more than they did if you hadn't thrown anything. Sometimes I'm too soft and too forgiving, although other people say 'well, sometimes some of the things you say are quite harsh, or the way you say them.' Obviously they know it's true – they need to be told when things aren't right, so you set a high standard. You've got to promote standards. But then, obviously, you've got to avoid orthodoxies and allow their work to come through.

Perhaps the particular practice demands its own particular standards?

A practice has to generate its own standards and has to define its own standards, to some extent. There are some standards I think that are important and unified; that are integrity and honesty, and what I'd call craft. Even the most sort of abject scatter-aesthetic work can have its craft. Try getting a 19-year old to understand why Raymond Pettibon's work is actually incredibly crafted and theirs possibly isn't yet. So generating standards and making them laugh, I think that's quite good. And taking them on trips. I take them on trips, I like to take them out. We did one to Cologne Art Fair last year; it was great. It was fairly hands off, it's like, 'Go and amuse yourselves, don't follow me around, figure it out yourselves'. I'd like to take them to somewhere like Tiblisi, or Tashkent, or something, or Beirut. I was trying to organise one to Beirut, but that looks like it might be a bit iffy now. Things like that are great.

Simon Lewandowski teaches at the University of Leeds.

Bjørn Melhus — an October evening in Berlin — a large open-plan studio — one other person is present in the background.

Can you tell me with whom you studied and what kind of influence they had on you as an artist or teacher?

I studied in Braunschweig, at the Braunschweig School of Art, between 1988 and 1997. The last year – my Masters' year, I studied mainly with the filmmaker Birgit Hein. When I first went to Braunschweig, there was this sign on somebody's door, in German. It said, "Macht doch was ihr wollt!" which means 'do what you want!' However you can read it in two ways; as either 'we don't care', or 'do what YOU want'. It can have both meanings.

And how did you take it?

I read it several times! The interesting thing was that I went there with things in mind that I really wanted to try out: studying art was for me a huge playground. At that time Gerhard Büttenbender was teaching in Braunschweig. He was the one that had put the sign on his door – but besides this, he had absolutely no influence on me. He had actually left by the time I arrived – so I mainly studied with Birgit Hein. She started to teach there with a strong, new, fresh energy. I maybe had no more than four or five individual critiques with her in the whole six years. But we met as a group once a week and learned to look at things and talk about work, and that was really important. From that point on, everyone was just left alone to make what they wanted to make – I made my work. It was completely different to what anyone else including my teachers were doing at that time. If you know Birgit Hein's work and you look at my work, you'd say, 'oops, it's something *completely* different!' But that was really important. It's important that you respect the work of your teacher; that you look at it, that you discuss it, but that you do something else. Birgit at that time was still making new work and we looked at it in a very critical way. I like her as a mind, as someone who has something to say, but that's not the way I wanted to work.

You looked at each other's work on a weekly basis? Is that what you were doing when you met as a group?

Yes, as a group. Everyone brought in something for the group critique once a week, something they felt was important – maybe someone brought in a work in progress or a new piece of work they'd just finished. We also had weekly screenings where we invited visiting artists to curate film and video programmes that we then watched. If you watch everything you can over six, or seven years, on a weekly basis, by the end of this you'll have seen a lot and you'll have talked a lot. This was really important for me … and it was actually a very simple thing to do. Of course, I joined other classes that were available at the art school, like art history and theory, but that's a whole other thing.

And did your experience in the technical college before coming to Braunschweig have any influence on how you worked?

Oh, yes, absolutely. Yes, that was really important.

In what way?

Good that you mentioned it. Because I was trained as a photographer at a technical college, I knew how to make film and video, and I worked on commercials in between schools. When I arrived in Braunschweig I knew how to organise my whole shoot. I didn't have to spend time learning the whole technical part. I walked in and said, 'OK, from now on I just want to do what I want to do, what I have in mind, I want to try things out. I have a studio, I have lighting equipment, I have a camera, it's all there, it's free – I can use it and I can do something'. And that was a wonderful situation.

So what did you think you were going to get by going to art school?

The one reason for going to art school, although it wasn't the only reason, was to study film as art, because at the time Braunschweig was the only school in Germany to offer this. Prior to that I was considering going to a film school.

Is there one in Ludwigsburg?

Yes, but that didn't exist at the time. There was one in Berlin, the Deutsche Film-und Fernsehakademie Berlin (DFFB) – I applied for that and got rejected. I've been working in film since I was a teenager, more experimental stuff and less to do with normal film. I made my first piece which went out to festivals in 1986. That was also how I heard about the school and how I met people studying there at the time and thought, 'OK. If there is a place, that's the place to go'.

What characterises Klasse Melhus?

What characterises Klasse Melhus? Very good! First of all it's a Klasse like all the other Klassen at the art school, in the visual arts programme. The funny thing *is*, when I started they gave me a very strange subtitle for my Klasse, which is *Virtuelle Realitäten*. You would translate it as 'Virtual Realities'.

Meaning you, or the …

Yes, isn't that wonderful! They came up with something like that because they said there was a need at the school for someone to teach moving images, or time-based art. Students come in from all directions; some study with other professors and other Klasse or Klassen, and at a certain point, if they want to work mainly with video or film, or computer-based work, video-installation and time-based work they come over to my place and my Klasse. Many of them will also do something else like photography and so on, but they do that with other professors. When they're in my group, they're working on their own projects. They come with a project. From the beginning it's very open. We have group meetings once a week and we make a lot of excursions, visits to exhibitions and museums, and I also try to bring visiting artists in. Basically, the whole programme is not just about time-based art or moving images – everything is possible. We went twice for example, to Istanbul and for the opening week of the Biennale. Not just to look at work as the students also presented their own work in Istanbul in a series of video screenings in a hotel room. The project was called ROOM 101 at the Büyük Londra Oteli – that will also be continued in the future. I think it's really important to encourage them to take the initiative – to encourage them from the very first moment to send out their own work because they're not just students for five years and then it ends, and they go out into the world. This was really important for me as a student at Braunschweig at the time; from the moment you arrive there, you make your work and if it's good, you send it out and suddenly you're getting invited to festivals, to exhibitions … The most important point is that when you're at the end of your time here, you're already a kind of recognised young artist, with your own position. These students need to find their own position in what they want to do. I don't tell them 'do this, do that'. Along the way I tell them what to look at, what to read, where to go, but they have to find themselves.

Can you teach art?

No, I don't think so. You cannot teach art in a way that says 'this is the way to make art.' It's something you have to discover. What you can do is show students a lot of work that was done before, which you talk about and discuss with them. They have to create an overview, that's really important, because otherwise they'll end up inventing the wheel 5,000 times. You can teach techniques; that's what I think is really important when it comes to this field. It's the same when you go into painting; it's important to know what it means to create an image and what it means to edit. There are some rules and it's good to know them, and it's good to ignore them at a certain point again. But to be able to ignore them, you must know them. Of course it's important to encourage people in what they're doing, and to give them self-confidence at a certain point, when you have the feeling they're not sure, that they're kind of afraid to do something. And it's important to get the work out, because then they can see it and you can discuss it, and say, 'OK, maybe that's not the way to do it'. When I say 'encouraging', I also mean encouraging them to make work, because working is so important. Making something – looking at it, and then making the next piece. Some people play around a lot and they just think, 'yes, I have this concept – maybe this is something I can do'. And then six months later they come up with a different concept and they never really make anything!

Can only artists teach art?

When you ask, can only artists teach art, then I answer you as before: you actually can't teach art!

[Laughs.]

It's important to learn with an artist and with their point of view on things. And maybe it's important to have more than one at a school and to have different influences. And not just artists, but artists are important at art schools, because they're the ones that make the art – living artists, artist's who are still alive with their work and in the market – who are getting out and exhibiting. Because that's the other point, the practical stuff; what it means to be out there. What it means to show work, to exhibit work. We need a little bit of the market … but not too much.

Does the market decide who teaches?

Yes, when it comes to painting, because all the successful painters wouldn't teach since a lot of them make so much money in the market. I did a few finding commissions in the last years, and a lot of successful painters just do not apply for teaching positions.

You did what?

Finding commissions, for other professors – how you bring in other faculty staff. And there's always the question of status; of market status, of the artist's importance. Why a school really wants to have this artist, whether it's just about name-dropping. And this artist might not have the time to be there regularly in the end, which I think is problematic. When you're given the choice of 200 different people who apply for a teaching job, of course the school always wants to have someone who has a certain international reputation. But then when you look at the work, you start thinking about what's best for the students. The most important thing is to see those applying in person, because that changes things; when they do their interviews, or make their presentations, and introduce their work and ideas about teaching. You look at someone, and maybe he or she is famous, has a much better art world reputation – is good in the market, but someone else is much more inspiring and open, and delivers something. Of course, this is the better teacher.

Was that the case with you? What do you think Kassel saw in you?

I think I just walked in and was really authentic in what I had to say. I just said it without pretending. 'This is my idea, this is what I have to offer, this is how I work and I think I can … yes'. It happened because I really wanted to teach at that point; this was after a few years of doing exhibitions, travelling around, showing in museums and art fairs and being in the market, and actually selling quite well. I got bored. Maybe that's the wrong word, but I really wanted to do something else. I thought 'maybe there is a responsibility'. Of course, later, when you're doing it, sometimes you hate yourself for this decision, and you say, 'wow, how stupid am I! What the hell was going on!' These ideas you have about changing the world, because you think, 'yes, if I go into teaching I would do this, I would do that …' You think you can invent things anew.

And can you?

At certain moments, yes, you can move things. I had this very interesting experience when we did a nine-day summer camp during Documenta 12 named OPEN SPACE. Something we did in Kassel with eight different art schools from all over the world, with students from Chicago, Singapore, Taipei, Tel Aviv, Istanbul, Edinburgh, Helsinki and Kassel, and two students from Belgrade. We created a temporary village in the park, close to the Documenta Pavilion – where 50 or 60 people could live. They didn't all stay there the whole time; some of them moved inside the building after a while, because it was raining the whole week. But some stayed out there in their little huts. We spent the whole week together. The students saw the show, we invited some artists over from Documenta, we joined some talks, we had our own meetings … many meetings. And while they weren't really supposed to do something, one day at the end of the summer camp the students were asked to deliver a kind of statement, and this was a really amazing experience. We also had a cook who cooked every day, we ate together, and we had campfires in the evening, and so much happened. There was so much energy that was created in that time, that at the end of the week it was an amazing outcome. That was an exceptional situation, of course. But after this experience I thought it would be interesting to bring in more experimental ways of teaching, having more laboratory-like situations. From this winter semester on, I'll really try to change my whole way of teaching into workshop situations: I'll spend six, seven or eight days in a row with the students, from morning till evening. And we'll look at work, we'll talk about it, we'll eat together, in the evening we'll drink together, and so on. Because if you just teach on a weekly basis, it can be like some of them are just taking a class.

It might disrupt the institution – this attempt to create an intense period of working with the students …

I've not had that experience yet, because it's something I have to try out. But I can imagine it could, of course, because … I mean we know how these institutions work.

How do they work?

[Laughs.]

They're like dinosaurs! How can you include a week like that? And how can students deal with that in their timetable? It might collide with other classes, or programmes. There's a lot of other stuff going on: that's a little problematic, but you have to try it. If you were completely independent and could do whatever you wanted, without an institution, it wouldn't be a problem at all. But with an institution it's … even with my part in the institution, with all these faculty meetings. We know that that is one of the darkest parts of teaching in an art institution: that you have to do the administration work, that there's a whole apparatus that has to function. That's another problem in Germany. All the artists who were hired as artists to come to an art school and to work with the students, suddenly they're working for the institution as administrators. It's probably like that all over the world, but that is a very problematic point.

And is it increasing here in Germany?

It's increasing, of course. Sometimes I have the feeling they just save money on administrators and you get more and more work on your desk. And you're the artists! You're abused, you're hired to teach art, or work with the students, but in the end, half of the time you do administration.

How many days do you teach in a week?

Let's say, on average, two full days a week. But then, since having started there, I've been there almost every week. I tried to teach every second week and stay a little longer but that didn't work out so well, because of administrative work, or faculty meetings, or whatever came up, which I had to attend.

What happens when you travel? You're just now planning to go to Argentina …

That's OK. We have the freedom to organise ourselves, if I compensate for the time that I'm gone. We have other faculty staff at the school who just come in once a month and stay there for a week or 10 days in a row and then leave again. They fulfil their expected teaching time but it depends on how much you can stay out of administration. Whether you say, 'OK, I keep my fingers out of this pot and I just take care of teaching'.

Can you do that?

It's very, very difficult, of course. When we sign our contract it says that we have to do the so-called *Selbstverwaltung* – 'self-administration' we call it. Because the school, or the faculty, make a lot of decisions, it's important to be independent, that there is no one else who makes the decisions. We, as professors at the art school, run the whole place. That's the good side. But the bad side is that you have to run it.

It's one thing having autonomy as an artist teaching in an art school, but if you want to teach in a particular way I assume that teaching extends to some form of administration because that's where you get to affect how things are run. What seems to be really important, particularly in Germany, is that this sense of autonomy is an implicit part of the contract, and that it's based not so much on legal terms, but on trust and privilege. And that the more administration there is, the more it seems to attack this place of privilege and trust, where artists should be artists in their own right and come when they feel they can, and then give their best because of having this autonomy and freedom. Is that how it works?

The autonomy – how often someone shows up – has always been a big issue in Germany, because as we know there are some art schools where the artists, the professors, just show up once a year, which is not right. Responsibility, self-responsibility, is a very important point. Someone who starts teaching should feel responsible for it. But there should be the autonomy and the freedom to decide how to do it. So if I would prefer to have only one day every week, but on a regular basis, because I think that's the way I want to do it – OK. In the contract we have a certain amount of hours we're required to deliver per week, but we still have the autonomy to deliver them in the way we want to. Although we are requested to be at the school, in our case four days a week, which is part of the contract of being there, and to do all the other work. But that's almost impossible. Then you can't be an artist any more. It's so important that, as a teaching artist, you are still able to continue your own work. Otherwise the whole business makes no sense.

Can you teach without having a practice? Maybe you went through art school, maybe you once had a practice but you don't have one now. Can you still teach?

Yes, of course you can teach, but I think it's really important to create new work yourself. Being inside the process – the practices and discourses in contemporary art – the renewal and continuation of your own work is important. It has something to do with the ability to … Let's put it this way: we're talking about contemporary art and if you're not contemporary … When I was studying, some teachers would sometimes say … yes it was like … remember the 1960s and 1970s, wasn't it amazing, blah, blah, blah'. And 'we did this, while these artists were doing that'. OK, but that's the past – it's much more thrilling – from the point of view of being a student – that the person you're talking to is also working at the same time as you are.

Do you think the student understands that you're still working even if they're not familiar with your work? Do you think the way you engage with a student means that they will have an implicit understanding that you're also equally engaged in something?

Yes, because you're engaged in a different way when you're engaged with your own work. Making art is always about making decisions, and if you just talk about the decisions you made in your past, that's maybe kind of boring. But if you're always on a level at which you have to make decisions for your own work every day, it changes something.

How do you deal with a student who wants to be like you because you're a successful artist?

[Laughs.]

It's a very difficult point. At the beginning I thought I'm not showing them my work at all. Just try to leave it out, but they see it anyway. You have to address that in a very open way. Of course, some of the students, while you wouldn't say that they're copying you – people see something similar in the work. But if a student comes out of my class and people say, 'oh yes, this person is so much influenced, or is copying his or her professor', this is a problem. Often they've already done this work before I even met them, and they'd continue to do it without me. It's difficult, because I cannot walk in and say, 'no, stop it! You have to do something completely different now because I did this!' But you can approach it by looking at and talking about work. I remember when I was a student, people said, 'oh yes, this is like …' Some people came up with Cindy Sherman, with Bruce Nauman … trying to find out what a student's position is, what is authentic, what is it they're going for when you work with them and both sides are really honest in looking at and discussing the work, that's how I try to help students avoid copying their teacher or professor. By finding out what they want for themselves. That's really important: what they want for themselves.

And are you in character when you teach, in the sense that you often appear as a kind of protagonist in you own work?

When I teach?

[Laughs.]

That I appear as a smurf?

Maybe another way of asking the question is whether you understand them to be separate discrete activities – your teaching and your art practice?

It's not easy to answer. There is my work, which is what you see; the whole surface of images. But behind the work there is a lot of research in looking at things, at certain images that are out there – in the media, the movies, TV shows, films – that comes before the work. Watching all that, and looking at mainstream culture, looking at trash and analysing that, is something that happens in my work before the artwork happens. It's really important to bring that into teaching, that something that triggers my work, to create a certain awareness that I had to make my work.

Does the art school also provide you with a way to be engaged with what is current and contemporary?

Yes, absolutely. That's a very nice element of teaching: you get something out of it for yourself, because you continue a dialogue. I mean the students have other generational questions: where they are right now, and what they look at. But in any kind of Klasse, or any system with professors and Klassen that we have in Germany, if it gets too specific, it gets really difficult and dangerous. Because then you create clones.

If what gets too specific?

What you're teaching. You want to be surprised. And sometimes I have these wonderful moments; it's beautiful, with documentary work, installation work, all kinds of work.

You look at things and think, 'wow, yes.' Not that you haven't seen something like that before, but that it's a very, very personal point of view on something. They found something and it's new to me, and it moves me. That's really rewarding when you get this kind of feedback. I've had really desperate moments and sometimes I'm really struggling with what I'm doing, because I went into the whole thing in a very idealised way. But then I've also had really wonderful moments, when you're really happy about the outcome.

Is it temporary?

The happiness?

The teaching ...

My teaching? You mean the position, or the contract?

Your own desire for teaching, is there a limit to it?

When I started teaching, I went into it with a six-year contract, as a temporary project. But I don't know if I'll leave. They'll probably offer to extend the contract for some more years, or even into a lifetime position, and I don't know yet.

Bjorn Melhus teaches at the Kunsthochschule Kassel.

Philip Napier — his office — The National
College of Art and Design, Dublin — mid-April.

Can I start by asking you where you studied and how that influenced you?

I left Belfast when I was 18 and couldn't wait to get out. I went to Manchester and after
a year there, I went to Falmouth in Cornwall and I had to leave there before … I thought
I might end up binding books and keeping chickens too early in my life, so I left Cornwall
and went back to Ulster to do an MA. I guess the kind of work I was making at Falmouth
was about a form of contested space, possibly within a pictorial tradition, but nevertheless
contested. So it made sense to go back to Ulster, because that was the real contested
space I was interested in and continue to be. There I was taught by Alastair MacLennan.
When I'm being cheeky about chickens and book binding, it's not that the teaching
wasn't interesting, the context just seemed a bit other. And I suppose the idea of
landscape being contested in Cornwall wasn't really happening as a context in a way
that I was interested in. So for MA purposes it seemed necessary to go back to what
I perceived to be the site of contest that still interests me.

Is there something about how you teach that has its roots in the way you were taught?

Possibly in the sense that the way I was taught, particularly in Ulster, was related to
ideas of how you might think about making work matter, or making work register.
Broadly speaking, because the market wasn't pronounced there, it really wasn't much of
a consideration. So in one sense it felt as though you were free to make what you liked,
because the market wasn't going to be an arbitrator. But also the effort to make anything
register in a context of war really seemed to be, at least in some sense, part of what the
job was. I also think that – and maybe we'll return to this – because of a failure of politics,
the use, or deployment of ideas was really fugitive. There's a sense of artists talking to
themselves a lot, because nobody really seemed to have a use for any of these other ideas
that might be emerging. And maybe at the time the effort of dialogue was just getting
underway; social dialogue, political dialogue, as opposed to art dialogue. Not that I think
that things should be seen in isolation, but in many ways they were in isolation. This kind
of effort, through the process of teaching, to be attempting to figure out how to make
work register is a persistent legacy, and something I'm still interested in.

**There's something quite particular in the way you talk about 'work registering',
which seems to carry a strong ethos. In your staff profile you introduce yourself**

not as an artist, but as a consultant lecturer/ manager. The language you use is around a negotiated, mediated practice or space, and I was just wondering how that particularity is found in your teaching?

All art is a conversation with itself, and with its antecedents, so to speak. But I suppose it seemed to me that possibly without sounding grand or rhetorical, there was another role or job that art could do, or needed to do.

Which would be?

Which would be that it might provide a way of acting, participating, or reflecting, that might find a way forward, if I say out of a warrior tradition, then that's much too grand, but, in a sense, I think that Northern society produced this kind of context where ideas of future were really fugitive. What I was interested in was that there was a form of vacuum, and I was interested in how a broad culture could have a role that wasn't only reactive. One might have also seen that earlier in the development of Irish independence; there was a form of vacuum that was filled by the Gaelic revival, and the legacies of that are still being worked out in contemporary wealthy Ireland ...

What place in the world should the art school have? And if we talk about this art school in particular, what kind of place ideally would you want it to have? Because you're talking about a kind of contested space, and maybe some notion of the art school and its relationship to a public space.

I am really talking about that. In rich contemporary Ireland, public space is being privatised in particular ways that are problematic, as part of a global condition but also as part of a wealthy society. But I also think that the last 15 years have been absolutely transforming Ireland, and I am interested in art and culture having a role in commenting, activating, articulating aspects of what could be, or what we could be within that. It seems to me that here might be a kind of expanded or extended role for art and its use, or deployment. I suppose I'm really speaking in broad brush marks here, but I guess Ireland's solution has been to say, 'we are Irish and we are art; we are differentiated from other people'. We're an island, we do cultural things, and we have this inheritance. We don't do art, we are it. And that doesn't quite work. So I'm interested in whether there is a role for artwork and art processes to be more engaged in this kind of debate and dialogue about civil space and future space, and what that looks like and feels like. So in terms of the teaching here, it feels that it's been about setting up possibilities and supported contexts where students at least might have access to some of these debates. Maybe not as the artist sitting on the sidelines being the critic, although I think that is a valuable role. Maybe not being the person who provides a symbolic something or other, even though I think that can be a really valuable role. But there might also be a role to participate, to be involved beyond those traditional roles. There's also a certain responsibility that comes with being part of and with … I'm interested in that transmission, I suppose.

Do you think there's only one way an artist can teach that's implicitly bound up with the kind of practice they have?

No, I don't think that's implicit. And I do think that that is a process of the teacher learning; that there are numbers of methodologies and enthusiasms and interests. It's taken me, and it continues to take me big efforts to learn this. But the other thing about the effort of practice, of whatever kind, is that it reminds you how difficult it is to make work. What seems to me to be one of the purposes from an institutional point of view of people trying to make practice, is the fact that it becomes a non-virtual kind of teaching engagement. It reminds you that these things are human, difficult, compromised, problematic and that making good things is really difficult. I'm stupidly reminded of this every time. Just ask me that again …

I was curious if the way one can teach is implicitly bound up with the kind of practice one has. Maybe I can ask it in another way – can anyone teach?

I'll have to come back to that … 'Can anyone teach?' is an interesting question. I might think in terms of whether teaching is also experienced as a number of voices not contained within the same individual, but in different individuals. And I presume that with somebody's engagement in an art institution, there are a number of voices that articulate a number of experiences. Some gifted teachers are certainly able to teach with a number of voices, and some clearly teach with a different kind of coherent voice. But I would have thought it was the matrix that made that rich. And I suppose that in a teaching circumstance, that should be the reality as opposed to the rhetoric. Rhetorically we all think that everybody can access everybody, but often the reality isn't quite that, so it is really important that that's preserved.

And can you teach art?

I think you can teach art … I think you might teach consideration of it, but it also seems to me that it's bound up with personal development, bound up with whether it provokes the personal development. Whether it is parallel, or it runs ahead, is another kind of issue. Certainly at undergraduate and postgraduate levels, I think there are forms of personal growth, experiential learning, that really matter.

What do you need to teach that?

Maybe this is glib, but I think you need to think that it matters whether you do it or not, you know. Not teach, but I think it needs to matter whether you make the work, or not, and I think that in a time of so much visual proliferation, trying to figure out who the work might matter to is kind of important. What was the question again?

What you need to teach art …

Some desire for the work to meet the context of its day, in some way or other.

You're thinking of setting up an MA in participatory practice. I'm interested to know how this intends to distinguish itself from an MA in art practice?

There are interesting debates around a participatory component, collaborative components; about whether it's the business of an institution to be educating around this practice. Whenever the nature of the practice itself may be and ought to be more fugitive than this, that the academy shouldn't be the place that consumes this. Sometimes it's like all art colleges are shot through with a studio to gallery trajectory, and it can take a very long time for people to even get a taste of other pathways, if that's what they want. So my interest is, can the academy, as part of its job, give a sense, or a taste, or access to that. Not necessarily as …

Access to what?

To other communities of interest, or dialogue, or engagement. There are other kinds of dialogues and agendas and observations that aren't art-based, where it seems to me there are interesting and dynamic things happening. How might an artist get access to those things? It can take a long, long time …

Is this about a pragmatic shift? Is this how we might distinguish participatory practice from other forms of practice? Maybe you have an architect in to talk about what he or she does, or a civil servant to talk about some form of legislation, or whatever?

I'm a little less interested in the coming in and a little more interested in how one might access these contexts and situations that lie outside. Unless that's being done, there might be a real virtuality to it that doesn't make sense. So, back to this thing about thinking that experiential learning is important in terms of trying to understand community, or other forms of engagement. I know 'community' is such a contested word, but the work should be out there in the field, as opposed to in here, only learning virtually.

Given that 'in here' there's a general consensus among teachers and students as to why we're here, once you want to leave this context and community and look for another kind of context and community, where do you go? How do you leave the academy, in other words?

We have an experience of this at BA, where we run a programme that works through all four colleges in Dublin – which is a form of participatory practice with various communities of interest. It is growing from communities of people linked by gender, or age, or addiction, or economic marginality, and moving towards other forms of communities of interest, that either wouldn't choose to call themselves that, or might be interested in another agenda completely. So I suppose we've been involved in quite a structured training and arrangement with communities that have established themselves as communities, and then there are lots of contested and different ways of thinking about what a person's personal community is; it might be their work colleagues now, not the people they live beside, not place-based, but work-based, or professionally based.

I'm interested in how art practice devolves to another kind of space outside the academy. There's a whole set of other agendas out there that see opportunity in what you're perceived to be bringing. Is there a threshold, or a limit to this engagement, where the work tips over into a form of bureaucracy?

Becomes a form of facilitation, you mean?

Where the work perhaps gets lost in endless meetings.

Is it a form of criticality that you think gets lost?

How do you maintain this criticality in the steps you take from the art academy into the community or communities out there?

I am interested in that one might embark on this with some sense of self-interest as an artist; how your self-interest is meeting a series of self-interests of others is where the dynamic might be happening. So it's less about going there and trying to shed a sense of self and gain another sense of self. It is much more about being aware of what those identities and power structures and sources are. And about who might be using whom? And the fact that this is problematic, sometimes contradictory, I think is a dynamic, human space. And I do want to retain this idea that community is a problematic phrase, in terms of what it indicates and what it means. It gets bandied about a lot, and it's problematic enough. The idea that 'it's just too difficult, so why would we?' that is the complex and layered nature of it – which is where I think the real learning can take place. We don't arrive as artists neutrally, or in any other way, but we arrive with a kind of series of empowerments and baggage. How that might meet the context, preserves issues of criticality and this real interesting process of making work that's dynamically informed by other kinds of agendas, or other kinds of experiences. But your point about endless meetings isn't uninteresting; the nature of that kind of work is that it takes time, and sometimes in a teaching capacity you know time is the commodity that's really fugitive.

Should we likewise be preparing students not to be artists? Is there a burden of responsibility to teach them to do other things as well?

Yes, and maybe I'm careless around the use of the word practice here, but I would have thought there's also the possibility of them understanding the forms and vehicles that would constitute a form of practice, and that this wouldn't be limited to art practices as we know them. There's a form of engagement and skilling here that allows people to be able and active in circumstances and situations, in terms of being able to understand and read and engage. I think we do want to train some people to be artists, but there's a realisation that not everybody will be an artist. There are forms of being culturally active that are interesting and that need to be understood. When you're sitting in a room with students, potentially within that room – within those students, there will be future artists, and there will be future writers, and there will be some future museum directors, and there will be some future journalists, and there will be some people who kind of do other things entirely, and some who will sell insurance. Broadly speaking, these people become your colleagues, people whom you'll start meeting in later life as cultural practitioners, who are part of the debate, who are part of the social and societal debate, and who are sometimes, in part, making decisions about what happens next, or commenting on what happens next. In a sense, this is a wider view of being part of a debate, as opposed to 'you're an artist or it's of no use to you'. We have some responsibility to be training people in the business of making visual art, but the vehicles and forms and contexts of that seem to be really up for grabs.

I'm curious where you think art schools will be in 10 years time, because the idea of training people to be artists seems almost at times to be something of an anachronism.

People come to art for lots of different reasons; some because they don't know what else to do, some because they're a wee bit bonkers, some because they're brilliant, some because they have specific agendas, and some because it's still an education that is perceived to be not so specialised. For some it's because they want to be in a band, and I think it is critically important that that kind of mix is retained, otherwise there's a form of absolute specialisation taking place that mitigates against what I think is rich within that kind of intake. I understand that there are some people who are looking for different kinds of things, but I also think there are people coming in who, in a screen-based generation, retain some media and romantic ideas of what art practice is, as well as those who have other ideas. I guess the interesting thing about this is that there are forms of scholarship around these things and that one can take those kinds of enthusiasms and locate them and expand them if that's the appropriate thing to do.

Can you say a little about *Soft Estate* – the work you did with Michael Hogg?

Soft Estate is ongoing. I'd heard the word in relation to a motorway; when you drive down a motorway and there's the hard shoulder, and then the next bit is called the soft estate, which is where plants grow, and then beyond that is the visual amenity. I liked this idea of the soft estate being the bit that's being overlooked.

What's the visual amenity?

It's the view beyond. In Britain there's an agency that looks after the soft estate, and because it's not trampled on; orchids grow there, and butterflies, and when you join up all the strips it's the size of a national park. But somebody has administrative control over it. In Ireland they're just completing the motorway from Belfast to Dublin, so they're late motorways, and the soft estate is taken very seriously. The way in the past you might have imagined there were bits in-between that were nobody's responsibility – under bridges, etc., and inevitably artists want to be in those places. It interests me now that these places are fully administered in-betweenness. In parts of Ulster these kind of layers are a very administered landscape. In fact there is somebody trimming the hedges and clearing the gutters. The *Soft Estate* project is based on a new town, the story of building a utopia and it descending into a dystopia. I don't think that's a new story, but what happens after the nadir of that dystopia, and the coming out the other side and that bit where the journalists have gone home? It seems to me that there are forms of effort to move from a warrior tradition to a form of civil society, where the tools, or the skills of that civil society have been a bit lost, but the place is nevertheless still kind of economically divvied up. All the other operational administrative functions take place, but civil tools have been a bit lost. It's not that I think my job is to provide any form of civil tools, it's to understand this moment of a post-conflict context, and this seems to be a form of soft estate. But I also think there's a time process required in terms of the practice, and this was one of the things we talked about earlier; how long is too long, and how long is not long enough?

I was wondering if, metaphorically, the art school is a soft space; an administered space but a space nonetheless where orchids and so on are allowed to flourish.

I think that's not bad, but the interesting thing for me is that we're not pretending that it's an abandoned space, or that it's a space in-between, but that it is covered. Part of the challenge is to tread a little gently in a funny kind of way, to not pretend that it's otherwise, but where these extraordinary things can happen. It's like I'm speaking in code to you and I don't mean that at all. It's not the romanticism of the abandoned space. Because I think that's a romantic place and it was once interesting, but I think everything is covered now. So therefore, can we create these kinds of spaces within what is covered, protected; spaces carefully constructed which allow for new kinds of hybridity and experimental forms.

How far do you understand your teaching to extend in terms of the bureaucracy around teaching? As acting head of department, you obviously have an administrative role however at this level, administration becomes a place to effect things. So there's a certain power that goes with that. To follow the idea of the soft estate and the administered space, you have a hand in how to preserve that. Does that also get included in what you understand as teaching?

Yes, it very clearly does. But the other side of the coin – and I'm sure everyone will say this – is that sometimes the amount of ... I do think the administration tool is a creative tool as opposed to being a tool of measurement only. And some of the effort, of course, is to try to keep the blunt instrument in some kind of abeyance and the creative instrument foregrounded. And, like everyone else, sometimes the requirements of one can seem more onerous than the possibilities of another. There's a form of responsibility to be creative though, that you want to take the responsibility of making it active and engaged and interesting as opposed to simply carrying it out. What I want to say is that responsibility and power can enable the construction of a flourishing space and time where students and staff are supported to create and communicate their own frames for practice by taking the responsibility to make decisions based on testing things out. This can be vivid and hard work and is about not sleepwalking into habitual ways of doing things. This is not just the protection of fertile space but expanding on spaces and places of practice. The alternative is a bit like that psychological experiment where, if I call you the jailer and myself the prisoner, we both can start acting out these roles very quickly. And with some of these kinds of structures of examination and so forth, one needs to be really careful that you're not becoming the efficient jailer in a sense.

How do you police that?

I don't know if I can answer that question yet.

Philip Napier teaches at the National College of Art & Design, Dublin.

Tobias Rehberger — Studio Rehberger — Frankfurt — mid-December.

In the UK many artists who teach in art schools are almost totally unknown as practising artists. What do you think about that?

It's possible because in my experience the most famous artists are not necessarily the best teachers. But, of course, there's automatically a lack of knowledge if you're not incorporated into a certain position within the system. There's some knowledge you don't have of how things work at a certain level.

What kind of knowledge?

If you're a completely unknown artist, you don't have a lot of experience of doing shows in museums, for example. So that might be a piece of knowledge that you're missing. But I think it's not such an important thing for students.

What is the important thing for students?

[Laughs.]

It's a very general question! What you can't do for students is tell them how to make art. You can't tell them what they should actually do as artists. But you can tell them a lot of things around that; from technical stuff, organisational stuff, to a way of thinking that may help them to understand what they actually need and want. My experience shows that a lot of the time younger students who are just starting, are so full of clichés and ideas about what an artist is, and how an artist should live and what he should do. A big part of the work is getting rid of these clichés and trying to look into what they are really interested in themselves, and not so much what they think they should be interested in.

I was interested in what you said to Mai Abu El Dahab about how you would never dictate 'that a particular model would produce a good artist'. You say 'the student has to decide themselves how to be a good artist because the school is about forming something that doesn't exist yet; something which the students themselves have to discover'. You go on to say 'the first thing you have to do with students who are just beginning is to destroy their expectations; this kitsch they enter art school with'. This suggests a strong ideological position, a strong sense of what art is predicated on,

which seems to go right through to the recently published Städelschule book *Kunst Lehren – Teaching Art*. It goes something like … we're open to everything here, but we're very particular about what that is …

No, it's more of a process. First of all, I think it's a very important to deal with the students – and I would rather call them young artists – in a very individual and personal way. It's not so much that you exactly know what it is and what it should be, but you know a lot of things about what it shouldn't be. That's straight away much easier, and then it's more about searching for something that fits. Of course, it's always based on your own expectations, on your own knowledge, and your own idea of what art could be, or what it should be. And then you try to offer that to somebody.

So if I were to ask the question in another way: what characterises Klasse Rehberger?

That it's very heterogenic.

That's what all the artists I've interviewed have said.

Yes, but it's true.

But why is there a Klassen system when everyone says everything is very eclectic and very heterogenic?

For me at least it helps to deal with people on a personal level, on an individual level, because the way I do it is more a kind of family thing. It's not necessarily only a kind of patriarchal power you have, it's also a kind of trust system. I have to be really tough with them. Sometimes I have to be allowed to say something to them that normally only their father or their mother is allowed to say. But that only works when you trust one another, and so that system helps me to really be hard and do something. Which on a more teacher-student level is almost impossible, because sometimes it's a very fragile thing. You have to be very sensitive. It's about the problem of understanding your abilities. I'm not interested in whether everyone who leaves the class, or the school becomes an artist. If someone is happy to become a rosemary bush grower, a farmer, or whatever, that's totally fine. I really think that it's more important that people who have done the course are happy with what they do afterwards. That's more important than that they become artists.

Is the difference you make between the teacher-student relationship and the kind of relationship you have with your students, or young artists, as you prefer to call them, a question of intensity?

I'm not making a difference about the professorial system, but about the way I'm trying to run my class, which is more like a family, or gang, kind of thing. I believe that has a lot to do with a certain kind of trust level. It's not just an inside outside thing, but it's like being on a boat. It sometimes helps to bring things out. Like last year we went skiing. We were in this hut up in the mountains for a week, and, of course, sure enough, one night something breaks out, and the next day it can all be fine again. But they almost beat each other up, and that's a method to raise the levels of intensity of communication and of interaction.

And how do you deal with being the authority?

They're not children.

I am thinking of your own relationship with Martin Kippenberger, which you said was also destructive, because he couldn't stand any other kind of authority or challenge.

I'm totally not interested in comparing it with what it was like with Martin, I try to keep myself, at least my work, out of the discussion in the class, because I don't want to use it as an example, and I don't think it helps them if they're too close to my own work. That's the big difference. I don't even know if you could say it was teaching with Martin; in a way we were more a kind of entertainment system for him. Everything we learned was not part of a pedagogical programme, it was more on the side, so to speak. On the other hand, he was a very generous person, with all his knowledge and stories. I just try to create some space for them to develop their own stuff, and sometimes I'm able to do that and sometimes I'm not so able to. It's also very much a matter of a certain level of communication; sometimes you have students with whom you try for two years, and you have to admit we can't find a level of communication. And then you say, 'maybe you better go to some other teacher, maybe you can talk to them, or maybe they can talk to you.' But sometimes it's just impossible; I can say whatever I want, they don't understand. And whatever they say, I don't understand. It just doesn't click. But with others ... as long as that works, I think I can offer them a little bit. And then they have to find their own way to deal with it, and that's it. I think there's not very much you can do.

You can't teach art then?

You can talk about it, or teach the periphery of it, or rather the circumstances, but it's almost by definition impossible for you to tell them what it is. Because it is always about what it is, and they have to do something about their knowledge and about their time and about their understanding, which always has to go beyond what I know. Every artist, young or old, who appears in the arena of discussion, has to make a different proposal of how to understand art than all the others, otherwise it doesn't make sense. How can I teach that? I can try to teach them a certain kind of strategy to arrive in some place like that, but I cannot tell them 'that's how you do it.'

If you can't teach it, how do you recognise it?

It's like an invention. You see something and you understand something about it, but a big part of you doesn't, and it still makes sense. I recognise it as I recognise it in a museum by an artist who's 60. I recognise it because it has qualities that at least fit in my system of what I want from art, and that's it.

In an article in *Artforum* you say 'a guy wants a classic suit and he goes out to get one. Maybe he thinks he's found the ideal cut, but years later he takes another look at his sample of eternal beauty and the whole thing seems grotesque – maybe the lapels are too wide, or the colour seems off. My work deals with these mechanisms: what at one time was seen as a classic form, something neutral or even timeless, is a construction. I'm interested in this whole process. I want to look at the context in which aesthetic values arise.' Does this also describe something about your teaching?

It describes my teaching, because it describes my way of thinking. Of course that's the only thing I can offer to the students, and in that sense, it's unavoidable that your own work goes into how you deal with people. But I try to do that as indirectly as possible. Of course I have my belief systems, and I have what I think is my knowledge, and of course that influences me. Obviously the system of what I believe in has something to do with exactly that change in time – not in the linear sense, but in the progression of ideas about what art is. I'm sure I've said something like that a couple of times to the class in the last couple of years. I'm sure that once a year I say something like that, because for me it's very important to think about that. Whenever a work appears that leaves something like that out of consideration, then I critique it. And of course they can either take the critique or they bring something that proves me wrong. I'm really interested in that too. So it's not that they have to follow what I think. I'm even more interested in them being able to prove me wrong in certain things.

In that sense, can anybody teach art?

Not anybody.

It sounds like it's really just about having a discussion …

Yes, but in a way they have to teach me as well. That's what I'm waiting for, that they bring something that teaches me as well.

But there's a difference: you're getting paid to teach, they're not.

They're getting paid a lot – one student costs 100,000 Euros a year.

There's a difference of interest and authority …

Of course, first of all they don't have to be there! And I think I can help them more than they can help me, because I have more knowledge and I've been through a lot of the things they are going through. And through that knowledge I can help them go through it in a more effective, or more comfortable, or more uncomfortable way. I think I can do that, otherwise I wouldn't do the job. If I weren't convinced that I could help some people – not everybody of course, but some – if I had the feeling the students didn't think that anymore, I would stop. If I thought they thought it a waste of time, then it probably is a waste of time.

You've been teaching a number of years now. How do you avoid repeating yourself?

You can't. Of course you repeat yourself. Sometimes it's necessary to repeat yourself, if you have the feeling something hasn't been considered that should have been. Of course, it's always fine if they say, 'no, no, no I don't think so. I do it in the exact opposite way', or whatever, that's fine. But if I say something, or I try to get something across, I do so because I think it's necessary; then sometimes you do repeat yourself. You're not a new person every year, you think things five years later that you've thought five years earlier. And I think there's nothing wrong with repeating yourself. It's not an entertainment system.

Why would you say it's not an entertainment system?

If you say, 'how do you avoid repeating yourself?', it sounds like a television show, or something. We always have to do something new, we always have to do something that hasn't been there before.

You say yourself they have to show you something new, they have to go beyond what's there …

But those are two different things. One is teaching and the other is what they do in their artwork.

Going back to the question of cliché, what is the cliché you have to destroy?

There's a lot of clichés. There's always things around that are more historical, like the nineteenth century idea of genius. Somebody who knows artists and who lives in the system knows that other people, who are not so much confronted with the art system, have a lot of these clichés. They have a kind of funny idea about the way you dress, the way you live, what time you get up. I remember myself. I come from a little village in the south, and my only connection to contemporary art was a rather bad magazine there in the magazine shop. Of course I was thinking of a lot of these clichés as well, because this magazine was a very clichéd magazine.

But you also felt yourself to be very different to everyone else in the village you grew up in …

But then I had to learn. The moment you were at art school and you were around all these people you had to learn that a lot of the bullshit you believed in was a complete joke. And it's very hard to understand that yourself if you don't have help from outside. It takes you much longer. And that's what I mean when I say that in the interview. 'Destroy' sounds a bit too macho somehow… Help them to get rid of the clichés would be better.

What do you think the student's responsibility is when they come to art school? Because, as you say, they don't have to come.

No, they can stay in bed for five years, that's fine. The only responsibility they have is a responsibility towards themselves. That's their only responsibility, besides not setting the school on fire and destroying all the equipment. But the only real responsibility is … I want them to try and find out what they like to do, that's all. They have the responsibility to do that; if they don't, it's just a waste of energy and of money and of time. I would appreciate if they would not waste my time and energy, so I want them to try to find out … to develop in a certain way. That's one of the fun parts of teaching. The best is when you see people develop their potential – that's fantastic. That's what I really like about it. You can really see a difference in three or five years, or sometimes faster.

Does the market decide who teaches?

Not necessarily, I think there's a lot of teachers who are not super successful in the market. No, definitely not. It's a little bit like the first question you asked; it doesn't mean you're going to be a bad teacher if you're not a super successful artist. But it definitely doesn't make you a good teacher if you sell a lot of objects. The market is part of your world if you're an artist for a long time, but I really do not think the market is part of the artwork itself. The quality of art has nothing to with the market, nothing at all.

And how do you think the art school is connected to the market?

It's connected through the fact that a lot of people are going to sell. It's just an economical system, and I don't think an art school is necessarily connected to that system.

But how should it, or should it not be connected ideally or, put another way, how important should an art school be when we think about art?

There's so many different systems of how people teach. If I look at the system in America, it's very school-like and you have to fulfil certain things in order to be able to finish it. I don't see how the market could possibly be a parameter for quality, so I think the market could only appear in an art school in a very, very peripheral way. You could share some experience you have in the market with the students, but it has nothing to do with what the school is actually doing.

You could say that the German system is very much bound up with the market and also mirrors the market through the Klassen system, in the manner in which students vie for the professor's attention, or want to be part of a particular circle around the professor. There also seems to be a lot of movement between the art school and the world, through professors organising exhibitions with students, having students help with the professors' work, and so on. I think there's something very dynamic about this ... rather than thinking about the art school as a safe environment.

The way you describe it as a 'safe environment' is interesting, because I think that's what an art school is; a kind of protected space. We've been doing degree shows now for a couple of years, which is something that comes from the British system. We thought it would make sense, because you don't get a diploma when you leave the school, you don't get a BA, or an MA. But you have to make a mark when you leave, and we thought that'd be really good, Which is of course also a way for some students to get a foot in the door of the market. That's a kind of parallel universe somehow. And if you don't want to become a cab driver, you have to sell your work, unless you come from a really rich family. Those are the two possibilities. The discussion that you have in an art school is not against the market, but it's a discussion about what art is – I really believe that. Of course the market can have an influence on what art is, on how it's discussed, but it's never a measure of quality. You can make work about art and the market, but what this work actually is about is not the market; the quality of the work comes from the way it talks about itself, and its position maybe in the market. But the market doesn't offer you any tools to measure the quality of an artwork, I think, and that's why it's not so interesting to have that in an art school. It's a protected space; to protect you from the art market, from critics, from the fact you have to stand up for yourself and say, 'that's what I really said'. You can try out things in order to arrive somewhere where you finally have to stand up for it. And I think that's very important, that an art school stays this kind of protected space.

You've spoken about some of the positive aspects of your time with Kippenberger, and what you describe as a kind of learning by default through doing things with him, going places with him, going to Vienna to his opening, meeting people, sitting down to dinner with other artists, gallery owners, and so on.

That's important.

What then are you keeping the students safe from? What particular thing is it that threatens them?

I had students who from the beginning were in like five shows a year. There's so many possibilities for somebody who has just arrived in art school to do shows, and to do shows all the time. What usually happens with these students is that it's a little bit about contacts, it's a little bit about fun, and it is always an easy mixture. It's always art, but it's never something that's really interesting. It has happened to me a couple of times that these people want a personal critique after three years. And then they tell me they're thinking of stopping because it's not so interesting for them anymore. And they're frustrated because they're only dealing with something from the outside, but they never take time to develop their own stuff. Of course, not everybody is the same; sometimes you have people who'll do it like that. [Snaps fingers.] They might not even need an art school. An art school is only really important for people who are on the verge of not being able to develop themselves. A lot of people use it because it makes it easier for them, but they don't need it so much. And then there are the hopeless ones, and where you thought the work might become something, but at a certain point it becomes clear it never will.

What kind of advice do you give to them? Do you recommend to the one that can do it that he or she leaves? And the hopeless one …

No, there's a lot of advantages to being in art school, on a social level. It just makes your life easier if you're a young artist going to art school, even if you are … finished. With the hopeless ones, I don't dare tell them to stop, because I'm not sure enough myself. There's always the possibility that BOOM … so I would not dare tell them to forget it.

Just to change the subject, can you say something about craft skills and how useful they are?

Of course skills are always good, whether you're able to cook a nice dinner, or make a table, or find your way through the city. But the problem is: what kind of skills, except for a well-functioning brain, do you need to be an artist? Should we teach them to work with wood? Or should we teach them to work with cotton buds? Nowadays art has been separated from the use of a certain medium, so it can be anything – the medium of art can be anything. You can only guess at what skill might be used over another, but in the end it's hopeless, as every artist is different. It helps me that I can draw a little bit. Not to make nice drawings, but to explain something with a drawing quickly to other people. That helps, but it doesn't mean you have to go and draw a lot of naked people.

So when you look at portfolios and you're interviewing students, what decisions are you making when you select one student over another?

It's relatively simple because 95 per cent of the portfolios you get are the same.

In what sense are they the same?

They look the same, you see the same attitude, you see the same clichés.

Why is that?

Because of these clichés. And then you see some that seem to be less clichéd and seem to have something original. Then you invite these people for interview, and some are more different than others, and those are the ones you take. It's just about difference.

How are you perceived in the art world, being professor Rehberger?

In Germany it's a bit different to other places in the world. In Britain it's a little bit the same as in America. I always had the feeling that if you're teaching in America it's because you haven't made it in a certain way, and when you teach in Germany it's the other way round. Because here it was the most important artists were always the ones who were teaching. But on the other hand, it doesn't help you in any sense. You might get a better room in a hotel when you say 'professor', but that's all.

But does it put you in a certain kind of historical framework?

I've never thought about that. Max Beckmann has taught at the school at which I teach, Courbet has taught there, but I've never thought about that I'm lined up with Beckmann and Courbet. Never thought of it, no.

Is this what the new book, *Kunst Lehren – Teaching Art*, is doing? Putting the Städel into a particular art-historical lineage? A kind of self-aggrandisement.

Maybe it's trying to show off a little bit, or advertise.

It is an attractive book … a book which says, 'this is a significant school, this is a significant moment'.

The book was done by Daniel [Birnbaum]. I've not seen anything of the layout, or any of the articles. I think he enjoys seeing it that way. Its also a little bit of an advertisement; we want to attract good students, because it's more fun to deal with good students than bad students.

Is it a good time to be at the Städel?

It's a good time, because there's a lot of great people there and there's a lot of good discussion, and there's a lot of good parties, and there's a lot of good craziness. If I were a student, I'd be there.

Tobias Rehberger teaches at the Städelschule (Staatliche Hochschule für Bildende Künste), Frankfurt.

Olivier Richon — late September — his office
— the photography department of the Royal
College of Art, London.

What was your first teaching job?

My first job was teaching the theory of photography at Bath for about a term. And then
I moved on to Derby, where I taught photographic practice, but always informed by
theory and criticism. Actually, Derby was an interesting place, because it was isolated,
so one felt fairly autonomous there. Somehow, one didn't feel like one was being judged,
as it were, by others, and as a result one could work very well with students. And it was
pre-university status, which I think was a different, much freer moment actually. You had
all these BA courses, which were fairly autonomous, and which didn't have to conform to
a set pattern of teaching methods. For me, the 1980s were a different period somehow
for art schools in Britain.

A better period?

Retrospectively, I think so. The shock of having to conform to university curricula and
modular schemes … A lot of these places, like Derby, suffered for about 10 years.

What was the main shift of emphasis from the polytechnic to the university?

The teaching became fragmented and turned into distinct teachable modules with aims
and objectives, and that basically doesn't work with art. It's not as if for three months I'm
going to do conceptual art, and then three months I'm going to do expressionism. And
I don't know … art is work in progress, as it were. It may work for humanities, or it may work
for studying literature, but as far as art practice is concerned, I think it's a red herring.

How did it work in polytechnics then?

Very simply, classes were smaller. They were based more on general development. That's
how I was taught, and that's changed a lot. Art schools always were in a funny position,
with this thing, actually.

You can't go back to that, can you?

No, you can't go back. No, because now the whole business of teaching has to be
accountable; we need to account for everything. We need to account for being transparent,
and how we deal with things, as well. So it's totally … I'm not saying the older system was

necessarily better, but it certainly enabled more freedom. And, perhaps, to some extent, it produced better results as well; students ended up after three years of doing a BA with a real sense of their practice. Yes, you can't go back, you're right. Now one has to deal with teaching differently, I guess. In Derby, we created one of the first postgraduate courses in photography based on the sort of polytechnic model, of merging theory and practice. Of course, here at the RCA there's been a course in photography for a long time …

Is that similar today at the RCA?

When I arrived here, it's what I did, yes. So, in a sense, I brought this model with me. It didn't exist before.

And it works?

It works if one gets the right tutors to work with it, but … yes, I think so.

What do you look for when you talk about getting the right tutors?

I'm looking for people who have this ability, of course, to make distinct work, but who are also able to reflect on their practice … and go outside of their practice. You have two modes of teaching; one is the crit, centred on the student's work. And the other one is the seminar, where it's centred on ideas, which may or may not inform their work. It's very classical, but somehow it's still a debated idea in fine art: is theory getting in the way of practice, or is practice sufficient by itself? It's still going on, this debate, these questions

If these questions were settled, maybe it would be more of a problem …

Yes, and one cannot really resolve them. Maybe if they were settled, you would have art that illustrates theory. Or, you would have really boring theories as well.

Is that what we might sometimes describe as a bad PhD?

Yes! The PhD in fine art is quite novel. Although it has been going on for a long time, the culture of the PhD is still being established. It's really interesting, because it's totally unresolved somehow. I find it quite thrilling, and quite bizarre as well.

Do you have any involvement with the PhD students here?

Yes. You probably know the Royal College is purely a graduate school, so we have an MA course, and a PhD programme. It's not a programme really; it's a research group, as it were, a PhD research group.

Was teaching for you always going to be something more than a means to pay the bills?

Well, it's a good way to pay the bills. My own practice is based on research. In a sense, I would say, it is based on researching a project fairly academically and then making work, which may diverge enormously from the initial project. But, in a sense, theory and practice inform my work. And, because of that, it constructs an interesting framework in terms of teaching; because I can share the research I do with my students. The research I do, in a very classical way, is what university professors do; they make their research public in the form of lectures and seminars, then they write a book. So, in a sense, this very classical model is partially adapted, partially followed.

So would you think of research as a kind of chosen area of exploration but without a preconceived outcome?

Not really, no.

It's examining something, and then the work kind of happens in relation to that ...

You're right, you're right, its more speculative, open-ended. Yes, it's true.

In the way we might talk about art practice?

Yes, absolutely.

There seems to be a tendency when we talk about research today, certainly at PhD level that it becomes more exclusively about a theoretical discourse.

Theoretical research must be foregrounded, definitely at PhD level. That's what distinguishes it from an MA for instance, where it's no longer necessary. It all depends ... it's also quite obsessive, PhD research, which is not a prerequisite of doing an MA. In a sense, good PhD people are people with serious blinkers; they don't diverge very much, they stick to one thing and quite obsessively go into it in depth. It's a minor psychiatric disorder, or it can turn into one!

How would you describe the way you teach? I'm thinking about this in relation to your interest in allegory and a text by Michelle McGuire in which she describes allegory as – another speech, '... an open declaratory speech, which contains another image or meaning'.

I don't often describe how I teach, because one doesn't tend to do that. But allegory is an interesting model, because it foregrounds 'incompleteness', speculation. The problem with allegory is that it can be all-encompassing, and has no end. There is no end to deciphering meaning, there is no end to reading a text. But it still gives us such a broad horizon to practice. I think allegory is very good, and it doesn't limit practice to either something expressive or something intuitive. Neither does it exclude it, but it enables a kind of complex edifice to be built.

And what kind of framework do you use to build this edifice?

The subject I teach is quite interesting in relation to what you might call allegory. I don't think it would be the same with painting or other, more sort of ... how shall I put it ...other more physical practices, because photography is very dispersed by its nature, and distant and fragmented. The production process is fragmented. So one could make a case for saying that allegory in its modern notion maybe lends itself more to the theory and practice of photography.

I was also thinking about allegory as a mode of speech, or a way to conduct a ...

It's a mode of reading an image, but it's a mode of making one as well. Images built on other images, quotations ...

Which is maybe how a lot of practice is developed today.

I think so. Or at least, at a more advanced level there is an awareness of that.

Even to the point of citing other kinds of practice deliberately and explicitly within your practice.

Sometimes it can be deliberately. One announces it; it's the content of the work. At other times, perhaps, it's more discreet, more implicit.

Can you teach art?

You mean how to make pictures?

Well, if part of the contract for working here is that you engage with the kinds of discourses and practices that constitute art …

I would say our students need a lot of teaching!

You're not answering the question.

If you want to be an artist and if you come here … we think that most people we have as students will need a lot of teaching. Maybe one can teach art to people who are already artists … I'm not really answering your question, am I? I wouldn't think very democratically that 'everybody can be an artist'. I would be a bit worried about that, actually, because it's a bit like saying 'everybody can drive a car'. Being an artist just becomes a set of instructions. It depends on what kind of art, and what you mean by practice. But I don't think everybody can be an artist, because we get 200 portfolios for 20 places, or less even, and it's quite clear; out of all these we retain perhaps 40 and we're just not interested in the rest. It would be professionally disastrous if we were taking everybody. I don't think everybody can be an artist, because it's a weird thing, to be an artist, isn't it? On the one hand, you have to be flexible enough, but you also have to be controlling enough to do what you do, and you need to be able to regress enough as well, but not too much. It's not about skill, it's not about being able to respond to a commission. It's more like being one's own master, which is not something everybody wants to be.

Can you see who the artists are among your students?

In a sense, it's easier in this place, because they've all been trained already. But I would say there's always a sort of risk; one never quite knows. Some people might come with very good work, but might be unable to continue, or do different work. And you may have people who come with the promise of good work, but the promise never arrives. So it varies a lot, and some change radically for the better. So it's very difficult to tell. In a sense, that's why teaching art is difficult, because we can't. This is clear; one can't really teach it. The students have to teach themselves to some extent; they have two years to rely upon their own decisions.

But it does, in a way, almost make a case for taking anyone … the whole 200 that apply.

In theory, yes … as an experiment. The only problem is that out of these 200, let's say 100 already have a notion of art in their head. Which would stop them from making good art, because it's quite a conservative notion of what constitutes a good image and that would be very difficult to shift.

This is something Beuys was interested in, wasn't he?

Taking everybody?

It seems that he would push students quite hard, and those who didn't want that would remove themselves from his class.

Yes, I can see it as being interesting, but I can see it as being quite intimidating as well, because it becomes a matter of group psychology. And, unless one is in love with Beuys, does it work? I don't know. It's interesting, but there is something a bit religious about it; the idea that everybody can be an artist is almost like saying everybody can be a believer.

Do you share Michael Craig-Martin's unease about PhDs, the Research Assessment Exercise and what he describes as 'the insidious growth of academicism in art education'?

Yes, I do share his unease, even more so because it's not as if we have a choice about it; it's a new ethos of teaching. So I do share the unease. It worries me that art as research might not need an audience anymore as what's tending to happen is a split between art practice and art as research. The audience is just the PhD examiners or other universities; that worries me. Suddenly art ceases to be in the public domain, somehow. That could be one of the consequences, because if one writes very good proposals for research through art, one will get the funding, and one will get employment, and it will generate itself irrespective of how the result is judged by the community of artists. I still think we make art for other artists, and if one makes art purely for research assessment, that gets very, very worrying somehow. On the other hand, unless one knows how to do these assessments, one is in trouble.

Does the RAE encourage teachers to think about their practice as artists?

I think so, but it feels forced … it maybe reminds, or makes sure that artists who teach are still artists. That's good, that's definitely good. Of course the specialisation that the RAE encourages might divide the community of tutors into teachers and researchers. I would find that worrying, because, especially where I work here, every teacher should be a practising artist. It might also encourage strategic people, people who always know how to find a result and discourage the more speculative work. But it's difficult; one can't hope to go back to the good old days, which were not that good anyway. In a sense, research wasn't at all acknowledged then, so what good is that? The RAE can have good aspects. It's just that the way it's conducted is such a heavy form of assessment; one just doesn't want to be assessed, I guess. In a sense, one becomes a student who's been mugged and has lost his privilege of not having to be assessed anymore, so it's bad news. That's why there's so much hysterical rejection of the exercise. Artists would like to preserve a sort of aristocratic independence, so they're not accountable for anything. In a sense, it's a modernist disdain for having to account for what one is doing.

Olivier Richon teaches at the Royal College of Art, London.

Karin Sander — after lunch — her studio —
Lehrter Strasse, Berlin.

Do you need to teach?

No, but I've always communicated very well with young artists, and my own work is in some sense reflected in the projects I do with the students and based on the ideas I explore with them. For example, this summer we went to Rome – close to Rome – the Sabina mountains, where we lived and worked in four little villages. I was invited to work with my students in and with these villages. Four artists worked in each village and we used rental cars to visit one another. I really like to create these kinds of projects – in concrete situations.

The benefit for you is that you're working with other people?

Not on my own work, but with a concept – almost a curatorial concept which will challenge the students to develop their ideas within a specific situation.

Do you get them to work to a project brief?

I just create the opportunity, and then they can do whatever they like. They study the situation, the history of these towns, for example, or their architectural and social context. And within these parameters each of them finds their own way to realise something.

Do you also work there?

No, when I'm with them, I just co-ordinate, orchestrate and support or … I don't know … challenge their ideas about their work.

While you were often invited to teach, did you also want to teach?

Not really. The first teaching situation I was in was very brief. I was invited for a kind of crit. I went to see what students did. We talked about their work and so on and even when I met them a few years later, they told me that I'd said this and said that to them. I never saw any results at the time so I thought it would be nice to be somewhere a little longer. [Long pause.] There's always a kind of connection between my own work and working with students. For example, I always work with things that are already there, but maybe not visible. I try to develop or search for something – I work with the background of a situation. So, in a way, that continues in my teaching practice. I work with the found situation of the class with the state of each of the students, who will ask questions within the context of their work. I am not pushing in any direction but rather supporting what is already there. Whatever I observe that comes along, I'll emphasise and support, and I like that very much. I really like what comes out of it – there's something that you can't quite see, and neither can the students. But they're really digging into something and you just help them dig a little deeper. That runs in complete parallel to my own practice.

But at that point they're clearly separate activities?

Absolutely … or maybe not quite. Because when I go somewhere to teach for a day, for example, my mind is in a creative mode and this continues in the class. It's a kind of living communication that continues with friends, artists, colleagues, as well as with students, but always with a different emphasis. It's not that 'now I'm a teacher' and 'now I'm an artist'. It's more like my working and thinking process as an artist continues in my teaching as well – or at least that's what I've tried to do and so far it's worked.

What do you think characterises Klasse Sander?

You can see that every artist or student tries to have, or already has, their own kind of handwriting. So their work is not defined by technique. It's not a conceptual class, it's not a painting class, it's everything at once. They work in different media and conceptually they work totally differently. Students also have different … what is *Vorbild*? People they admire. It could be Christoph Schlingensief or Helmut Federle … they go through periods in which they admire certain people. I always try to invite those people in whose work they feel connected to.

Is there anything else that might distinguish it as your class?

They're very good students! I can only talk about those I've had in the past, but I'm always astonished by how quickly they come to a point where they really find something. When they've reached this point, they're usually very closed to any other artistic practice. It's then I feel they can really go and exhibit, or publish. Firstly they make this kind of nest in which they feel protected through the institution, but then there comes a time when they are ready and can leave the institution. You can really feel exactly when this happens, when it matters less what you tell them. When we do things outside the institution like, for instance, in these villages near Rome, they still have the protection of being part of the institution. And while OK, it's not a Documenta, they are in a public situation, and they have to defend themselves, they have to defend what they do even if, as I say they're working against the background of being students.

Oliver Koerner von Gustorf, writing about your work said, 'the subversive question concerning the "framework" within which we view art not only applies to the material quality of the means Sander uses and the spaces she selects, but the socio-cultural relationships they refer to as well.' I was wondering if this observation could be extended to your teaching and to an idea of 'public' you seem to be interested in. There's something about this framework being challenged, for instance, when you take your students to Rome. Or that something unexpected can come into the framework, as in the case of your patina paintings, or your work in Lodz, Poland, where something unexpected 'occurs' like the balcony, which can then be made or claimed as your own.

Exactly. It's as if the unexpected which 'occurs' becomes an extension of your original idea and you have to be ready to acknowledge or admit this, and to understand and take it into consideration. And, of course, this challenges the practice of the students in a very positive way.

Are the students alert to these opportunities?

Not really, because when they're here, when they're in the institution, there's so much distraction. There are so many things they have to do. It's important to take them out of the institution, which is the same thing as when artists take themselves away to withdraw from everything – in order to think about something. It's the same as taking time off from your job, your family, or whatever, and being concentrated on something particular, but also being in communication with others. In the Middle Ages it was called a symposium, where you ate together, you talked philosophically and it's said that this had to happen in nice surroundings, with nice-smelling flowers. You would walk between the trees and philosophical ideas would come to you. So this is the kind of environment you create when you go somewhere and exclude certain distractions for a week or two, when you take away the day-to-day duties – this allows you to be ready for something else to happen that challenges you in some way, and that leads to a door opening. And no matter whether you're a student or a world-famous artist, you search for something like that to happen – something to develop and extend your ideas. In the academy, or any other kind of institution, there are certain rules and rhythms to it, and to break these is very important to your art practice.

So it could be anything really that breaks these rules or conventions?

Yes. I also do this by teaching here in my studio. When you go to the academy, on the way you'll meet this or that teacher and you'll think, 'oh, I need somebody's signature', or 'I have to pick that book up or I have to drop this off'. Here in my studio we're in a separate environment, outside of the academy and as soon as you enter a different environment like this you open up in another way. All the conversations and discussions I've had with students here at this table have had a totally different concentration than those at the academy.

And how many students do you normally have in your class?

We're three professors, and between us we have 90 students. What I did for the Rome trip was I asked all 90 of them who'd like to go. 40 wanted to and had time to go. So each one developed a project for these little villages and then we presented them to one another and the students themselves selected the best projects and hence who would go. I'd have made the same choice …

Tough.

It was very tough. I thought, 'oh, how am I going to do this now!' The students voted and I accepted the result. I was very, very surprised. 15 were selected – it was a very good group. They said it was the hardest test they'd ever had.

Because they had to make the choice?

Yes. But it was also interesting for them to see how they gain acknowledgement amongst themselves. It was not about who's a nice person, or who's the cleverest person, or who can speak better than the others. It was really about the work they presented and how they could imagine that being realised there.

Can you teach art?

Can you teach art? I think you can teach techniques. You can help a personality to develop and from there you can see who will stay with their art practice or do something else.

And what do you think are the signs?

The signs are that you stick with something, that you really – how can I say? – you can really see this development; at a certain point they really make the decision. If that decision is made at some point then they will continue.

The decision being …

Being an artist and living like an artist, and being focused on what they want to do. Others are more distracted; they do this and that, and then tomorrow it could be something else. You see this very early on. But there are some who are very interested and they want to find something …

How do you deal with students wanting to be like you: a successful artist and teacher?

I don't think of myself as a teacher in the first place. I'm an artist, and I try to work professionally as an artist. My teaching is completely different. I don't teach them anything, I just open a platform of possibilities, and they can grab them, or they can leave them. They have to be responsible for themselves from the beginning. If they want to present something they can't really stand by, it's their choice. They have to please themselves and nobody else.

Can anyone teach art, or can only artists teach art?

It's a certain way of thinking, a certain position you take. Only somebody who's really actively developing their own work can transmit this experience.

Can you say a little more about that?

If you are actively working as an artist then you live a certain way and this can be transmitted and a student can pick up on this.

Is it more a question of demonstration, when you say you don't teach them anything;

they see you there as an artist with an active practice?

It's a kind of *Haltung* – an attitude, taking a position in your social field, in your surroundings. Someone can see that and pick up on it. But that's only one way; maybe there are others.

Without a practice you can't do this?

Practice in a broad sense; practice could be in curating, in writing, in whatever.

It's about taking a position. A strong position …

Yes.

And if you take a strong position – maybe students want to be like you?

That's more an idea from the 1960s and 1970s; a teacher has a certain kind of charisma, walks once through the class and the student soaks up the air and the smell and that is how he learns. That is not what I mean. It's more about the way you think through strategies, think through ideas; it's about communication. An academy opens a field that everybody can be in for a while, and you learn much faster being in that field for a while, than when you are a self-taught autodidact. Even if being in the academy environment is in a way self-education, because you decide what you'd like to do. I don't think it's good to teach students etching, sculpture, or whatever – all the techniques. I think you learn them when you need them. Of course, you can have a look into them and you can try them out to see what they're about, and your ideas might be influenced or challenged when you begin to explore them, but you don't need to take that all in. If you want to make a video you look at how the camera works, and then you just do it, you learn it when you need it. If the interest isn't there, it just doesn't make any sense. I'm not against education, I think it's very important to have art history and all these kinds of things.

What is your involvement with the institution?

Very little in terms of politics, more though in terms of future direction and conception.

Do you have any administrative duties?

Yes, of course, you have meetings and you see which artist, or whatever, has to be organised for the school. But that has nothing to do with teaching; it's just an organisational thing.

And do you co-teach as well?

Sometimes we meet and we develop a new idea, or we develop a concept, what kind of exhibition projects we could do together, etc., but the teaching is separate from that.

Artists teaching in the UK sometimes talk about teaching in terms of bureaucracy and organisation; it's often quite heavy and dense. There seems to be a much lighter emphasis here on administration and maybe a less burdened approach to teaching.

This is a question of organisation. In Zurich, for example, the school is very well organised in the sense of secretaries, assistants, and so on. They take away all this administrative stuff from you, so you can completely concentrate on the thing you were asked to do – teach. The more you keep the administrative element to a minimum, the more creative you can be. But that's the same in a studio, where there's always a certain amount of administrative or organisational stuff. One can do it very efficiently, or one can make it their main job.

And how much teaching are you prepared to do? You teach in Zurich one day a week. That's it? No other teaching?

That's all. Teaching is most successful when the main thing is still your artistic career, your artistic ideas and working method. If you have that as your main focus then the effect will really flow into your teaching and ultimately the teaching will be more successful and the students are right at the source of that where the most interesting thinking happens. As soon as I have to recall to students what I thought 10 years ago, it's not alive any more. They have to get the most recent thinking, the most active thinking, because that also makes them active … if these two elements come together then teaching is most successful. That's my experience of it. The students are so sensitive, they feel it right away. I remember when I was a student and the teachers that had given up on their practice … its just not vivid …

You could feel it?

Yes. Absolutely. It doesn't matter if a teacher comes every day; if he doesn't have a successful working process in his studio any more you don't have such an encounter. You challenge each other much more if this communication process is active from both sides and everybody throws in equally and honestly what is vibrating in them some place.

If this relationship is working well, is vivid and vibrant as you say, what do you take away from your students?

They also discover things on their own. They bring in music or for example, one of my students was very interested in performance and he brought Christoph Schlingensief and his kind of thinking into the class, and it was very fruitful for everybody. My students also travel, they're everywhere. For example these two students – one was working in New York and one in Japan – did an exhibition together, and it was very interesting how they chose each other and the work they showed, which fitted really well together. I managed to get an exhibition space for the school here in Mitte so they can do exhibitions that they curate themselves. I'm really pleased when something like that happens, and the level it reaches. One of them had done performances using himself, but for this exhibition he invited a mother and daughter and asked them to sit next to each other in the exhibition space. He had their biographies printed and put on the wall. That was the one who came from New York. The one who returned from Japan – from Hiroshima – asked two security guards to come with him into the woods and asked them to protect a tree for a couple of hours, which he then filmed. It was a very small video on a flat screen on the wall. You see these two security guards with uniforms and guns protecting this tree. And you think, 'why just that one?' There were tons of trees, but he decided on this one: this one should be protected. It's a really beautiful image and metaphor. It's a pleasure to see such a successful exhibition.

Is German art education in a good state?

At the moment, yes. Germany has this tradition where, for example, Polke, Richter, and all these really famous, incredibly great artists are able to teach at an academy. To be able to teach so successfully you have to have the freedom to work on your own, to come and go as you want, and this relationship has to be very open as it was always a position of honour, of trust: 'you are an artist we admire, we really appreciate your professional career, you get this job.' There are lots of attempts to change this freedom to the point where you'll not be able to continue your own professional career, but then artists won't take these teaching jobs any more, and then you'll only have artists teaching who need to teach, and that's a different story. This kind of position has to be as free as possible, not only for the good of the artists, but also so that students will get the most out of it. Too many requirements would disturb that structure. Stan Douglas, who had a position here at the Universität der Künste Berlin, came here according to his own schedule. And when he did he gave it everything he had. He organised an incredible symposium about film, film history and film theory, for instance. It lasted two weeks. It was so intense, he organised screenings of films that you can hardly get, and so on. Some students said it was so intense that these two weeks replaced two years. He could do that because afterwards he could continue his own thing again. This is what I mean by freedom. You have an idea in the academy in the same way you have your artistic ideas; I do a project, I do two weeks of film screenings now, and I give them as much as I can get together. I invite the most critical art historians, film critics, and so on, so it's very concentrated. There's a discussion in Germany at the moment that they would like to change the contracts with the teachers, so that you have to teach 20 hours a week, for example, every week, and have a rigid schedule. It's not been realised yet. The new contracts are more hours per week, and so on. Not that I want to discuss if it's one hour more or less; that is not the issue, since you put in much more anyway. But this system is so against the artistic process. The amount of freedom the teacher needs to develop his work is the same amount the student needs for his. It doesn't make any sense to tell a student every day what they should do. If you tell them something, they need two weeks to think about it, to realise something …

Then that kind of proposed structure really is opposed to practice, and not to a particular kind of artist?

Exactly. The freedom to withdraw to reflect, to travel, to come back, to bring something into the class that you have experienced, that would be destroyed.

Why create the bureaucracy if you know it's going to damage the system?

That is a good question. I don't know. After Bologna, everybody thinks, 'OK, more structure; the teaching is not good enough.' So one starts to improve it without taking into account what was working well.

What is it they thought wasn't good enough about the teaching?

People took advantage of the system. If you have total freedom and you have a career that requires 100 per cent of you, then you just don't show up. That has happened in the past. But there are just a few examples, which doesn't justify changing the whole system.

Karin Sander teaches at the Eidgenössische Technische Hochschule, Zürich.

Christoph Schlingensief — the office of the director of Hauser & Wirth, Zürich — while Schlingensief prepares for his solo exhibition.

How did it all start?

I started by myself with my father's camera. He was really my first teacher, and this was also when I made the first 'mistake' and understood the possibilities of it. I started making films when I was nine or 10 … This was in 1967–1968. I began imitating television series, or feature films. I made a film called *The Secret of Lady Florence*, based on one of those cheap novels.

Was it about Florence Nightingale?

[Laughs.]

No, no, no.

Hotter than that?

Correct. The story was very complicated and not in chronological order. I learned about telling a story when something is in the past and in the future. The problem was that I could only shoot the film at weekends because the money wasn't there. So at one point you see the criminal boss coming down the stairs and he has long hair, and at another point when he comes into the police station he has short hair. I think this was my first moment of learning … Every time I showed the film I was unhappy because it wasn't really the story I wanted to show. So I decided to learn filmmaking in the film school in Munich, but they wouldn't accept me. I was really depressed … my father wanted me to become a pharmacist so I decided to study philology in Munich. I don't know, I was never there really. I was there six semesters, but I only ever attended a seminar in *Hörspiele*, audio plays, and one in film, and the others I never went to. I went to the cinema and film museum in Munich every day. There I learned about Werner Nekes, he's an avant-garde experimental filmmaker. Coincidentally, when I shot my next 16mm film, we met in the cutting room; he was cutting his film and I was cutting mine. I was watching him working on his film, when I noticed his face in a row of frames and I told him to stop, I pointed out that there was a picture of him and we went back to it and it was. He was surprised I could see it because it was running at 24 frames per second. Anyhow, he phoned me the next day and asked me if I wanted to be his assistant, because he really liked that I could see this so fast. So we had a meeting, and I became his assistant for the next three years. He has one of the biggest collections of historic film paraphernalia, books and dioramas in Germany; he researched the origins of film. So Nekes was my second major teacher. He was also a professor in Offenbach in the Hochschule für Gestaltung where I then began to teach. I got a job teaching people, who were sometimes older than I was, how to use a camera. I was 22 and the thing was that I didn't really know how the camera worked. So when I had a problem I'd run to the toilet and look at the manual, come back and give the information to the student. This was the third kind of learning I had, because these were fantastic students and there was a lot of emphasis on drinking, sex, drugs, fighting and films. Nekes was at that time becoming an alcoholic and only sometimes organised things for us. But we made these films. They were really great, because they were powerful and against things, against people and sometimes against Nekes. After this I became a freelance camera assistant, and was second camera assistant in a number of big films in Munich ...

How long have you been teaching and were you invited to teach at Braunschweig?

I've finished my second year.

Were you invited?

Yes, they asked me to come.

Why do you think they asked you to come?

They have Birgit Hein there, she's an experimental film-maker. I don't know her well but I have known her for a long time. She comes from Cologne and was president of the Film Bureau of Nordrhein-Westfalen. She's very loud and aggressive and we'd sometimes fight, but I like her and maybe she talked to people about me. I also think Braunschweig maybe needed names in order to be talked about and to attract students which is a bit the problem, the students already think they're artists when they start, free artists and very crazy artists, but they don't have a very strong position, or way of fighting. The problem for me is that I can't stand at a blackboard like a teacher and explain things to students; it's just not possible. I've tried but I'm very egocentric. I want to show students my films, tell them how they happened and that's all. I'm not very interested in looking at their work. I'm really not. When a student wants to show me something, I look at it very briefly, very quickly. Although it's only like this recently. In the beginning I thought I had to sit there for hours and hours in order to understand what they want, but now I look very quickly. When I feel that people really have the energy for doing ... I really need to feel the energy coming off them, then we'll do things together. We'll have a coffee, look at their work, fight with each other, call each other asshole and so on. Then I really begin to engage with them. But if students want to work with me, then they have to come with me and work wherever I'm working.

You mean physically or conceptually?

During the last two years I've had up to 15 students working with me on my work, whether it's opera, theatre or film-making, though this wasn't possible when I did Bayreuth. Wagner made sure of that, very closed ... like a concentration camp. But the work in the Burg, the Wiener Burg Theater, that was interesting because students came with me and they painted, they built, they ate together and the power of all this came together in the end, when they made an installation re-telling the narratives I used, but telling them in their own way, telling them against me.

This was a form of teaching?

And creating new stories and new narratives.

This is how you include the students? How do you avoid creating a small and rather privileged circle around you?

This is really a problem. I can't work with 50 people, it's not possible. In the Burg it was between five and 10 and in the Amazon, in Manaus, it was four. One student even said to me on the first day of being there that he didn't want to work with me after all, that he wanted to go into the jungle by himself. And I said 'OK then, go into the jungle and come back after six weeks, because I want to see you, and call me sometimes so that I know you are there.' I didn't tell the university that he wasn't involved in the process with me, that he was developing his own process, which I think was even better ... Because when the students are sitting there, and you feel they're not having any fun, then it's better they go away.

At this moment what are you giving the students?

When I work with them I want them to share in my process, show them how I work, how I get depressed, how I get excited, how I get sad, how I cry. Not down to the last detail of when I go to the toilet, but more that I can share my experience. I don't necessarily know how to tell a story in the right way. I don't know how to make a picture in the right way. I only know that I can combine things in certain ways, that you have the possibility to learn that things transform themselves through this combination. So students can't be involved in this process thinking they are going to learn through me giving them the recipe for success, whether it's successful art or successful theatre. When they're with me, we have ideas, we have fun, and we fight about the work. They can see that 10 days before a premiere or an opening I get really down, because I'm afraid and anxious. They can see all of this. Then there's the opening and after the opening they can read in the newspaper what critics think of the work. 'Schlingensief wants to provoke but he has no chance', or 'he's boring', or 'this wasn't interesting', or 'he's not a political artist', or 'he is a political artist', or whatever. And this is always changing; the positions are always changing. This is what students can't be taught but can maybe live or experience.

And can you teach art?

Nein, nein! I have no idea how it works, I've now been in the art world for four years and things grow slowly. It's interesting that my gallery, Hauser & Wirth, see my things, they talk with me about them, but I think they don't really understand what I'm doing. They give me the chance to transport things and to put things in storage. But ... I can't explain it, when my gallery claims something is art now! It's art now! Now! Now it's art! Now! Now! But before, it wasn't art. I don't understand the process and I think in the museum and in the art world, a lot of the time the frames are on the walls in order for people to understand that what is inside the frames is art. Even when there's nothing there, the frames as still there, so you think there must be something. I can only ground things through my family.

In what way?

I can only endure this world through exposing where I come from, because I'm a bit like this, and I know it. In 1976, my father was in the Lions Club, in the Ruhrgebiet, in Oberhausen. Once a year there was a big event for the Lions Club members, when an invited speaker, an artist or teacher or whatever would come and speak. This time it was the artist-teacher Joseph Beuys. I was 16 years old and I was watching this man with the hat, and he was talking, and I could see my father and all the other people falling asleep in their chairs. Within half-an-hour everybody was asleep, and at the end of the talk Beuys said '... and this system of society will be destroyed in seven years ...' and whoosh! At that moment everyone woke up collectively and barked like dogs. I asked my father three years ago whether he remembered this moment, and he said he remembered it well. And after Beuys's visit, I wrote every year for seven years in my calendar that society would be destroyed, and after seven years I could see it wasn't going to happen. Beuys was wrong, but then I said to my father that I thought it was good that Beuys had said this, because you write it down.

And you think about it ...

You think about it. Groys, Boris Groys, a friend of mine – and I find this very funny – he explains how Joseph Beuys said a lot of things and that he was a big teacher, but what we remember is that he talked a lot, we don't know what he was talking about. We know that he was a teacher and he talked a lot, this is Joseph Beuys ... nothing more.

Is this something to do with the power of charisma?

Yes, I think so. Do you know Rainer Rappmann and the Freie Internationale Universität, the FIU? Rainer Rappmann teaches Beuys's ideas. I was in Achberg at one of his seminars and it was so incredible how he explained Beuys. Everyone in the seminar had this kind of arrogance; they wanted to be like the apostles of Joseph Beuys. I actually think the apostles killed Jesus. It's always the same; they'll say, 'yes we know him and he was like this and this, and blah, blah, blah'. That is the problem of teaching. A good teacher is like my teacher in high-school. He irritated me at just the right moments. When we'd get our marks back he'd say 'ah Christoph, this was fantastic, this was great, this was really good – Magritte, Cézanne, very good, very good, this is a five ...' A five is the second lowest mark! At other times he'd say 'ah Christoph, this is completely wrong, this is wrong, and this is wrong', then he'd give me a one! A first! He changed everything all the time and that was very irritating. He also used to give us manifestos to read, manifestos of Futurism, Surrealism, or whatever. I found them very interesting because people claim in manifestos 'Now we have it! Read the manifesto! You're for me or against me! Read it! For me or against me!' It's good when you can see an artist fighting for his ideas, he's fighting for or against something. This teacher of mine was not really an artist, even though he made art, I saw some of it. A bowl, a triangle and a little bit of sand. He wore a Joseph Beuys-type jacket. A good teacher needs to stay longer than I do at the blackboard; needs to go away, come back, clean the blackboard and write down a new formula. I can't do that. I go somewhere and leave my mark, and then I go somewhere else, and the students have to come with me.

What's your particular interest in teaching and in the world of the academy? Is there a target, an enemy, something that brings you into teaching, brings you to Braunschweig?

It's the arrogance of the teaching and learning process. I dislike students because they think they're on the way to becoming something. They do little things ... I think of students as being unwashed, as smelling, students stink ...

When does the smell go away?

It's more the attitude.

How do you lose this attitude? You seem to suggest that students smell because they think they're somebody, because they don't understand anything?

They have to pretend to be the artists they might become one day. They're playing at being something that they're not. That's why they smell.

And how does the transformation happen, when does the smell go away?

This year my father died while I did Bayreuth. I learned that every time, not every time but often when I show my work, it isn't the work I really want to show, its not really it. I think, 'OK, I have to organise the situation in another way, so that people can live with this "wrong result".' The other thing I learned was that when my father was dying I was living in a film; he was dying for four weeks at home and after the first week I thought, 'OK, he's dying now, so I play the music I've prepared'. It was *Ave verum*, heilig, heilig, heilig. And we were sitting there and everybody was thinking he was dying. Then the music finished and my father wasn't dead. He had three more weeks. So I learned that I don't have the power to decide that we have a good ending, the music is playing and the titles come up; 'Hermann Joseph Schlingensief and Christoph Schlingensief, camera and music ...'

Your father wasn't following the script?

He was not! This is the thing I really learned more about this year, than at any other time before in my life. Now I accept more that I can't determine or control progress, but then I'm more political than before. When I'm ready to accept that things are not clear, then, I'm not a fatalist and I'm not crazy, I'm highly political, I'm really fighting. This is interesting for the students when they come to show me that they are living in the film of 'I'm an artist' [Laughs.] Then I have to cut this film, I have to put it in the wrong development fluid, and I have to turn off the lights so that nobody can see it. I have to destroy it. Actually one of the best things to learn as a student is that critics want to destroy you, that they're not really interested in the progress of your work. You have to learn that everybody wants to destroy you. You're like a fly that lives for one day, that's what it's like. And the fly says 'oh, is that all!' I was in New York and saw the Roselee Goldberg performance. She took money from Rockefeller to do this big performance festival and it was unbelievable, the worst performance I've ever seen. People I know were crazy for it and they asked me whether I liked it, and I said 'put this person's mirror away' so that when she comes home there is no mirror in her room for at least two years. 'She has to do the performance without a mirror and then we'll see it again ...' This is the problem of Prenzlauerberg in Berlin, and maybe London has the same problem. A lot of people are acting the artist, the performance artist, and the fight is against themselves. Jonathan Meese is maybe not the best performer, the galleries want him to paint more, he wants to act more and his mother says; 'No stop it! Stop it!' I don't think he's pretending; he's really crazy, he has to do it. That is more fascinating than the people who attempt to imitate a performance artist.

Till Briegleb said of you that 'you create a permanent state of insecurity by blurring borders between reality and fiction, art and offence, intention, and action'. Are you

making these so-called borders clearer when you go into teaching and when you go more concretely into the art world? Schlingensief the provocateur, the teacher, the artist …

At the moment I'm in a process of learning, of having a look at how everything works. When your main actor is ill, the director stands in for him. He reads from a script because he doesn't know the text and he doesn't know how to act. He wanders across the stage reading from the script and in the end the audience clap louder for the director than for the main actor. But when the actor says, 'now I'm the director, I'm going to direct a play', everybody says 'oh no, you're an actor not a director.' But maybe the actor knows more about what has to happen on stage, maybe he has more influence. Now I'm working more in the museum or the art world, people are saying 'No, you're coming from theatre. This is not art. Art is when something can exist alone. You come from theatre and theatre is about being with people and you have to stay there.' I'm trying to take myself more out of the picture, I started doing theatre in 1993, so 14 or 15 years ago now. I forgot that I come from film-making where I was behind rather than in front of the camera. Once the film was finished, it was shown and I didn't have to be present in the cinema while it was showing. There was no Christoph Schlingensief in front of the screen saying 'Hello, ich bin Director!' You look at the film on your own, which is something I'd forgotten for the last 15 years, because of the stage. Theatre is at its most interesting when you have those metaphysical moments where you suddenly think 'is it really theatre?' 'What just happened there?' Maybe what just happened is very shameful, shameful for me. This is where I think reality and art, my work and my person are now coming more and more together. After the death of my father I can walk out of the picture because I still remain in the picture, even if I don't remain in front of the camera.

There was a moment in *Wien-Aktion*, when 600 people were demonstrating near the work. A woman walked up to someone and asked if it was real because she no longer knew what was staged, what was directed by you. There's something about your work in Documenta and Venice where it's easy to know what's happening, to know what's yours. Is this a problem? It seems the power you have is to create this space where we, like this woman, are not sure what is real …

The morning of the Wiener Festwochen and *Wien-Aktion*, the organisers put up very big posters on the street, saying that it was a theatre play. When I saw them I phoned the organisers and told them to take them down. I was screaming down the phone that they had to take them down. A lot of things that happen are more real than we can see … There's the problem that Schlingensief, the provocateur, comes in front of his projector. Then you can't see the real picture – and I'm thinking in terms of film-making and picture making now – what happens when Schlingensief is not there. For example when I cut my films and do stage design, my name is Thekla von Mühlheim, and there's also Peter Deutschmark, who makes a lot of the art … not Schlingensief. A lot of people will come here to the opening of my exhibition on Friday and they'll say 'oh, he now makes this … but where is the political aspect of the work, because he claims to be fighting against Blocher?' That is true, but for me it's very important to do it now in this way. In São Paulo I saw a lot of political artists, but is it really political, all this art that you can see in the Arsenale and so on, where they call themselves political …? If someone paints all the dead people in Iraq, it's more about art itself.

Maybe what I think is interesting about you going into the academy and into the museum is not so much about whether art is political, it's more about different fields that you get to enter and leave, that you get to play in. Each of these fields have certain kinds of protocols, certain kinds of politics, certain kinds of limits and exclusions …

I'm a little bit like Doubting Thomas, who puts his hand in Jesus's wound, and maybe he goes so deep into it that he kills him. 'I don't believe, I believe, I believe, I believe, I can't believe!' And then ah, hah, hah. Buff, Kills him. And maybe that is what's going on here, I want to try it for myself, to do it by myself. I had a political party, CHANCE 2000. I really fought for this party and in the end I was completely destroyed. My brain was completely empty and after CHANCE 2000 it was the Church of Fear. By going to Braunschweig or the museum I can learn new things because I have to. Bayreuth was a new thing and maybe I'm looking for that moment in the opera, *Fall of Potici* … when during the break people go out and start a revolution. Maybe the moment I'm looking for is when people get to the point at which something kind of crosses them or hits them, and drives them to do something.

Speaking of CHANCE 2000, how do you think making politics artistic and art political takes place? This is after all what you wanted CHANCE 2000 to do …

When art gets political then I'm looking at it and thinking, 'OK, now art has political aspects … very interesting …' So [Santiago] Sierra's piece … the truck on the street … it is a fantastic image to see, and you maybe learn something about the actual provocation on the street. But the image is something more than the actual provocation on the street, something for the future. When Sierra closed the [Spanish] pavilion in Venice, I was in the same Biennale. There was a moment when I thought 'OK, now what happens next? Blond hair for black guys, it's all the same … he's labelled'. But the image he left is different, you can transform this in another situation, it's not finished. My job is to find all the images that say they're not finished, because that shows me that this need not be the end. Things are transforming the whole time and the image I see is not the image you see; we digest things in different ways and sometimes shit comes out, sometimes not. This is the way in which I want to be freer than before … this is the information for the future. I'm learning to say 'no' to things, that I'm not part of this, or 'I won't participate in that'. I have to learn to say 'no' to all those people who pretend to organise the truth of life. I want to teach people to say 'no', 'do it without me, I'm not part of it'.

You mention something like this in CHANCE 2000 and its motto 'Aktion Aktion Aktion: do something, anything'.

I have to learn and remember that everything is communicated above my head all the time. This is a view of the future, because I'm looking into a cinemascope, my view is cinemascopic.

Daniel Birnbaum writes, 'sense is not Schlingensief's ambition, rather it seems he is suggesting that higher forms of lucidity are to be found in delirium rather than in normal coherent discourse'.

Yes, I think so, but this is not to say I'm crazy. I really think there are possibilities in my mind that I've forgotten, I have possibilities that I've forgotten and I have to remember why I've forgotten these.

What are the dangers of inertia and do you see much of this in the art world and the academy?

Inertia breaks out when you use art as a recipe to be more interesting than before.

[Schlingensief's Mother rings.]

My father died and six weeks after my father dying, my mother got a brain attack. Now she's speaking again, but her voice is a little bit higher than before, and she can't walk so well. But I like her very much, she's very funny and she always wants to know where I am and if I'm OK …

Inertia.

You talk about the need to do something, whatever it is …

For four years prior to and one year after the first Bayreuth, I was thinking all the time 'can you do the same thing next year? Is it possible to work again? Do you have enough power?' Sometimes when you have success, you want to hold on to it and say, 'yes, I have the recipe for success.' Then you do something again and nothing happens. Maybe in art it goes so fast that artists feel 'OK, I paint in this way, and I do the next and the next and the next painting, and maybe I can earn a lot of money.' But after three years, or whatever, people say 'oh, there's nothing new here.' That is maybe when I look at artists and think there is no real fight behind their work, but more a working with success. I'm happy to come into this new area to learn and to go into opera to learn, and to work in other countries to learn. Because to always live in Germany is really sad, it is very depressing, because everyone knows everything.

When Till Briegleb describes what he calls provocative art, he includes you in this description, and thinks that once we understand a particular kind of irritation, then the artist or performer has a sympathetic audience who come for the irritation, so you no longer have that fight that you seem to be interested in.

When I did *Kühnen '94* at the Volksbühne, Berlin in 1994, it was I think the best play I'd done and it was a very, very powerful evening for people. But for the critics it was a disaster, and after that I didn't work at the Volksbühne for two years. Castorf finished

it for me; the play was too powerful, too heavy, but now you go to the Volksbühne
and Jonathan Meese is screaming 'Heil Hitler, Heil Hitler, Heil Hitler, Heil Hitler!' and
Prenzlauerberg is fine with that, is happy with it! 'Yes! Heil Hitler! Wow, wow, wow, wow.'
We have to accept this, we have to accept that this is the death of the ... Maybe I was
lucky that the Volksbühne opened their doors to me when East and West came together,
and Castorf is maybe also a little bit tired, and Prenzlauerberg is so hip! There are
galleries everywhere on Auguststrasse and the place is full of tourists. I was away
from Berlin for eight months and when I came back I stayed in a hotel for one week in
Prenzlauerberg – I don't have a flat, I live in hotels and in my caravan. I walked through
the streets and it was 'waah!' It was really like a shock. I'm talking a little like an old man
who says 1968 was a good time. Well, 1968 was a good time, but the thing is that I really
don't like the imitation of things. This is maybe Hermann Nitsch's problem. It has been
said that Jonathan Meese and I imitate him, even if there's no relationship between
Hermann Nitsch and my theatre, or between my work and his. He came to have a look
in Area 7, and after the show Nitsch was very relaxed and happy. I can accept that things
are changing and this is the way it is. In art, as in theatre, the Volksbühne and all this, it's
too easy to have success. It goes very, very fast and it's not aggressive in any way, the
reactions are not really aggressive, and the people don't come. There are some theatre
plays and nobody goes.

It doesn't matter?

No! The Volksbühne is there, and nobody comes.

**This would be the absolute failure of the work, when everything fails, when it doesn't
matter, when nobody cares ...**

I don't think we'll have a new revolution in the next 20 years, and I don't think that
everybody is only stupid in Prenzlauerberg. But they can surf over things and things don't
touch them in an essential way; it's just a play and everybody knows that now. I feel that
in Vienna, Zurich and Berlin we look at something, it finishes, and then the next thing
comes along. It's happening to everybody now; it's not giving them anything to talk
about, they just think, 'OK, we've done that. It's just repetition.' It can be more of an
irritation today that Hitler painted flowers and landscapes than the fact that he killed

millions of people, 'Oh yes, this is interesting, yes, yes. It's normal Hitler killed people, but um ...he painted flowers and landscapes? Ah, that is very interesting!'

Are you tired of the enfant terrible label?

I hate that label! You know Werner Shroeder, the film-maker? He is an enfant terrible too but he's 64 now, or whatever. The label is bad because I don't really know what an enfant terrible is. When I use things from reality in a way that I transform them, people actually find the reality the provocation, it's not Schlingensief. There's really much more provocation around me than I can represent; the handicapped people in my work are a fantastic provocation but nobody talks about it. The label of provocation is sometimes the death of thinking. We have a cabaret artist in Germany, a comedian, Harold Schmidt, he's 54 or 55 now. He had a lot of success and everybody liked him very much. Once when he was in a restaurant and ordered a glass of water, the waiter thought he wanted to provoke him because such a successful comedian surely only drinks champagne and whiskey, not water ... I was flying from Vienna to Berlin during the time of the Wien container, or the television show and I was sitting in business class. The steward, who knew me, said 'ah, Mr Schlingensief, hello, what would you like to drink?' So I asked for a coke. Then the businessman sitting next to me and the man sitting next to him recognised me, and one of them bent down and picked up this little can of coke, shook it and opened it over himself and the other businessman and they're all covered in coke. I was sitting there watching this and then the businessman turned to me and said 'ah, this was typical Schlingensief!' I only asked for a coke! Another time, I woke up in a lot of pain with a lung infection. I was living in the little flat at the Kunst-Werke and I phoned Klaus Biesenbach, who was living nearby. I said 'Klaus you have to come and help me.' I was in really unbelievable pain. Klaus said 'OK, lets get you to the Charité.' I'm in the car bent over in pain and screaming as we drive to the Charité. When we arrive a nurse tells us to go upstairs, and while I'm waiting there in a lot of pain, one nurse after another came and just looked at me before going away again. Then a doctor came, 'ah you have pain ...' He had a look and also went away. Eventually Klaus Biesenbach started shouting! 'You have to help him! You have to help him! What's happening here? What's happening here?!!' In the end a nurse told us they thought that I was doing some kind of candid camera thing. What's been happening in the last three or four years is that people are actually looking again at what I'm doing, even if journalists still write that 'the provocateur and enfant terrible Christoph Schlingensief is coming to Zurich.' I've asked them why they write this even if we've had a good chat and they're interested in my work. They say 'we have to write it because people can understand who you are.' So I get the label of provocateur. But it's better to be a provocateur than a loser.

Christoph Schlingensief teaches at the Hochschule für Bildende Künste, Braunschweig.

Jon Thompson — Queen Elizabeth Hall,
South Bank, London — 10.30am.

When did you stop teaching?

I stopped teaching last year. I stayed on four years after retirement at the request of the university. That was Middlesex.

Is there anything you miss about it or has this interest been taken up in another way?

I miss nothing about it, because I think that art education has changed so much … from something I adored doing into something that became a nightmare, basically.

Can you say something about how it changed?

I'd have to say that it is the mechanisms of academic surveillance and control that have completely destroyed what was best in it. There is no trust anymore between the different levels. They call it quality control, but really it's a form of policing. Everyone is made to check on somebody else. Nowadays, when you ask a young teacher to come in and teach, half of his day is spent writing reports to be submitted in two or three years time to a surveillance body of some kind. Half the day is lost before they start. The real exchange between the experienced artist and the artist/ student is curtailed; systematised to very little end. At Middlesex, all teachers were asked to make each tutorial 15 minutes long because of the number of students and the general rule that all students should be seen at regular intervals. Even visiting staff were required to write tutorial reports within the time that they were being paid to teach. Now that seemed to me to be an utterly stupid and wasteful process … and it's only one example.

Was there a time when it was free of this control?

Oh yes. In the 1970s at Goldsmiths we quite accepted that a student might not be seen formally by their tutor for four or five weeks, and that was the right thing for them. We discussed it of course – as a group – and we decided that this person was best left alone for a while.

The key being that you decided rather than managers deciding?

Yes, we decided as a group. Because something had to happen in the students' heads before they could make the progress that we thought they were capable of. Until that happened, we were wasting words, wasting their time and ours. This was the revolutionary aspect of the Goldsmiths approach: that you treat students as if they are artists. They might have less experience than you and as teachers you have some responsibility for their overall direction and to ensure that nothing goes disastrously wrong … but ultimately and before all else they have to learn to take responsibility for their own thoughts. Only then can you help them to translate those thoughts into a practice of some kind. If they are not having the thoughts you can't sow thoughts in their heads that will be of any lasting use to them. In this sense artists have to make themselves: I've always said that. What you can do, however, is provide a context in which vital developmental moves can be made by a young artist and that is what we tried to do at Goldsmiths. We did our best to provide a context which strengthened self-awareness; where the emphasis was on taking responsibility for your own ideas and actions. There was also a purposeful communal dimension to the way we did things. We felt that the way in which students related and gave ideas to one another was almost more important than what a member of staff might deliver at a seminar. We did do seminars, of course, and we did critical seminars at great length sometimes, but the teaching mechanisms we were trying to foster were communal and not top-down.

Michael Craig-Martin, when speaking of his time at Goldsmiths, said that he felt that he had little or nothing to do with the development of the so-called Brit-Art generation that came out of Goldsmiths at that time.

He wasn't there. He wasn't there at all for the whole period.

He wasn't there, but he said that he felt some of his best teaching was done when he was working one day a week.

I've heard him say that before, but I don't know how true it is. With the right students he is always a good teacher.

He talked about this complex coincidence of social conditions, people and so on. I was thinking that whatever he said about this, you and Michael had to create the conditions that allowed for this to happen.

We worked very closely together and I love Michael dearly, and I think he likes me too, but there is some untruth about this. By the time Michael arrived at Goldsmiths I had already begun to make the important changes … in the staffing especially. I had brought in Glen Baxter, Andrew Brighton, John Tagg, Yahuda Safran and Richard Wentworth. They were there to set the tone for a new approach to teaching. At that time Michael was still teaching in Canterbury and I had to poach him from there. I was looking for somebody at the highest level to support what I was doing. At that point, there were still quite a few resistant staff who wanted to go back to the old departmental structure … you know; painting, sculpture and print, that sort of thing. The sculptors were particularly resistant, determined to act as an independent unit even though I had abolished departments. Eventually, of course, this ended up with Bobby Jones resigning. I needed Michael then. I had worked with him before at Canterbury, briefly. I'd been a visitor in his teaching group so I knew him as a teacher because of that. We'd also been with the same gallery, so I knew that Michael was the right man. I knew that we shared a similar philosophy and that he would help me knock Goldsmiths into shape … but he withdrew from teaching for a couple of years while Damian Hirst and that crowd were still there. The important thing is that … I mean he and I both agree that they weren't the best students that we taught. Did he say that?

No, he didn't say that.

We did a public seminar recently – about a year ago – and I was quite surprised as I expected him to be very supportive of that group. But, in fact, in the discussion that followed he entirely agreed with me that they were not the best students that we taught. They were a couple of years earlier, before he took his time out. Because his own work took off in a big way and he wanted to concentrate on that, he took two years out and then came back. It was during that time that the so-called Brit-art group – Angus Fairhurst, Damien Hirst, Simon Paterson and all the rest – graduated. That is as I remember it anyway. Sometimes your memory plays tricks … but he and I both agreed that in some ways they were not the best generation of Goldsmiths students. We were thinking of the years that included Lisa Millroy and Julian Opie through to Michael Landy and Liam Gillick. For all sorts of reasons some of the best young artists have not really surfaced. There was Hamat Butt, of course, I think he was a year earlier than the Brit-art lot. He got some public attention … briefly. And we both think he was potentially a really good artist, but Hamat died of Aids. He was in Michael's group at the Millard building before we moved back to the main site in New Cross. A lot of good young artists from that time seem to have got lost … it's very strange … who knows what makes for success in this crazy art world. Such a lot of very talented, very interesting young artists simply lost from view … I like to think … possibly because they didn't conform to any stereotype that the art world is looking for.

Would you agree that good teaching is something that you, the teacher, or academic, has in a sense little or nothing to do with, a lot of the time?

I would have to agree with that. I believe it to be true. The mechanisms of transference in teaching fine art are still pretty impenetrable to me even after 40 years of teaching and so I can't trot out a definition of good teaching. Good teaching happens and you know it when you see it. It's a mystery too, why some people can do it and some people can't. It has little or nothing to do with training – leastways where fine art is concerned. There is something very odd about it: it's something to do with rapport, openness, being prepared to receive projections and being capable of producing a response that's useful. And it is something that you do almost without knowing that you're doing it. But it certainly registers with students. I mean bizarrely, I went to do this seminar at the Whitechapel yesterday and the place was full of my ex-students, going back years, all coming up to me afterwards to say 'hello, I'm glad to see you'. I don't know why that should be, it's weird … I mean I don't stay in touch with them. It's something … I don't know what it is. It's hard to explain why you have that degree of projection.

What's the best that you can do then as a teacher?

There are two levels to be thought about. The direct relationship with the students: remaining genuinely attentive to them is the first requirement. Knowing when to talk to them and when to keep silent. Knowing … having an instinct about when they're in trouble. That's one aspect of it. I remember with Steve McQueen, for example, he came to Goldsmiths as a painter, very much in the Chelsea mould. But you could tell his heart was not in it and quite quickly he got into a terrible mess. Finding the right moment to talk … well that was something else. He became very defensive – he was like a bear prowling around. Knowing just when you could go to speak to him was absolutely crucial. That was at eight o'clock in the evening, or something, because I used to stay on late. He used to refer to that moment … that it was just a curious moment when you could really talk. But I could give you lots of other examples.

You couldn't really do that now could you?

You couldn't. It would be absolutely impossible. That's why when I was at Middlesex I was so unhappy. I thought, 'this is ridiculous, because I know how to operate as a teacher, I don't need to be told.' I've been doing it for God-knows how many years – 40 years or so, I think - and then there are all these rules and regulations. You have to see students, whether it's useful to them or not. I mean you can say the right thing to a student 50 times, but if it's not the right time, you may as well forget about it, it's no use. You can see the blankness on their face. They're nodding their head, but they're performing by rote – you're performing by rote. It's of no use to you and no use to them. I was very disillusioned when I got back. Things had changed so much, and not for the better. I think if I were absolutely honest, I'd have to say I taught far too long. I should have dropped out after Maastricht, really.

This is the Jan van Eyck Academy?

Yes. You see, my experience at Middlesex was a disaster pretty well from the outset. I soon found out that I didn't respect the man who ran the institution. I didn't like the academic structure. As a place of work I didn't like anything about it. It was a university in name only … certainly not in spirit. But even at Middlesex I had good relations with the departmental staff and students, some of whom are now doing very well. You always have this satisfying payback from individuals, and, I guess, that was the tantalus that held me to teaching for so long. But I still think I should have finished after Maastricht because the system in England was, and in fact still is, changing at such a rate. The objectives … the general educational objectives… have shifted from education to training in the university system as a whole, without there being any proper reflection on anybody's part. It seems to me. It has just been imposed by successive governments. I agree that we should all have a broad range of skills, including IT skills, but that shouldn't be the central educational objective. Education is about more than that. It was these things happening in English education that made me go to … mind you I was running into the same difficulties at Maastricht with the Dutch government beginning to model its thinking on the English system.

How is art education in the UK now, as far as you are concerned?

I think it's ceased to exist.

Why do you say that?

It's not centered on art anymore but on some weird version of cultural and social theory. I mean, the thing we tried to do at Goldsmiths was, yes, to embrace the latest thinking, but to keep the focus absolutely on art at the same time. This was the Goldsmiths model. It was picked up by other schools and it worked as long as artists were running them. Now there are very few artists in charge of these places, certainly not at faculty level. More and more it's people with a cultural studies background because they have the administrative skills and institutional no-how for setting up and running the surveillance apparatus ... the blanket tutorial systems and all the rest. They have a vested interest in such things because their career focus is within the institution. This is seldom true for artists. They have little or no interest in systematising things in that way because they know that it's about a model of accountability which is antithetical to the way artists develop. What we have now – by degrees – is a system wherein those who are actually running the departments are no longer artists, so you can't really expect them to keep their eye on the question of art. Many of them are trained teachers too ... products of a training system which is more about education than it is about art. It's amazing, some of the art school people I was helping to supervise for PhDs during my time at Middlesex, didn't think like artists at all, but like a curious brand of hybrid educationalists intent on ticking all the boxes. Artists are just not like that.

That can't be good for art?

No, it's not good for art. The thing I always used to say, and Michael always agreed with me about this, is that it's the easiest thing in the world to teach people to make something that resembles art, without being art at all. Anybody can do that ... there are ways of doing it, and the art school education system in England did it as a matter of course for more than 100 years. It's what I call 'art school art', and there is a lot of it about. Much more difficult to produce is somebody who makes something that not only looks like art, but feels like art and is art. Some of the best schools began to get the hang of this in the post-Coldstream period, but it's disappearing again now. You see lots of … it's kind of fake, it ticks all the boxes of what art practice – current art practice – might be, in a studious sort of way. But it doesn't have any feeling to it; it doesn't have any real depth.

Is what you consider good teaching going on anywhere in the UK, as far as you're concerned?

It's going on more in Scotland. I've been examining in Dundee and the general ethos was healthier … although it's now getting ironed out there too. They are being forced by the system to adopt the kinds of funding strategies and teaching tactics that we are using down here. For a time they resisted and very successfully too in places like Dundee. They managed for a long time to hold on to some notion of what art is … its real demands … and they managed to keep a degree of academic flexibility, more than we did at Middlesex. I guess they won't hold on very much longer there, either, because the current system is driven by financial constraints and the necessity of raising research money. And this is why I disagree with the whole research ethos in art education. To my way of thinking, it's the wrong kind of duress. Funding practical arts subjects and institutions like art colleges through research money distorts their whole purpose; drives them in entirely the wrong direction.

It's driving them towards what?

Towards a kind of orthodox university-type of view of what practice should be. And so few places have resisted that … in fact, none of them have resisted it. Even in Dundee they're talking all the time about how to capture more research money.

Is this the Research Assessment Exercise?

Yes. But it goes much deeper than that. Of course all artists do research, and that's important, but they don't do research in the way that a sociologist or a scientist might. They are concerned with interpretation too, but not in the way that historians or scholars of literature are. Artists are not in any sense concerned with plugging gaps in a known arena of knowledge – not by disposition anyway. But you asked me about the Research Assessment Exercise. Not only is it corrupt, but because – in its university grounded form – it is inappropriate to the activity of making works of art, it is also corrupting. To my way of thinking it is corrosive of the very purpose of art. Art is about chance-taking; about holding certainty at bay long enough to discover something. You have to feel that you are risking something when you start a work. It may be a miniscule risk, but still a risk. You're trying to do something that you haven't quite managed to do before, or you haven't tried before … an idea, a move that you don't know is viable. The only way that you can ever know whether it is a sound move is by carrying it through to completion. That is why the study of context – its elaboration via the traditional methods of research – gets you absolutely nowhere, because what that tries to do is predicate an outcome, more efficiently, more economically, more directly, or something. In fact it doesn't help in any of those ways, it short-circuits the essential process, basically. Process means making physical – bringing into existence and that cannot be achieved discursively. It requires perception harnessed to intuition … the lightening to strike. I've just written a book on modern painting … painting after Courbet … and I started to look at artists that I hadn't really looked at before. Their biographies were fascinating … you know, the when, why and how they started doing the kind of work they became known for. Often the thing that triggered it off was quite a minor event in their life, or something totally unexpected … sometimes from looking at other works of art, but rarely if ever from the exploration of context. A moment of revelation accompanied by a weird kind of certainty. I was writing about Patrick Caulfield, for example, who I knew for years and years, and I remembered the fuss that surrounded the early paintings that he made at the Royal College … in 1960, I think it was. He was the only person at the College who thought they were any good. None of the staff liked them, nor the students neither, but he was absolutely sure they were good. They were taken by the Young Contemporaries, but the hanging committee hid them away in a dark corner because they were embarrassed by them. Yes, they hung them in a dark corner … it was the Slade lot as I remember. Anyway Patrick Caulfield marched in on the day of the opening, said 'I'm not having my wonderful paintings treated in this way' and took them away. So where does that come from, that absolute certainty? It comes from having done something and recognising what you've done. And that seems to me to be the key to the whole of art education; how do you get someone to do something, and not just to do something, but also come to a full recognition of what it is they have done?

There seems to be a current interest in notions of teaching and pedagogy – you have Manifesta in Nicosia, the Shedhalle in Zurich, the debate over the Bologna Convention in Europe, etc. I was wondering if this current interest in teaching is a reflection of an attempt to think through and get out of a certain kind of academicism, or is indicative of a prevailing and even growing academicism in art?

This is a difficult one for me to answer, because I haven't really been involved. As soon as I stepped out of teaching I refused to think about all this very much …

[Long pause.]

I heard about the Convention and I heard about the failure of Manifesta …

[Long pause.]

I've never liked Manifesta, because I always think that it pretends to do something that it doesn't actually do. It pretends to show diversity when in reality it represents a consensus – conformity – about where certain people in the opinion-forming bit of the art world think contemporary art is at. It's a kind of 'hip' academicism, if you like. I've known a lot of the curators and I know very well what they think and how they position themselves in relationship to current art practice. They are all of them trying to make a name by aligning themselves with what they see as progressive forces and they nearly always get it wrong. They move from country to country, picking out certain things and rejecting others and they end up with a mess of a show. So I've always been rather sceptical about Manifesta. But then I'm wary about anything that's programmatic. By which I mean where there's an unstated critical orthodoxy at work shaping the direction of things, and this is very much the case in today's university fine art departments. You know the sort of thing … the agenda-setting that goes on under the guise of curriculum design. This is why I would like to see the schools and departments cut loose again. It seems to me that in art you can do that, in other subjects you can't. You can't cut people loose who study English, because English has a canonical set of texts which have to be studied, etc. Art doesn't have that, and the pretense that it does is often very dangerous. It's a university type thing, which is why I've always thought that the great mistake for the art schools was to go into universities.

They should have remained polytechnics?

They should have resisted incorporation, the polytechnic was a better place for them. But, of course, the polytechnic directors were so ambitious, they wanted to become universities at all costs. To my way of thinking the whole business of dissolving the binary line in higher education was a huge strategic error ... but that's another story. As far as the art schools are concerned, though, the polytechnic was a better place for them. It's interesting that the only place where I enjoy teaching –and I still do a little bit of teaching there from time to time – is the Royal Academy Schools, where there is none of the top-down policing that goes on elsewhere in the system. They're coming under some pressure to comply now, but at present there is only the lightest of academic superstructures there. So you can talk to people on the basis of some kind of equality of exchange, and you can concentrate on the values and quality of the practice rather than spending your time writing spurious reports. You do feel that there is still a spirit of adventure there, in the limited way it can exist in an institution of that kind. So I'm always suspicious about any ... you see, having been brought up as a teacher by Harry Thubron ... Harry was one of the great trickster figures ... and I suppose I modelled myself on him, really. He was so schizophrenic about teaching that there was something rather marvelous about it. On the one hand he liked teaching courses, with rules of procedure and clear objectives, and on the other hand he only ever praised the students who broke the rules. And this became so apparent to the students that the courses almost failed – failed by default. Students were so desperately trying to break the rules ... it's a form of schizophrenia, but a very interesting one. He didn't say 'well there's nothing to be taught', because he did actually fundamentally believe that you could teach. But then he never praised the things that answered the exercises that he set. And it was this which led me to the idea that it's much better to cut the individual student loose and not have not have year structures and the like ... not have any of that nonsense. In other words, make the institution's interference as light as possible, so as to maximise the exchange between individuals.

What courses did Harry Thubron teach?

With Victor Pasmore he invented the basic course which he put into practice at Leeds, and from there he went on to be head of fine art at Lancaster, where I first worked with him, and afterwards at Leicester. Then he came to teach with me at Goldsmiths. But ... ah ... he was a difficult man in all sorts of ways. Michael hated him because he was so up front ... sometimes outspoken to a fault. Michael was quite low-key in the way he operated, and he was a gossip of a certain kind ... like passing on secrets. But they were both essential ingredients in the early days of Goldsmiths. You needed someone who was a bit like a bulldozer, and that was Harry, and you needed someone who was more serpentine.

Does the academy or the art school today provide a certain kind of network and affirmation?

Yes it does. But the degree to which that network is properly reflective of cultural value – any notion of lasting cultural value, that is – is open to question. Thinking of the people I have taught, I sometimes wake up screaming in the night, because I find myself asking 'what do they actually represent? Do they represent those lasting values that I feel should be represented? And I don't think most of them do. They represent the values of the market, as it stands at the moment. And the market values of today have the power, over time, to atrophy the development and the progress of young artists. Take Damian Hirst, when did he last make an important work ... a work that explored new territory. Most of the time it's market fodder. I'm not saying that he has never produced good work, but that was some time ago, much of it formulated at Goldsmiths or soon afterwards. What has he invented since that time. Very little ... I would say. And this is the problem with today's 'academy' as you call it – which also harks back to the Goldsmiths model for which I am responsible – it has become far too entangled with the concerns and values of the market. This fact alone makes the issues surrounding art education highly complex. The market driven idea of success leads to a whole lot of improperly considered demands being placed upon students ... it slews the creative objectives. One of the most successful things I did at Middlesex was to do a talk each week about painting. Very simply, without a lot of theoretical clap-trap. At the time I was writing a book about modern painting for non-specialist, interested adults. So I thought, 'why not just give them my thoughts about some of the people I was working on very directly', and it worked like a charm. I mean it was quite idiosyncratic ... talking just about who I was thinking about at the time ... say the mirror paintings of Pistoletto or the Achromes of Manzoni ... whatever. They were amazing these talks. Their popularity really took me by surprise. The students adored them. It wasn't that they were a great intellectual tour de force, just that I was talking about works of art ... as a practitioner ... in a very straight forward way rather than about sociology or cultural theory. They were so relieved.

What do you think might be an appropriate model of teaching for today?

I've thought about this a lot. And at rock bottom I think we should abandon the pretense of a professionally inclined undergraduate fine art education and leave that to the postgraduate level. Especially if we are required to work with academic processes that imitate the university style of degree course and if, as time goes on – as I suspect – courses are going to be made to conform more and more to that model. It would mean major changes throughout the whole system but it would be more honest than what we have at present. Then, we could really cut to the chase by setting up new kinds of post-graduate departments, staffed by artists, and focusing entirely on the practice of art. You could assume a certain broad range of knowledge and a commitment to professional practice at the point of entry. They would be places where artists meet and exchange ideas about art. I mean, if you look closely at the history of modern art, say from the mid-1850s on, you find that so many artists either didn't attend art school or the academy at all, or they left after a short period of time. You know ... they decided, 'this is not for me, these people have nothing to teach me'. In fact it is a very peculiar idea, that only the academy can produce artists. It harks back to the eighteenth century. It's an eighteenth century idea – a pre-modern idea.

Could you expand a little more about the idea of abandoning undergraduate programmes in art?

My point is very simple. If you increase the numbers in the undergraduate programmes to the degree to which they've been increased, then you've already jettisoned any form of really meaningful selectivity. The Coldstream model was intended to be highly selective on the basis of aptitude. By now that has completely gone by the board. But still the pretense of specialisation towards professional practice remains the raison d'être for nearly all departments and schools, it's an untenable situation. I had to do a lecture on this just before I left Middlesex and hard statistics were hard to come by, but I worked out that taken altogether there were 13,000 graduating fine art students – single honors and majors – in each year. There can be no justification for such numbers, unless you restyle the degree as a broad-based, education-through-art type of course. A fine art studies program with a more structured curriculum – teacher rather than student led – and without any specifically professional intentions. There can be no justification at all for training more artists each year than doctors. That's absolute baloney and nonsense. My solution would be to get rid of foundation courses by incorporating them into these new, carefully structured, broad-based fine art degrees. They have tended more and more to imitate the free-wheeling type of fine art program and in this respect have long since outlived their usefulness. You could then deal with professional practice in an expanded post-graduate provision ... longer courses and some increase in overall numbers would do the trick ... carefully controlled, of course. This would encourage a much more varied intake at the professional level by attracting students from very different academic backgrounds into a much more varied range of courses. It's always struck me as highly significant that so many American artists of the post-war period had first degrees in other subjects ... philosophy, social anthropology, psychology and the like. But nobody is going to allow this type of postgraduate development to happen here. There are too many vested interests ... and the freedom to experiment would not be there. The government and the universities would want to maintain the kind of institutional levers of control that they've established over courses in general ... it's suffocating this university thing ... certainly not creative ... a form of normalising totalitarianism from which nothing is allowed to escape.

So what are you offering then at postgraduate level?

You would have to make it a genuine specialist, professionally-focused postgraduate course, but along very free-wheeling lines. As I envisage it, these courses would be staffed by fully practising artists, not by occasional or pretend ones. They would be absolutely student centered, even shaping and reshaping the year program and the staffing according to the changing needs of successive cohorts of students. The intention is very simply stated: to help able, aspiring young practitioners to emerge as artists. It sounds simple but not so simply achieved. Freedom is at the centre of any significant model of art practice ... the freedom to act imperiously ... to change direction willfully ... and to fail abjectly where there is a lesson that needs to be learned. This type of freedom can only thrive in an atmosphere of mutual trust where there are no over-riding, external academic constraints in place. 'Failure' then would be an outcome of the working process itself rather than a product of some phony examination regime. But what university is going to go along with that. None ... I fear. But I want to say something about Art-based PhDs. I have been thinking for a very long time now that we shouldn't be giving PhD's to artists. It is entirely unsuited to art as a practice-based endeavor. It devalues it. More importantly for the long term, the PhD is, itself, likely to be devalued by the growth of this type of hybrid qualification. The PhD is a written document, a summation of speculative thought grounded in research ... purpose, to provide new information to a known area of study. That's what its function has always been ... and what its function should remain. It is important to recognise that fine art is not a subject in the normal sense of the term. It is not defined by, or beholden to, a body of knowledge in the way that subjects are. It is essentially a traditionally-grounded, artisanal, sited activity. Despite its increased involvement with technology, conceptually speaking it belongs in the studio and studios – even virtual ones – are not studies. Artists do not go to the studio to study or to do research. They go there to explore their intuitions and test out their relationship to the visual (not the visible) order. If you want to have degrees in the practicing arts, then they should recognise this crucial difference. For fine art there should be something like a DFA where the emphasis is absolutely on practice.

What's a DFA?

It doesn't exist yet ... they were going to set one up at Middlesex. I'd been arguing for it from the moment I got there. It's a doctorate in fine art and to be honest, it was not my idea. Originally it was put forward by Christopher Frayling at the Royal College of Art and then dropped for some reason best known to him ... political pressure I suspect.

OK.

So you would have a doctorate in fine art as an entirely practice-based degree.

But why would you need that then?

That was the question I asked myself when we first started to talk about it. Why would someone who was doing reasonably well in their own practice want to risk breaking the flow by going to do a DFA? There is, though, at least one sound reason why that might be the case. Some people find that their feeling of isolation is a problem and they want to get back into a community where there is a broad but intense discussion of practice. That is a perfectly valid … entirely reasonable objective at a certain point in your career … to decide that you have thoughts you want to share with other people, and to hear what they have to say about them. That's a very different to saying, 'well, if I really elaborated the study of my context I would be able to improve my work'. That's the way it is at the moment … you know … endlessly elaborating the critical context as part of the PhD. I'm still advising a couple of schools on PhDs and I'm so embarrassed because I have to say, 'look these guys couldn't write a PhD thesis if you gave them 100 years … why have they been registered?' The usual reply is that they are interesting artists, but that is no reason to register them for a PhD. Whether they are or are not interesting artists should be of little interest if you are registering someone for a PhD where it must be the research project in the form of a written report that counts. It is this kind of obfuscation about what the qualification actually is and what it represents that is really bedeviling the whole system. If they were interesting artists and enrolled on a DFA alongside other interesting artists, it could be a very productive situation … probably a very interesting one.

And that would be purely practice-based?

Yes. If they chose to do some writing that would be up to them. In the past I have examined postgraduate work at a number of schools in Europe: Zurich, Brussels, Amsterdam, Antwerp and others. Many of them have what is called a jury system. Three or four practicing artists who have been agreed with the students in advance. And the examination takes the form of a lengthy critical interview with each candidate in the presence of their work. It can be half a day or a whole one … but it's very very serious … a complete engagement with the work. It's a level of seriousness which is not achieved here – not at the point of examination anyway. So you know, I think we've lost it here … its all about academic standards rather than the quality of the work and the potential of the candidate as an artist.

Going back to the RAE for a moment. There is a certain school of thought, depending on who you talk to, that the RAE is good, in that it forces people in institutions that have been there for a while to think about and focus on their practice. What do you think of that?

Personally, I have seen no convincing evidence of this, but it may have had some marginal effect. People who really want to practice have always found ways of doing so without the need for institutional carrots and sticks. As for the rest it may be better – academically speaking – to let sleeping dogs lie. But I was never an RAE assessor. Chris Frayling recently asked me to be an advisor for the Royal College of Art RAE submission and I said no because I think the whole system is quite immoral. I don't want to be involved in any way. But I have talked to people like Adrian Rifkin, who was an assessor in the last round, and it is clear that unless you have a much more astringent form of monitoring submissions on the practice side, the process is fairly meaningless. People list galleries that they have done exhibitions in that you've never heard of and the picture that you get is that they are all rushing around Europe – extended Europe – showing work right left and centre. Mostly though they are small, non-professional showing places where they go to spend their holidays or something like that. It's crap. If they had proper exhibitions at known venues – public spaces or well-known commercial galleries – that would be something else. Then you could take them seriously. Furthermore, a small exhibition in an obscure village near Brit-San-Meritus ... that shouldn't even come up for listing in an RAE submission, never mind score points as an indicator of international exposure. You would need a much more serious and professional type of scrutiny to drive up standards in the way they are intending. It's the old how-to-fill-in-forms-syndrome, isn't it? Some people are good at it – make a little sound a lot – and some are not. There are people who spend a lifetime learning how to do it while others stumble. Usually, in our business, the ones who stumble are the most interesting people. From a practice point of view the whole process is scandalously off beam anyway because it focuses on printed material – catalogues, statements and essays – not on the work itself.

Jon Thompson taught at Goldsmiths, London; the Jan Van Eyck Akademie, Maastricht and Middlesex Polytechnic and is now retired from teaching.

Richard Wentworth — The Other Side Restaurant — Pentonville Road, London — 10am.

I want to begin with a visit you once made to Manchester for a meeting.

I went to Manchester for lots of meetings.

This was to do with curating an exhibition: you got a cab from the station to the museum, you don't say which museum …

The Manchester Museum.

You say that 'a large part of Manchester had been rebuilt since the war'. You drive past a 'pretty derivative 1970s building with a big enclosed courtyard area and overly designed steps that were probably five or six-sided.' You describe the steps and then you see that 'balanced on these steps were four chairs and that there was a tape that went incredibly, laboriously from chair to chair … what caught my eye was the precariousness of the chairs.' The problem was that you thought you'd be late for your meeting, 'all those heavy people from government [...] it won't look good.' But you also thought ' … bet it'll be there later [...] It will be all right [...]' So you say you went to the meeting. Eventually you got out and went back to the steps and of course 'it was gone.'

I remember that. Something similar happened again yesterday, in France actually. It's to do with this funny new ruralism: you recognise this in Ireland as well. It's petty bourgeois, but still very attached to the earth. It's not really urban. The whole of rural France is full of rubbish farmyards with electric gates because they don't cost very much. I'm not even quite sure what they do. Maybe they have some symbolic value? I have a filter system that only sees what I see, which of course is one of the worst things about being an artist. You ask yourself 'will I ever get out of this habit?' And you don't. You're stuck and you see it in the patterns of other artists' behaviour, good or bad. You can see the filter is there.

What's particular about what you saw?

I'm amazed at what I can't not see, or can't avoid seeing. In this case, what I actually saw was a row of posts, poles in fact. And it's interesting that that's such a different word. At the base of each one were two traditional roof tiles: the curved kind, which used to borrow the thigh as a template. There was a row of them and they were all leaning. I'd be really interested to know how long it takes to do this work with mature knowledge, how many fractions of a second it takes you to do this: what the child sees, what the adult filters. We need a psychologist.

Fractions of a second to do what exactly?

To select and recognise and shoot it to the centre of attention. I was driving at maybe 50 mph...! I yelled F-U-C-K-I-N-G!!! and my wife yelled, 'WHAT!?' And I said 'never mind, we'll come back.' So it was a row of poles in a newly tended garden, with vegetables, beans, or whatever. And each pole had two of these tiles, maybe three, in the manner of a sort of tepee. The mutual leaning had a wonderful sense of intention, a wonderful repetition. There weren't hundreds, maybe a dozen or 20. More than one and it becomes a conversation. It vaguely occurred to me that they might be supporting the poles temporarily, so there was a question of primacy, a question of who was doing what to which. It's not that I'm interested in good photography. I just need that little memory trigger, a modest record. It's like a really bad stamp collection this thing I'm talking about. I don't see it as something to be displayed, or something I'm going to show to somebody. More like a note, a shopping list ... not a train spotter's log.

This is the *Making Do and...*

Getting By. It's a private thing. I don't even know what it is. It's a whole big category of things, which is probably much larger than people publicly realise. Fundamentally it's really architecture. Anyway, yesterday there's time pressure because we have to leave, and I'm thinking 'well, I'll say nothing, and then I'll be able to sneak by and it'll take three minutes.' But as we approached, they'd gone. I said, 'FUCK FUCK FUCK fuck fuck fuck'. BUT the really beautiful thing was that they weren't actually gone. They were just lying on the ground, like a nut that'd been cracked open. Maybe the first five were lying on the ground and you could just see a little shoot above ground. I think it was, quite literally, a temporary roof. Two roof tiles, earlier leaning against poles now resting on the earth, made of baked earth, protecting beans or whatever. Of course for me they'd lost that decisiveness. Suddenly I had got all their meaning and then understood that piece of innocent syntax. They'd lost their visual weight, which was partially the power of the leaning, with the pole coming out of the top. I love leaning, a sort of purposeful repose.

I said to Jane 'that's the point. That's the failure.' There's more pleasure in seeing what's taken place and failed, than in having captured it. It's this thing about where the acquisition is. It's desire. It's the fact that it was registered, though not registered so intensely that I would deliberately go back. And I'm quite good at not going back. In fact I think deliberately going back is a sort of death. I think the encounter is what it's really about. The encounter is incredibly important.

The initial, primary impulse …

The event. I always assume that on the other side of the road, there's probably something more interesting, but I didn't see it, and I think that is erotic. That is really quite erotic.

The going back is to rationalise the initial encounter, the spontaneous, engaged; the erotic encounter. You talked to Stuart Horodner about going out to take pictures and about your resistance to go out deliberately 'to take pictures'.

It's like coming to see you here. I had the camera lying around, I could have brought it but I quite like the failure of not bringing it too. I like what I've just described in a way. So, in fact I did see something that struck me very much and I wrote it down on my hand. It says 'wooden tree'. Shopping list to hand …

Does this work take place as a kind of peripheral activity? You're coming to meet me and this stuff happens along the way or you're driving from A to B and something happens?

Yes, I think it's to do with being diverted. It's an interesting word in French, *divertissement*, also *déviation* – but humans are ridiculous because we're so centred and peripheral simultaneously. Watching the cat sleeping on the printer before I left, I was thinking that I hadn't seen her for weeks so she's slightly more gorgeous. Then of course I was wondering whether the cat also thinks I'm slightly more gorgeous, or is more interested in me. Judging by last night I'd say 'yes she does', because she woke me up four times to say 'I'm here'. It's a bit like watching wildlife in France. One of the things that happens is that you become quite humbled by what they can do. And although it might sound ridiculous in print, you do discuss how a wren makes that much noise, and ask yourself 'what is it doing?' My wife saw one doing some sort of mad ritual process and it was just like 'what on earth is this?' We're so horribly further up the evolutionary ladder. At this moment, the cat is probably not making a phone call saying 'they're back!' Yet when you're with the cat you look at its eyes, and you anthropomorphise it. You know it's absurd, whereas when I'm talking to you I know it's not absurd.

Is it the same kind of approach that you bring to teaching, a conversation where art gets talked about almost by default?

For me, absolutely. I never want to talk about art and I think I never use the word 'teach'.

Why not?

It would really frighten me. It would sound like I've got something to say.

But you do, you have a lot to say …

That's different, that's like being a radiator in a plumbing system. Hot water comes through and goes out the other side. I have a kind of urgency to do what we're doing. I really like young people. I don't know why, but I really like them, I really like their desire and curiosity. It's probably a biological thing somewhere after 12 … after 15, until say 30. It's really brilliant. I think I learned that through Jon [Thompson], who invited me to Goldsmiths. I don't think I had any idea really. I mean, what would I know, I was 24 …

… about being a teacher?

Yes. I was recently thinking how extremely difficult Oxford can be and that I'm only really interested in what I'd call a 'coming alongside students'. It sounds sexual but I think it's a good term, which you have in the language of shipping. You come alongside, so there's something of a mutual recognition. Maybe one is a tanker and the other is a little Somali pirate boat, but there is this thing of coming alongside. There are lots of people I can't relate to because I simply can't. It doesn't matter whose fault it is, but I can't 'come alongside them', they can't 'come alongside me'. That's not to say that the coming alongside is like friendship, but it's got a lot of trust in it. It's got a lot of vulnerability in it, so that both parties can feel 'we don't really know what we're talking about but …' There are people you could go into a dark room with and it would be quite companionable when you're looking for the light switch. Then there are other people where you go

'I really wish I wasn't looking for the light switch with them.' This has nothing to do with having known somebody for a long time or not. It's a very odd space. It's not a comfortable thing, but it can't flourish in a menacing atmosphere.

What happens to the people you can't come alongside?

I'm sad about it, but I'm not really a missionary or somebody who thinks 'it's all got to work for everybody'. With people that have graduated – 150, let's say, in the time that I've given to Oxford – I suppose 30 per cent think there's some point to me, or I think there's some point to them, and we communicate that. There's a middle 30 per cent, where it's fine but we're not so alert to each other. It's not clubby but it might be a bit tribal in the sense of recognised mutual comprehensions. And then there's 30 per cent that don't want to do it. One of the things that's become quite interesting to me is the question 'who are students?' They're speculators. All they know is that they're not doing half a dozen other things that they might have done. Then, some of them start to heat up in really interesting ways and you think 'bloody hell!' And people say stuff like; 'remember we nearly didn't take them', or 'the most important person in their year!', or 'I don't know what they're going to do but that student's an artist!'. Then there are other people who you thought were so talented, and they actually are talented, but they don't seem to have any of the other kit. I think it's back to this thing that people who function well as artists probably function out of desire. They don't really function out of talent.

What did Jon teach you?

I think Jon taught an extraordinary and slightly risky sort of permissioning ... I once asked Peter de Francia about Jon, because Peter ran Goldsmiths for three years, maybe four years, before Peter went off to run the painting school at the Royal College. Jon in fact worked for Peter and they'd also known each other at Saint Martins. There's an incredible narrative that came out of Saint Martins in that period: Peter Kardia, Aaron Scharf, Philip Jenkinson teaching film and Michael Williams who was also part of the varied group Jon brought to Goldsmiths. There was a really powerful thing at Saint Martins other than the Caro myth/ missionary thing.

Gerard Hemsworth was there at the time.

My wife was also there and I probably saw Gerard's first show, somewhere in Piccadilly, but I never knew him. With Gerard it feels like there was only a short overlap at Goldsmiths, a long time after Jon had set out the stall. I met Peter de Francia, with John Berger, by chance in the summer of 1966. I can see countless threads now, which go back to that. I cringe at the thought of my immaturity! Quite separately I met Jon around that time, through Saint Martins' friends. I lived near Peter at the Elephant. Like all of us, Peter can be quite a troublemaker. Around 1971, I can remember him saying 'the thing about Jon is he's neither fish nor fowl'. I don't think I'd ever heard the expression and I went away thinking 'what does that mean?' Obviously it's about sexual orientation and I think that's actually quite central to Jon's accessibility at Goldsmiths. I'm not aware of actually having voiced that before, but I think it's very interesting that people need something between a sister and a brother, a mother and a father and an aunt and uncle. They need a handrail and they needed Jon's availability and his intellectual desire, which I don't pretend to have. Jon never appeared to take against anybody. He never seemed to say 'I can't bear so and so in the second year', and all that sort of tribal rubbish that goes on. I think that's probably to do with the shape of his ego. He was also very young, something like 31. There was a big joke that he only employed handsome young men. Everybody seemed to have long hair (there's a picture somewhere). I remember Tim Head, Michael Craig-Martin, Nick de Ville, and a lovely South American called Enrique Pardo who now lives in Paris, I think.

And Harry Thubron?

That's a bit later and something of an old debt. It was quite a complicated thing, where Harry had been important in Leeds. There was a kind of avuncular thing – Harry was very broken down. I mean Harry was very old school, puffing away – made of smoke. I once stayed at his house in Ronda for Christmas, next to the painter Peter Richmond, who had been taught by Bomberg. I think that's another thing that's very important: whether you become sort of dedicated to, if you like, a kind of regimental stripe. Whether you're taught in a way that is not very catholic and you become overly loyal to some kind of painting, or method of forming sculpture. I could never do that. Just because you see someone felling a tree in France doesn't mean you're going to become a French woodsman but you can appreciate they know how to make it fall this way or that. When I do it, it's more of a gamble.

What you're describing is a bit like the professorial system in Germany, where you're dedicated to a particular artist …

Of course we're all attracted to being 'that artist'. I mistakenly thought that's what I was being invited to be in Oxford. I think I just picked up some misapprehension. Maybe I needed the misapprehension in order to get through the barricades, because it's such a jolly weird place.

What was the misapprehension?

It was some idea that I was to be Tobias Rehberger, who is at the Städel with Daniel Birnbaum, except I probably didn't know Tobias then. And of course Oxford plays to all that. It plays to the idea that Richard Dawkins is over there. But actually it wouldn't suit me. I'm not like that. I'm no messiah. So it wouldn't suit me. But I think I needed it in order to justify whatever I thought I was doing at the time, seven years ago exactly, on April Fool's Day.

What did you think you were doing at the time?

I think I was doing something quite ordinary. I was sort of steadying economically the high ups, the low downs, an incredibly dodging life. I was 'exhorted' by my wife who said 'you are really good at doing that, go and do it'. I'm a depressive, so there's that as well. I don't mean of the broadcastable variety, but most of my time I'm quite maudlin, so I need to be with people because then I can go 'look I'm alive'. This is far more fun than looking at lots of emails or bags of paper I've got to sort.

And she meant you're good at teaching, 'go and do that …'

I think she did, but she's far too tactful to say that. She'd never say 'you're good at teaching'. She probably said something like 'it needs picking up and you're good at picking things up …' I'm very good at starting things, I'm not good at ending things. I don't mean I'd start them and then walk away at the wrong moment. I mean the refinements all get rehearsed in here [points to his temple, self-mockingly] so I sometimes project the impractical delusions of the perfectionist. Art will forgive this, life will not!

Is that what being in an art school context gives you? It gives you a community of people to work with and a certain amount of power to enable things to happen?

Through Oxford I've become incredibly interested in power, because I've started to become interested in how it enables or disables. What's power for? Jon's achievement in the 1970s and 1980s at Goldsmiths was a kind of enormously enabling ... It's ridiculous to say he was lucky, he made the luck but the scale was right, the building at Myatts Fields was incredibly important, and it was not at horrible New Cross.

Camberwell ...

Sort of, near the Oval. The number and variety of people who were teaching, the fact that the economy worked in such a way that people came and went. Tim Head wanted a better job and went to the Slade. You know, things moved around. Not this 'you're going to work here forever', which I knew nothing about when I first started at the Ruskin as I hadn't really been involved with a school for about a dozen years. I'd worked at the Architectural Association, but I was amazed that schools had become a terminus. Teaching had become a terminus! And it's a terrible vile example to set the students. Everyone appeared to be my age and I thought 'Oh my God!' I'd become part of the problem, and I don't want to be part of the problem. This is a real political issue. You can't run this constantly favouring, 'foot-in-door – you're here forever, these are your rights' kind of thing. Q.E.D., everyone else hasn't got any rights. Recently in Oxford someone wrote something about the school and they kept using the words 'permanent staff', and, of course, what was implied was the disposable staff, in other words the real engine of the school. These people are the biometallic strips and metronomes, yet they seem to not exist, the people who we'd call part time, the people who come in a couple of days a week. They provide a continuity, people get excited about them coming in and this isn't celebrated. These are big structural issues, the privileged western world going to sleep in a hammock, late Soviet style.

And what's the Ruskin connected to, and how do you allow for this, or even think about this architecturally? When you talk about the original building in Camberwell you talk about a building which was 'teeming, intimate, cramped. A creative environment in which good work could be done. It was like a little public school, very knowable with a nice sense of being independent.'

The imagery of the defunct chapel as lecture space, the defunct gym as studio, the general Arts and Craftishness of the Myatts Fields building helped, perhaps even moralising the place. A thriving art school often feels like a superior squat. I love watching, I love patterning. I think that's the story of the roof tiles, really. If there was only one tile I might not have seen it, but with a lot you get 'intention' and implication of intention, but also extrapolations like recognising why that Camberwell building had parking out front – so you could see people had arrived and left. It's a case of semi-domestic registrations. It's a Michael Bracewell idea really that art schools are essentially suburban and that they're made up of people who are desiring urban heat and actually end up in a Victorian suburb, off Camberwell New Road. Clearly Damien is not Liam, and Liam is not Lala Meredith Vula, and Lala is not Matt Collishaw, and Collishaw and Stephen Park are not Sarah Lucas and I think that's really important, that you're in this conversation and that the sparking gaps are interesting. Of course, if you're right-minded you're always trying to make those sparking gaps bigger. You know I've got a million prejudices, but it's not my job when somebody turns up with a portfolio to make social judgements. But if you can't attract a broad slice, it's a dull thing. National Service!

And what do you do when a 17-year old turns up with a portfolio?

I'm always very clear to give it time. I never flick through it and say 'this is no good'. I say 'well, why are you interested in blue and brown, and why do you like bilateral symmetry', and 'is it annoying that the cup has only got one handle. Would you secretly like it to have two handles?' I just do something that gets somebody going, sometimes I stroke, sometimes I jolt. 17-year olds never know which is which, anyway.

What are you looking for?

I've no idea.

But you know it when you find it?

I know it. I might be on the lookout for the crossroads where resourcefulness and resilience meet. What's actually awful is talking to people who are either not convincing because they're bullshitters, which is very shocking when they're young. Or, they're not convincing because they appear not to have thought about the most elementary things in their own compass. This could be anything, but if they don't appear to be sentient, how can you develop a relationship with this person? You can't say 'you're very boring, please go away', although sometimes the door closes and you say just that. I've got a very nice 1920s, maybe early 1930s drawing of a section through the Central School, and it's got printmaking, life drawing, and everything else you can think of in it. If we were builders it would be 'oh they're the wet trades, they're the dry trades', or 'here comes the sparks'. When you walk into a building where there's no power, no water, no gas, it can be a perfectly serviceable place but it's not energised and of course, us modern people expect this. I think an art school needs that as a metaphor. It needs somebody who brings gas, and it might be some new kind of gas called propane that comes in a special bottle. It's not a tidy thing. It's not as simple as 'who's teaching life drawing?' Because the great thing about all of those things is that anyone teaching anything really well is great. I don't think it even matters much what it is being taught. Somebody teaching something badly because it's on the curriculum is terrible. Some of us can still remember things we can't ever look at again. Because it was damaged by somebody who 'delivered' them. Milk! Coal! Newspapers! Better to think about the people or the product? And I think that's why Goldsmiths was interesting at that time, because London was between two wars, between the big war and this funny 'we're all regulated, GCHQ knows we're here' kind of war ... We thought we could have it all and we can't.

The 'we' being?

This conversation is not an academic conversation, but it is obviously academically informed. But it's also haptically informed. I can register power, choice, poverty, which is more and more complicated to do, because clearly we don't live in a tidy class system. The pivot is understanding how to put the critical mass together. Being present in a school I think is really important. I mean really important. Doors are the enemy. Open doors, even, do not guarantee 'accessibility'.

When you were in the Camberwell building, did you recognise that it was working?

No, I think I could feel it.

You knew it was working?

I couldn't have said what I say now. But that's because I can see that we become what we become. I don't want to sound too determinist but you start to see surprisingly assured patterning. The school prefect becomes the head of the minor art school. The troublemaker goes into the music business. It's very interesting I think, very funny too. Do we become our temperaments?

Who becomes the artist?

Very hard to say. Not the person who gets the chances. I don't think it's as simple or tidy as that. Anya Gallacio comes to mind, partly because I told her not to leave Goldsmiths. And she always quotes the fact that I told her not too. Whereas normally when someone decides to leave art school I think 'so decisive!' That's really good and there should be much more of that in education. 'I have eaten in this restaurant and I will not be coming back', or 'can I see the menu again, please?'

Why did you tell Anya not to leave?

Entirely instinctive at the time, I'm sure. Didn't feel right. I'm pretty instinctive and I trust this. In fact I was once congratulated at one of those great and good money give-away jobs, where I was in with very high-powered scientists and I, the artist, felt like a complete charlatan. Jesus, these people are so smart. I knew who some of them were too, and I thought I'd just sit quietly and represent my corner. It was one of those science-art things and I was sitting next to Richard Gregory who subsequently has become almost a friend – 80 years old – highly celebrated, brilliant near-polymath psychologist. I said something after somebody went out of the room, like 'well they definitely haven't got it', and Richard turned to me and said 'you've got the most marvellous instinct, I can feel it coming off you'. And I just thought 'wow, you're meant to be a scientist! You're not meant to be talking about instinct.' I spent quite a bit of time encouraging Anya to go to the theatre, which is where she's really from and why the work is like it is. She's got a proper decorative, theatrical intelligence and there's absolutely no criticism in that at all. I'm sure she will do opera one day. She'll be asked and she'll do it. But I remember thinking that she should keep going ... I would never say one of those crushing things like 'you want to give all this stuff up', because that's a killer and it's always remembered as the killer. It's an abuse of power because it's not a consultative space if you do that. Their clock is ticking too, so is mine.

[Phone call for Richard.]

I realise that one of the things we're talking about, or that you're asking me about, is a really important idea about picking the right person. We perceive availability in people. I tested it on some students the other day. I said 'you're late for a train, you're in a town you've not been in before, you've got a vague idea that you're not far from the railway station but you're lost. There's an old lady crossing the road with a Zimmer frame, there's a fat drunk, there's a baby in a pushchair coming out of a door, there's a dog walking towards you and there are three other people. You don't ask the old lady with the Zimmer frame, you don't speak to the dog and you don't consult the baby or the drunk, but you pick one of the three other people. Very quickly you go 'shit, they want to talk to me all day', or 'they don't have any sense of direction or whatever' or 'they go "yes love … turn left where that red van is".' That's not about an art school being a nice and cosy place, which is death. You need lots of positions and this constant sense of fertility. This fertility is legible the very moment you walk through the door of any institution.

Can you create that?

I think you can foster it. I don't think there's a formula for it but I think I've been in enough places where the order of the day is to crush it whenever it appears.

Why?

Because it reinforces somebody's position to crush it: 'this looks dangerous', or 'I've never met this before', or sentences which begin with 'yes, but …', or 'the problem is', which I won't have said in the school, 'the problem is' and 'yes, but …' In institutions, perhaps, everybody is a refugee. The motives for being there, for both students and staff, needs to be discussed openly. It's not an efficiency thing, it's an effectiveness thing.

When asked what goes into a good art school in 'Towards a free art school', you say 'Art schools are made of people. Some mix of premises and gumption is the fire lighter. It's a sentient being thing, not a correspondence course or a chat room. It needs buckets of goodwill and trust to work, because without that, you can't generate the essential atmosphere of vulnerability and the pleasure of risk. Lots of give = lots of take = a perpetual motion machine. Art Schools are places of desire amid the occasional wonders of recognition. There needs to be openness to get the necessary frankness. The verb "to confide" leads to the warm noun "confidence". The useful people are probably often not artists in the hidebound sense. Reliability helps a lot if it doesn't recoil into jobs worthiness. There are terrible models to witness. It can be contagious so wear a mask. Cowards should not be tolerated. Art school should be a testing place, not an assault course.'

I haven't said anything better than that in the entire time I've sat here. I think that was probably written very early in the morning.

What constitutes a coward in that context?

All forms of backsliding. I think it's the opposite of generosity. Generosity is a funny thing because we all want something so none of us humans just give. We're giving because it's to do with our own survival. We're drawing a space in which we figure by relating to people. So I'm wary of the word 'generous' meaning 'they always took us to the pub'. I think people with permanent jobs should really do that actually, they should really do it, take people out to dinner.

They should take people out for dinner?

Yes. Shell out and don't claim it back. They should do it for the privilege, the sheer privilege, not because everyone then goes 'oh, we all had a kebab', but because they might talk to each other in a way that is so not about meeting around a grey table. If you turn the coin 'generosity' over, on the back it says 'mean'. When you put it down again, the offprint of 'mean' is usually 'cowardly'. Old-fashioned words like spineless, gutless, and so on. World War I stuff of course, but often surprisingly close to mindless and careless. Scaredy-cats.

Did it matter you went to Hornsey?

I think it mattered. I walked past Zoë Wanamaker's house on my way here. Funny, coming to discuss all this, because she was a student with me. She was part of this massive acting dynasty, all that American refugee power living a perfectly modest mid-1960s life in Highgate, looking to become Zoë Wanamaker. There's no accounting for what becomes of people on a good foundation course. There was Zoë and a hundred others, I am in touch with about half a dozen of them. They were the people who went on to do the sit-in in 1968. I remember Kim Howells's Welsh fervour and his excitement that he hitched a lift up the new M4 with the young Michael Foot. Howells ended up being grumpy in the Blair government, but what an achievement when the British political class is nearly devoid of culturally engaged folk. Anyway, Zoë … The parent child space is God's great joke. My eldest son was a sort of chemistry child, always blowing things up. Always wondering how to siphon the petrol. He worked out at school that perhaps those things weren't deeply interesting over time for him, so decided to become an engineer. He even got a place at Oxford but nothing to do with my subsequent involvement. And I remember being slightly horrified by the whole process, because clearly I've got a problem with that because I know I'm not clever, I'm just criminally smart.

You've got a problem with what process?

With institutionalised cleverness. Anyway the son got a place and I remember asking him, 'who are they? Who's at Oxford? Who are they?' And he said 'they're clever and they always have been, and then they turn up at Oxford and discover there are other people who've always been clever too and they're all in the same place and then it's a very anxious atmosphere.' That is definitely not what an art school should be.

What do you think your responsibility is towards the students? And what's their responsibility towards you?

Their responsibility is to absolutely take me seriously, realising that I'm not very serious, or ponderous. I hope I'm not ponderous. I tend to speak like a Möbius strip. The front and the back are a bit confused, but artists deal in meaning, and meaning is fugitive. My responsibility to them is attached to energy and stamina. I'm not going to tell them, 'if you're not here at nine and don't stay until five you're no good'. It's getting them to understand how to use their energy. Some artists don't work, don't do anything for three months. So what are you gathering, harvesting, putting together? Who are you meeting, reading, and looking at? And they're different for different people because different people function very differently. Some people are tidy-minded in how they work and have an absolute fixed set of procedures. They're admirable, I haven't got them, although I think if someone really followed me around they'd say I join the dots.

Can anyone do this work, can anyone teach?

No. I read something that William Boyd said about teaching at Oxford and he said 'I did but I really hadn't the patience'. So polite. It's so clever. But actually of course a lot of people haven't got the patience, genuinely haven't got it in them, though having patience at Oxford is something else. There's an intimacy to what I'm describing. There are other kinds of teaching: great, good and bad. I think a lot of people are amazingly controlling and somehow not tolerant in the right sense of the word. But I think there's another model we're overlooking, which is the moment when the school should really look after people, that's what the schools should be doing at the moment.

In what sense look after people?

Today things are very hard and I don't know how long it's going to be like this, or whether it's going to be like this forever. But I think the whole thing about the permanent and the disposable is that the schools should be vigorous about seeing themselves as cultural agents and be very respectful of the ducking and diving that we're all involved in: to see it as a dynamic and argue for it. Say, 'look this is what we want to do'. In a way that's what this 1970s and 1980s period at Goldsmiths was about. Also urgent for students in this life/ hinge growing up moment. They need models of complex lives, becoming parents, two timing in art and life, whatever. Their suggestibility must not be abused, ever.

Is that argument being made at the moment?

No, that's why I feel a bit vehement. I think the forces are absolutely the other way, very tidy 'yes, they're all signed up for their annual review'. It's all perfectly good, but it's all about functionality. I think we're not curious about the subject. We're not even talking about the subject; we don't know how to talk about the subject. We haven't talked about painting, sculpture, whether printmaking will survive, and what it is, who invented it and where did it come from. Was Goya a printmaker? I don't think so ... delighted he made some prints though. We're so bad at talking about what the whole thing is. What on earth is photography, nearly 200 years after it surfaced?

Do you think artists are best placed to do this work, to teach art?

Not really. My greatest regret during the last few years in Oxford is that I just so wanted an economist to teach, I just didn't know where to find one. It's like saying I want somebody who knows how BMWs work, it's not in my compass, but I was hoping if I said it enough someone would say 'you have to meet so and so'.

Why did you want an economist so badly?

What I thought, obviously it's a thought that must have incubated in the late 1990s, was that we needed somebody to talk about how choices are made and the consequences of our choices. Somebody who could tell us what a market is, nothing to do with professional practice. I hate professional practice. If someone asked me to teach professional practice, I'd give each student a compass. We're removing the opportunity to be decisive which is part of a much wider educational crisis. It's lovely to know when to cross the road. I don't want to have to go to where it's got black and white stripes that tell me where to cross! I'm not frightened of being decisive. And if you're going to make a work of art you better know how to be decisive at some point, because it isn't about walking in fog.

Richard Wentworth previously taught at the Ruskin School of Art, Oxford and will teach at The Royal College of Art, London from October 2009.

Erwin Wurm — mid-January — Café Englander
— Vienna — the interview starts a bit late.

Can you say which professors taught you?

I first studied with Rudi Arnold and then Bazon Brock.

Did they have a lot of influence on your subsequent practice?

Yes. Definitely, yes.

What part does teaching have in your practice?

I think it's interesting to work with students and give something back. For example, when I was studying it was difficult to ask such questions as, 'what is quality?', 'How can I define quality?' I never really got a good answer. Nowadays, when I look at all the students, there are so many! Everyone wants to be an artist, and I don't know why, because it's such a difficult profession. Sometimes I think maybe I was too idealistic and I should give it up again, because teaching takes a lot of work most of the time.

I was wondering this as well, because you live between Vienna and New York.

No, I live in Vienna. It's a mistake often made; I lived in New York for one and a half years, a long time ago.

Does teaching benefit you, in that it keeps you in contact with young people and connected to new ideas?

Yes, but I find this rather disturbing in a way, because when you're together with young people, you also feel old all of a sudden. When I'm together with people my own age I feel much younger.

In relation to what they're talking about?

No, not what they're talking about, just their physical presence.

How would you describe the teaching methods you use?

I am lucky enough to have a group of teachers behind me – six assistants and nine teachers, so we are 16 altogether and everybody has their own role. I'm the one who speaks just about the work of the students and the work as related to the art world.

I do this once a week in the morning with all the students, and in the afternoon there are private lessons, private talks. Because many of the students are shy about talking in public and want to go deeper.

So is this similar to what they have in Germany, that they're dedicated to your class?

Yes, that is the Austrian system, they're dedicated to my class. The class is called sculpture and new media. Basically they can do anything. The only thing that I'm not talking about is painting. Obviously I'm not a painter. 'How do you make the distinction?' Just two days ago a student said, 'I'm only painting now and I don't want to do anything else.' 'OK, no problem', I told him, 'but you better go to someone who's a painter, someone who's dealing with the issue of painting, because I could talk about it, but maybe it's totally wrong, it's just the perspective of someone who's been dealing with sculpture and new media for many years.' He understood that and has changed classes now.

Do you refuse students who apply to your class or do you take everyone that applies?

No, we cannot take everybody. But it's difficult to decide whom to take. I'm not just counting on so-called talent, I'm also counting on will. I want them to have a very, very strong will, because that's so important when you want to progress as an artist.

Is that another way of saying ambition?

Alright – ambition – maybe that's the right word. And struggle. And the possibility to all the time rethink your position and to be critical within yourself. I think that's very necessary.

Can you teach art?

Can I what?

Can one teach art?

I try to find criteria for what we are looking at, what we are talking about. Criteria to describe the work in relation to other artworks in the class, or I'm more or less trying to connect the work to the rest of the world.

You mean relationships with other work and to the world?

With other work – to the world – to philosophy – to psychology – and to the art world.

Are there clear distinctions between your practice and your teaching, or do they become one and the same?

I try to keep my practice out of it, because I don't want to influence the students. I would never want to tell them that they have to do what I do. I want variety, I want to relativise, I want to show the students there are many, many different options. I try to explain that they have to define their own criteria and the body of work they're doing. Whether they're making minimalist work or very opulent work, I don't care about that.

I was thinking about the strong performance theme that runs through your practice and the relationship this might have to your teaching?

I think it's not right to put me into the discussion as an artist. I try to step aside, I try to analyse their art. I mean, what I have done, all my failures and all the not so bad things I've done, that's the point from where I am able to speak to them.

Just let me pursue this for a moment. As a student I sign up for your class, what am I signing up for? This must bear on what students think they're committing to. So your practice is there, is present ...

There are of course different possibilities. Some students may know my work and be interested in my specific language, others come from school and have so far no specific idea about art and also don`t know my work. This is a coincidental meeting which can be very interesting. But from the beginning it is obvious that there are also other people in my class – my assistants and the teachers – who will work with the students. Some of these people working with me are active artists and others are theorists or in the curatorial field. Students get involved in curatorial aspects as well as art theory and they also learn for example how to make a cast or work in wood.

So what it allows you really is to bring different disciplines and moments together?

Yes.

Without heavily influencing the outcomes?

Yes.

It's like a mini-institution?

Yes, in a way. It's not a master class like in the old times. The master being at the centre and all the students trying to work more or less like him. That is not at all what this is here.

Do you make connections with what is outside the academy?

Yes, very much.

In what way?

Nearly every month someone comes from abroad, like a writer or an artist or someone who makes film. They all talk about their work, so the students get as many different perspectives on these themes as possible. And then we have exhibitions, we do workshops; we've had workshops in Bangkok, in France, and we're going to do one in Cairo. Over the years we've had more or less two or three exhibitions each year.

John Armleder was talking about his connections to Volkswagen, where he did a project with the car factory. He had the idea of placing students in an unfamiliar environment with the demands, curatorial concept, and organisation that comes with this, and then actually making work as well …

That's very good. One of my assistants has a very good relation with the city and he had the idea to organise the possibility that students could make billboards for the city. This was a commission where some of my students along with several artists were invited to apply and my students actually won. There was a little show of all the concepts, all the models. And finally the students' work was realised for real.

What about the Bologna Declaration? Does it have any effect on your Academy?

What's the Bologna Declaration?

The Bologna Declaration is an intergovernmental initiative that aims to create a common European Higher Education Area to enable students to study across Europe. It's another piece of European legislation, which attempts to rationalise higher education.

Of course this is very important. I'm very interested in the students actually going somewhere else. We have the Erasmus system – that's an exchange for students between art schools/ universities in different countries. And many students are doing this.

You've spoken in relation to your work about 'laziness' and I was wondering whether this concept informs how you approach your teaching in any way?

Well, it's difficult because I can tell you I also use things in my work from a very theoretical point of view. I am very interested in laziness. I always need the feeling that I've nothing to do, otherwise I can't work. In order to have this feeling I never open the post, I don't answer e-mails. Yes, I answer the phone, which is a nightmare, but I am trying to work on this. I have a lot to do, with the teaching job, with my shows, with creating new work, but I still need to have the feeling that I don't know what to do. I can walk around, I have spare time, I need this kind of attitude. I try to tell students that first they need time, they need a lot of time. And I always try to tell them that to work is like a kind of exercise where failures are an important part of this. It happens to me often, and has done so for a long time, and it still does. And it's important to learn by making mistakes and not believing in yourself too much, because that makes you too sure, and that makes you bad in a way. I see many of these so called big artists and I see many of this big 'sureness' in the art world, but the art is weak. So I also believe very much in doubt, constantly doubting what I'm doing, and this I try and teach the students; don't be so sure, constantly ask questions about what you're doing, how you do it – try to constantly ask yourself questions and be critical!

It must be difficult to create a moment of uncertainty, because, with the students being accepted into the academy, there must come a feeling of being part of something, of a certainty …

The first thing they do is to change the outfit. It's really fantastic …

I assume you don't need to teach in the academy for financial reasons?

Right.

You want to give something back to these students? But teaching also creates a set of structures and rules which your own work can react to, can play with and so on …

There is another reason why I teach, because, when you work in the art field, you're constantly in this field, you're constantly relating to these, not always great, worlds; dealers, strange dealers, writers, critics, and I wanted to be able to breath apart from this. To have space somewhere, just to get things out of my head, and not to be constantly preoccupied with it. I realised to be lazy does not necessarily mean that you forget things, because if you don't work it comes even more into your head. I had to think about all this and I wanted to have something else, and teaching really works. I have no wish to make a career in the academy; I don't need that. Some colleagues of mine say they would like to be rector of the academy. That is not my intention …

Which is probably why you'll become rector …

No! No way, absolutely not . I would refuse it. I would deny it. No, I would leave …

Is there a limit then to the teaching commitment you make, as distinct from the life you want outside of that? Is there a limit to how much work you put into the academy?

Absolutely. I do this one day a week.

That's enough?

Absolutely enough, if it's all getting too much I have to leave.

What happens if it's too much?

I leave.

No, what happens at that point?

Because then it's destroying too much of the rest of my life. It's so interfering, it's pulling me in too much, and then I have no free time, I have no space to think about the rest, to deal with my work and the rest of my life. It's overwhelming then, and I don't want that.

Erwin Wurm teaches at the Akademie der Bildenden Künste, Vienna.

Published in 2009 by Ridinghouse

Ridinghouse/ Karsten Schubert
5–8 Lower John Street
Golden Square
London W1F 9DR
www.karstenschubert.com

Ridinghouse is the publishing imprint shared by
London gallerists Thomas Dane and Karsten Schubert
producing books, prints and multiples.
www.ridinghouse.co.uk

Distributed in the UK and Europe by
Cornerhouse
70 Oxford Street
Manchester M15 5NH
www.cornerhouse.org

Distributed in the US by
RAM Publications
2525 Michigan Avenue Building A2
Santa Monica CA 90404
www.rampub.com

British Library Cataloguing-in-Publication Data
A full catalogue record of this book is available from the
British Library

ISBN 978–1–905464–13–5

Ridinghouse Editor: Rosalind Horne
Copy-editor: Gerrie van Noord
Design: Marit Münzberg with the assistance of Martina Dahl
Print: Lecturis, Eindhoven

Generously supported by:

AHRC

The Henry Moore
Foundation

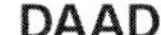 Deutscher Akademischer Austausch Dienst
German Academic Exchange Service